Robert L. Moore, editor

Carl Jung
and
Christian Spirituality

Paulist Press
New York ◊ Mahwah

Acknowledgements: The Publisher gratefully acknowledges the use of the following: "The Cross as an Archetypal Symbol" by M. Esther Harding from *Quadrant* (Autumn 1971): 5–14. Reprinted by permission. "Jungian Psychology and Religious Experience" by Eugene C. Bianchi from *Anglican Theological Review* (April 1979, 61): 182–199. Reprinted by permission. "The Self as Other" by Ann Belford Ulanov from *Journal of Religion and Health* (April 1973, 12): 140–168. Reprinted by permission. "Jungian Psychology and Christian Spirituality: I-III" by Robert M. Doran, S.J. from *Review for Religious* (July, September and November 1979, 38): 497–510, 742–752 and 857–866. Reprinted by permission. "The Problem of Evil in Christianity and Analytical Psychology" by John A. Sanford from *Psychological Perspectives* (Fall 1980, 11): 112–132. Reprinted by permission. "Rediscovering the Priesthood through the Unconscious" by Morton T. Kelsey from *Journal of Pastoral Counseling* (Spring-Summer 1972, 7): 26–36. Reprinted by permission. "The Archetypes: A New Way to Holiness?" by Patrick Vandermeersch from *Cistercian Studies* (1975, 10): 3–21. Reprinted by permission. "Jungian Typology and Christian Spirituality" by Robert A. Repicky, C.S.B. from *Review for Religious* (May/June 1981, 40): 422–435. Reprinted by permission. "Persona and Shadow: A Jungian View of Human Duality" by Thayer A. Greene from *Chicago Studies* (Summer 1982, 21): 151–162. Reprinted by permission. "Jung and Scripture" by Diarmuid McGann from *New Catholic World* (March/April 1984, 227): 60–63. Reprinted by permission. "Psychologically Living Symbolism and Liturgy" by Ernest Skublics from *Eglise et Theologie* (May 1970, 1): 205–228. Reprinted by permission. "Jungian Types and Forms of Prayer" by Thomas E. Clarke, S.J. from *Review for Religious* (September/October 1983, 42): 661–676. Reprinted by permission.

Copyright © 1988 by Robert L. Moore

Library of Congress Cataloging-in-Publication Data

Carl Jung and Christian spirituality / Robert L. Moore, editor.
   p. cm.
   ISBN 0-8091-2950-7 (pbk.) :
   1. Spiritual life.   2. Jung, C. G. (Carl Gustav), 1875–1961.
I. Moore, Robert L.
BV4501.2.C297   1988
201'.9—dc19   87-37480
                                                      CIP

Published by Paulist Press
997 Macarthur Blvd.
Mahwah, N.J. 07430

Printed and bound in the United States of America

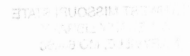

Contents

DEDICATION

This book is dedicated to those who have pioneered in the field of Jungian psychoanalysis and Christian spirituality and to those who continue providing leadership in this challenging area of endeavor today. We wish to honor especially three men who have been spiritual masters to untold numbers of us through their lectures, workshops, and writings: Robert Johnson, Morton Kelsey, and John Sanford. Together they have set a standard which will be an inspiration to us in the decades to come.

Others who deserve our gratitude and who have graced us with their leadership include Chandler "Chink" Brown, founder and director of Centerpoint, and Annette and James Cullipher, founders of the Journey Into Wholeness conferences.

Without the examples of these pathfinders this volume would never have been conceived.

APPRECIATIONS

I wish to express my thanks to the many who have in significant ways contributed to the task of making this book a reality. First, and most important, I am grateful to the authors of the essays that make up this volume. Their generosity in permitting republication of their work in this new format will be appreciated by the many who will now have access to this work for the first time.

The excellent editorial staff of Paulist Press has provided not only enormous support and encouragement but also a challenge to look beyond this volume to the series that follows it. I am especially indebted to Kevin Lynch and Lawrence Boadt for their interest in and vision for this endeavor.

My research and editorial staff has been invaluable in this work. I am indebted to Kelley Raab, Carol Montgomery-Fate, Patrick Nugent, and especially to my Chief-of-Staff, Daniel J. Meckel. Dan has carried the primary responsibility for coordinating the many different facets of this complicated project. It is my hope that our collaboration will continue on subsequent volumes of this series. Max Havlick, Faculty Secretary at the Chicago Theological Seminary, has provided much advice, assistance, and encouragement.

Margaret L. Shanahan conceptualized the beautiful and evocative cover design and Tim McKeen found a way to execute it.

Finally, I wish to thank the many persons of different psychological and religious traditions who have over the years been spiritual directors for me. These Soulfriends continue to provide me with inspiration and encouragement as I seek to live my life without cynicism and with a hope grounded in the Divine Mystery of our faith.

R.L.M.

Robert L. Moore

Introduction

Why a new series on Jungian psychoanalysis and contemporary spirituality? There are a number of important reasons why this is an extremely timely endeavor. Significantly, the popularity of Jungian psychology and psychotherapy has continued to grow rapidly and attract more attention from both laypersons and professionals in the mental health field—especially among those disillusioned by the more narrow and simplistic psychological theories. The number of accredited Jungian training institutes has continued to grow and certified Jungian psychoanalysts are now available in many of the major cities of the world. Books on myriad topics from a Jungian perspective are being written in growing numbers and are being read by people from all walks of life. Interest in the implications of Jungian psychology for the theory and practice of spirituality and spiritual direction has been growing over the past few decades in both Christian and non-Christian religious communities. It has become widely understood that a Jungian perspective adds a substantial amount of depth and insight to inquiries regarding the dynamics of the human experiences of the sacred. Throughout the world men and women are gathering together in small groups to study the writings of Carl Jung and to reflect on their implications for human society, human psychology, and the human religious pilgrimage. To what can we attribute this rapidly increasing interest in Jung's psychology and its implications for contemporary life?

First, informed people today realize that tribalism and pseudospeciation in human culture, politics, and religion must be transcended. A way must be found to help people find and affirm their common humanity and their common human spiritual roots. There are very few resources available today to assist in facilitating that process. Jungian thought is one of the most important. Its presentation of a "collective unconscious" is hailed by increasing numbers as a basis for seeking communication and understanding between different cultures and religious communities. Interpreting out of a Jungian perspective encourages an "appreciative consciousness" with regard to the symbolic and ritual forms of traditions other than one's own. The work of two great scholars, Joseph Campbell and Mircea Eliade, has been an important contribution to the interest in the importance of Jung's work for cultural and religious interpretation. Their writings on folklore, world mythology, and the history and phenomenology of religions were influenced by depth psychology in general and by Jung's thought in particular. Increasing numbers of thinkers from different disciplines have been seeking to encourage a new understanding of the importance of cross-cultural studies and a wider appreciation of the human "symbolic trust" as it is preserved in the many cultural and religious traditions of the human race. Though Campbell and Eliade are no longer with us, they continue to inspire many to follow in their footsteps in seeking to understand the many facets of the human religious quest.

This increasing interest in human spirituality is clearly not merely an academic or socially marginal activity. Nor is it simply an activity and concern of those who are religious professionals. There is an increasing realization among concerned people around the world that the human race is in the midst of a deepening spiritual crisis and that no less than the future of the planet is at stake. The nuclear arms race, the worsening ecological situation, the deterioration of the influence of traditional moral and religious values—all cause great concern among those who are interested in shaping the human future.

There is an awareness, however, that traditional approaches to this spiritual crisis will not suffice. Premodern approaches to the life of the spirit were usually characterized by tribalism, authoritarianism, and imperialistic attitudes toward other traditions. Culturally modern approaches are usually reductionistic and do not emphasize the value of symbol, myth, and ritual for contemporary human life. Modernity as a cultural configuration cannot affirm that meaning is discovered—rather it emphasizes the importance of the "heroic ego" in the Faustian creation of meaning. The challenge today is to find a means to create a postmodern approach to culture, psychology, and spirituality which affirms the importance of tradition—foundations in the riches of myth, ritual, and religious symbolism—which does not resort to an authoritarianism or coerciveness in interpretation. An adequate postmodern approach to culture, psychology, and spirituality would not condone the exploitation of religious tradition for narcissistic, egoistic purposes, the diverting of human spiritual treasure for narrow "tribal" political, ethnic, racial, or economic ends. Jung's psychology is founded on the assumption that at the deepest levels human beings are already connected—and that it is through these "deep structures of the psyche" that we make our most significant connections with spiritual reality. From a Jungian point of view, all religious forms and formulations are partial, yet precious—all deserving of careful receptive scrutiny in hope of gleaning the insight and illumination which we need to push back the poisonous veil of unconsciousness which both in past and present leads us across the planet to commit atrocities in the name of the Divine Reality.

What about those critics who decry the appropriation of psychological resources of any form for use in spirituality and spiritual direction? Many of these critics have good motives and important cautions which deserve our careful attention. Certainly the use of psychoanalysis and other psychological resources does not eliminate the need for careful philosophical and ethical reflection or for the maintenance of one's centeredness in a stance grounded in spiritual theology. Uncritical appropriation of psychological approaches as a substitute for more rigorous theological and ethical struggle should be unacceptable to us. Why, then, draw so deeply upon the resources of Jungian psychoanalysis for contemporary spirituality and spiritual direction, both lay and professional? There are a number of important reasons in addition to the powerful cross-cultural appeal which was noted above. Let me cite some of the most important:

(1) The Challenge of Spiritual Discernment—There can be no responsible approach to discernment of spirits today which has not availed itself of the resources of contemporary psychoanalysis in illuminating areas of probable self-deception and related "splitting" in the psyche of both the individual on pilgrimage and the individual or individuals who are attempting to serve as a guide for their journey. The contribution of psychoanalysis to a spiritual "hermeneutics of suspicion" is paralleled only by that of the contribution of critical sociology to liberation theologies. If we are to be serious "lib-

eration theologians," then we must use the most powerful tools at our disposal to help us find the areas in which we remain in bondage, to understand the dynamics of the bondage, and to break its enchanting power. The concepts of the shadow and shadow projection are very important here as are both archetypal psychology and the psychology of the autonomous complex.

(2) Spirituality in Social and Political Transformation—The problem of shadow projection underlies not only individual spiritual problems, but is at the heart of the causes underlying many of the social ills of our planet. The nuclear arms race, the poisoning of our environment, the easy acceptance of poverty and oppression, inter-religious hatred and violence—all are grounded in a falsification of the human consciousness which can be illuminated through the appropriation of resources from Jungian analysis. Evil, both personal and social, thrives when it can make itself invisible to those who would challenge it. If we are to confront the demonic as it is manifest in our social and political realities, then we must be able to break through its "cloaking devices." Psychoanalysis in general and Jungian analysis in particular offer powerful resources for the exposure of painful and transformative truth in our attempt to extend our spirituality beyond the realm of the private.

(3) The Importance of the Jungian Psychology of the Self—The uniqueness of the promise of Jung's psychology for contemporary spirituality, however, lies in the very structure of its metapsychology, in its fundamental conceptual structure and related clinical assumptions and technique. Jungian psychoanalysis is the only major school of contemporary psychology which grounds psychological maturity and fulfillment in the cultivation of a relationship between the conscious mind and a source of ego-transcending wisdom and guidance which lies beyond the realm of consciousness. Jungians acknowledge that the unconscious mind is more than just a storehouse of discarded unconscious memories too painful for the conscious mind to tolerate. The importance placed on the cultivation of a relationship between the ego consciousness and the deeper reality of the Self is an indication that a source of inner guidance is considered to be a psychological reality and one that cannot be ignored if psychological maturation—individuation—is a goal. The Jungian emphasis on the importance of the development of an "ego-Self axis" is an acknowledgement from the point of view of psychology of the

importance of the relativization of the pretensions of ego consciousness in human life and the location of a trans-egoic source of guidance for the individual on pilgrimage. This acknowledgement is unique in contemporary psychology. While a Jungian psychoanalyst speaking from within the disciplinary horizons of psychology cannot pronounce the manifestations of the Self to be manifestations of a Divine Reality, it is clear that the psychological reality being described corresponds to what, from a spiritual or theological perspective, has been called the God or Spirit within. From the point of view of the spiritual quest the essential truth attested to by both Jungian psychology and human spiritual tradition is that human life must find a center of guidance outside of the ego. Here Jungian psychology stands with spiritual tradition against the arrogant pretensions of the modern consciousness.

This series has been conceived to provide a forum for this important dialogue between Jungian psychoanalysis and contemporary spirituality, both Christian and non-Christian, in the hope that an important contribution may be made through this dialogue to the formation of the postmodern spirituality envisioned above. Through the series we intend to publish the writings of those contemporary leaders in human spirituality who have been the most creative in the utilization of perspectives from Jungian psychology in their analyses of issues confronting human spirituality and spiritual direction today. We will make available both collections of outstanding essays and creative monographs which are significant contributions to our topic. This first volume is an example of the former. Over the past few years my research staff and I have carefully combed the existing literature on Carl Jung and Christian spirituality with an eye toward finding those important essays which up to now have been available only in the form of journal articles and which, therefore, have had only a limited readership. It is our belief that the important work of these authors deserves the wider audience which this book will provide. The excellent essays included here cover topics ranging from theoretical reflections on important issues to essays on the application of Jungian concepts and techniques to religious practice. A second volume of these classic essays will soon be forthcoming.

We are also putting out a worldwide call for the best essays currently being written on topics relating Jungian psychoanalysis and contemporary spirituality, both Christian and non-Christian. It is our intention that in the years to come this Paulist Press series will provide a primary forum for those involved in the creation of a post-modern approach to human spirituality equal to the challenges of the twenty-first century.

Part One

M. Esther Harding

The Cross as an Archetypal Symbol

In its simplest and most obvious form "cross" refers only to a geometric arrangement of lines. That this form carries for all of us many underlying and overlying meanings depends first on its general usage. For instance, when we see a cross set up as a sign by the roadside we know it means: "Look out, there is a crossroad ahead." Or when we find it at the bottom of an arithmetic paper we know that we have got the wrong answer to the sum. In both these cases the cross is a sign carrying a well-known meaning, it is a sort of shorthand. But for all of us brought up in a Christian culture, the cross also reminds us of the crucifixion of a man nearly 2000 years ago. Though perhaps I am wrong about this. It would have been true in the tenth or twelfth centuries perhaps, but now when we see a cross set up over a building, we know the building is a Christian church, but I doubt whether most people recall immediately that its cross used to be a gallows, and so they do not feel the impact of the particular execution it commemorates.

If, however, when one encounters a cross in one's dreams, or sees it in a picture or a shrine, and its appearance produces an inner emotional experience, an impact that fascinates, awes, holds us, then we have to say that something beyond the mere sign, beyond the evoked memory even, has happened to us. For such an experience is alive *now*, in this very moment. Then the cross has become for us a symbol, and a *numinous* one. So here we come close to the meaning of the term archetypal. For the archetypes are the unseen patterns of psychic life on which, indeed, all psychic life is based, and they therefore carry the meaning and energy of life itself, while this symbol is the form in which its pattern is expressing itself. We can put this a little differently and say that the archetypes are the forms or patterns of a psychic nature, inherent in every man, that correspond on the psychic level to the patterns underlying the instincts that determine human behavior on the physiological level.

The term *numinous*, which I used above in connection with an impressive symbol, was brought into general usage in psychology by Rudolf Otto who described the *numinosum* in *The Idea of the Holy* as a dynamic agency of effect not caused by an arbitrary act of will, an experience of something that causes awe, fascination, dread and wonder. In his lectures on "Psychology and Religion," given at Yale in 1937, Jung, in speaking of the experience of the *numinosum*, pointed out that it seizes and controls the human being, so that he feels himself to be the victim of the experience and by no means its creator. When one encounters such an experience, whether one is confronted by it in a dream or in an objective situation, one cannot speak, one is helpless as a bird fascinated by a snake, or a rabbit caught in the headlights of a car on a dark night. Jung said there that "religious teaching as well as the *consensus gentium* always and everywhere explains this experience as being due to a cause external to the individual, whose presence causes a peculiar alteration of consciousness."[1] Indeed, Jung explains the sense in which he uses the term "religious" as referring to such numinous experiences. If one has never had any experience of this character, one may hold a belief, follow a creed, one may believe in the reality of religious teachings, but one does not *know*. It is to this that Jung was referring when, at the end of "Face to Face," the BBC filmed interview, he said, "I do not have to believe—I know."

Indeed, Jung defines a religious attitude as consisting in a careful and scrupulous attention given to such an object or value, for as he has pointed out, "Man is a religious animal." We can go a step further than this. For there is no people, no tribe, that we know of, that does not possess more or less organized religious teachings and rituals. And although today these sacred teachings may be in the possession of a priestly caste, yet obviously they originated from the *numinous experience* of individual men, that is, from individual subjective experiences. For there exists in man a genuine religious function in the unconscious, a function that manifests itself in dreams and fantasy images and in an inner attitude to symbolic pictures and happenings. It also reveals itself in certain urges and ritual acts and can be so powerful that it compels people to participate in or practice certain activities that are not concerned directly with visible objective situations, but rather with unseen potencies—spirits or demons, and above all with deities or gods.

It is with this side of human experience, or rather with certain aspects of it, that the archetypal nature of the cross is concerned. And in pursuing this question—this search, really—we have to explore the deeper layers of the unconscious, for this is where the motives and drives arise that underlie our conscious behavior, much as the instinctive behavior of an organism, whether animal or human, stems from unseen patterns inherent in the protoplasm of which it is made, and which cannot be bypassed or contradicted by an act of will, but can only be changed by a mutation occurring spontaneously—we know not why.

So long as we act and feel in the way that is customary in our society we do not usually inquire about the source of our motives. We take it for granted that the way we act is the way that "of course" anyone would act, assuming that our reaction is or should be universally recognized as right and valid. But surely this attitude means that we do not consider ourselves to be individuals, having a unique and individual experience and also a unique individuality that will necessarily meet every situation in life in a unique way. Rather we are regarding ourselves as merely one item in a collective group, one ant in the hill, one bee in the hive. Consequently we consider any action that is general, common to all, as necessarily right and indeed inevitable, for any normal individual. When this is our attitude we are slaves of the collective mores.

When we try to determine what in us is individual and what is collective we find ourselves facing a problem. For some of the experiences we encounter in life are universal, the small ones and the more significant ones too. Everyone meets them at some time or other. These can, of course, be discussed in a perfectly general way as part of the universal lot of mankind. Where then does the sense of being individual, that we all have, come from? When viewed dispassionately from the outside, most experiences seem to be alike for everyone, but this is not really so, for it is exactly these general or common happenings, like birth, marriage, death, joy and pain, that *feel* to the individual concerned to be the most personal, the most intimate, the most secret. That is to say, it is his *reaction* to the common happenings of life that distinguishes the individual from the herd. In *On Aggression* Konrad Lorenz says in effect that it is the unreasoning, emotional appreciation of values that adds a plus or minus sign to the findings and dictates of reason. And at this point there enters the possibility of making an individual choice. But it is just these emotional reactions about which the individual is most reticent. He cannot talk about them freely. "But why," asks Jung, "shouldn't he be able to talk freely? Why should he be afraid or shy or prudish? The reason is that he is 'carefully observing' certain external factors which together constitute what one calls public opinion or respectability or reputation. And even if he is in analysis and trusts his analyst and is no longer shy of him, he will be reluctant or even afraid to admit certain things to *himself*, as if it were dangerous to become conscious of *himself*. One is usually afraid of things that seem to be overpowering. But is there anything in man that is stronger than himself?"[2] Jung is talking here of cases of neurosis, where an unknown power has caused symptoms of physical illness or psychic anxiety. But his observations refer equally to individuals who are not neurotic. For there is, indeed, something in man that is stronger than his conscious ego, and in any deep exploration of the psyche sooner or later one encounters inner secret fears and anxieties regarding powerful factors beyond one's control—in other words one encounters the *numinosum*. These experiences, while they are universal, are yet extremely personal. They are not the same for everyone, for they are profoundly modified by the temperament and type of the experiencing subject, as well as by his sex and the outer conditions of his life, and perhaps most of all by his personal reactions to them, which depends so largely on the quality of his moral fiber.

Now the academic psychologist, and more especially the behaviorist, is content to observe how an individual reacts, overtly, to a situation. He makes a judgment of this person's psychology based on the data obtained in this way and disregards entirely the inner subjective side of the individual experience, as if the person were a robot. This, of course, is done in the interests of creating a so-called "scientific" psychology, capable of being checked by experiment and dealt with by statistics. It is a method that has proved useful in "industrial psychology," for instance, where the objective is to determine an applicant's probable reaction to definite conditions. It has also been used in education to set up "norms" of behavior at various age levels and unfortunately to judge the abilities of students by their reactions to the test situation.

But while these methods may be useful in classifying human beings, if one looks at them only from the outside, one is actually treating them as if they were mechanisms. Behaviorist psychology does exactly this. Jung calls it psychology with the psyche left out. Behaviorists disregard the inner subjective side of the experience the psychologist is studying, and so long as the study is confined to the "other fellow" it may seem to be quite satisfactory. On the basis of such observations one feels quite justified, in any quarrel or differ-ence of opinion with one's neighbor, in saying "Well you *are* like that!" giving him no chance to explain or justify the action under criticism because of his inner subjective attitude or condition. But, I think most of us would object most strenuously to having our own attitudes and actions, our thoughts and above all our feelings, ap-praised by such a method. For we each know, without any doubt at all, that we live an inner life, that we are motivated by unseen and indescribable factors—in effect, that we possess a psyche or spirit that is *not* to be measured by any external measure. Our greatest resentments, our deepest hurts, have resulted not infrequently from just such a judgment passed on us, for instance, by an unrealizing parent, when we were too small and insecure to protect ourselves.

So in writing about a common, even universal symbol like the cross I shall be obliged to refer to the subjective side of the psyche, about which people are usually very reticent, and this is especially so in its relations to the deeper layers of psychic experience, which depend on the not-personal elements of psychic or spiritual reality, which are mediated to consciousness through symbols—symbols not just of a personal nature but having a wider, even universal sig-nificance like the cross. Such symbols underlie the stories of folk tales and mythology, as well as the dogmatic teachings of religion, indeed especially of religious teachings, for the source of the symbol is unknown and so just because it is powerful, even numinous, man naturally anthropomorphizes its origin and feels the symbol is a rev-elation from a god. In passing, I must point out that folk customs are usually, if not always, the last secularized remnants of a ritual that was formerly part of a religious structure.

These are the symbols that Jung has called archetypal because they are based on ancient (arche-) types or patterns which exist in the unconscious structure of the psyche, corresponding to and also underlying the instincts which control physiological activity. In the psychic realm too, they exert an inescapable influence on the motivation of human behavior and inner subjective experience. Down the ages they have been expressed in legends and myths, and religious stories which have had a great influence on individual people and more especially on cultural development.

Now of course we do not know when or where these customs and stories started, but we do know that they must have arisen as creative inspirations from an unknown, that is an unconscious, part of the psyche of these earliest "first men."

We also know and can observe how similar myths arise and are lived out today in individuals who are facing apparently insoluble problems in their outer or their inner lives. So we are surely justified in postulating, as Jung does, a source of wisdom in the unconscious—a wisdom acquired through ages of experience transmitted to us through our inheritance. This inborn wisdom represents itself in the form of patterns of adaptation and of behavior. Such patterns have been observed and are now recognized by biologists as occurring regularly in the simplest living structures no less than in the highly organized ones. So it does not seem to be such a tremendous step to turn from unicellular organisms, for instance, to the psychic organization of highly developed mammals. It is these patterns that Jung calls *archetypes*. They are naturally unseen and unknown as such, but their presence and their power can be observed in consciousness through symbols—images and symbolic actions—which appear in consciousness, though their source remains unknown.

It is as if in the unknown protoplasm of the cell, or in the unknown, unconscious layers of the psyche, there were certain sparks of light illuminating tiny fragments of the mysterious happening. The Sethians, a gnostic sect, knowledge of whose writings we owe to Hippolytus, held that within the darkness was a spark of light,[3] a scintilla, an idea that occurs also in Meister Eckhart, who called these scintillae soul sparks, while many of the alchemists used this same image in describing their experiences of the dark abyss, the chaos in its aspect of *nigredo*, darkness or depression, when they said that it contained sparks or scintillae of light like "fishes' eyes."

These sparks we are told are like a light within the darkness, which illuminates it from within. Jung has suggested that these light-sparks can be equated with the symbols that arise spontaneously in the deep unconscious in the form of archetypal images—images that illuminate the dark and hidden depths of the psyche. So that an archetypal symbol in a dream is to be understood as a spark of light illuminating an otherwise completely dark region of the unconscious psyche. I have occasionally observed dreams in which globules of light rose like bubbles out of a dark pool and broke through into the air. These dreams occurred at the end of a long period of introversion in which the dreamer had gone down deeply into the unconscious and emerged with a new understanding.

Jung's suggestion that the light sparks are like the archetypal images which we meet in the course of a deep introversion is a most helpful analogy. Eckhart called them "little soul sparks" and Dorn, a sixteenth century alchemist, said the soul sparks were like fishes' eyes, and that the fish's eye is none other than the shining eye of the sun which plunges its center into the heart of man.[4] So that to Dorn, the spark of light "in the heart of man," corresponding to the unconscious, comes from the sun, which to Dorn was a symbol of the diety.

Surely this corresponds to the teaching that God created man in his own image, so that *his* image is to be found within man and not only outside in the outer universe. But *that "within"* is also in one sense outside, for it is in the unconscious realm, which is just exactly *not* the conscious part of the psyche, the ego, which man calls "I."

One of the difficulties we encounter in trying to bring the findings of two different disciplines together stems from the different use of terms. This is especially true of the attempt to correlate the data of religious experience and the findings of psychology. For instance, in religious teaching an inspiration, an inner voice, a revelation, that is, a new understanding or enlightenment, is explained as coming from a being—God, or a spirit—external to man. While experiences of this character are not disregarded or considered untrue by analytical psychologists, they are yet not ascribed to a being outside man, but rather are considered as manifestations of the unconscious, that is, of the objective psyche. The psychologist does not ascribe them to a person or being but leaves the question of their origin to the metaphysician, and confines himself to their observation and the exploration of their meaning. For inspirations and similar phenomena, regardless of what may be their source, are experienced by man as an inner occurrence, that is, they are psychological experiences and as such are available for study by psychology. These, too, follow certain patterns which are themselves unseen and inaccessible to observation except through their manifestation in dreams and visions. These are the psychic patterns that Jung has called archetypes, and their typical manifestation is in symbols and mythologems occurring in dreams and other unconscious products, including rituals spontaneously produced by individuals or groups to deal with situations where unseen powers are felt to be active, or when it is beyond the power of the conscious ego to control some situation effectively. For instance, the American Indian danced the bear dance to attract the bear when he wanted to hunt him, and at the same time the bear dance put the hunter himself into the mood for hunting. A similar method is used when a psychological danger has to be met, and liturgical prayers and ritual acts are used to mobilize the right attitude in the devotee, though they may be explained as attempts to change the attitude of the deity, who is believed to have been offended. In these cases it has always been felt that the ritual acts must be performed in the ancient, well-established way. The ritual must be faithfully observed or it will not be effective. Of course this means that an archetypal form has to be followed—only so will the unconscious take note, or the deity be appeased—this is what is expressed in the deep feeling of the necessity to perform the rite correctly. It is part of the religious attitude.

I hope that these few examples will demonstrate sufficiently what we mean by the archetypes and the archetypal patterns. Now these patterns of psychic life which we call archetypes are, so far as we know, universal, being the very basis of psychic functioning. Some of them can even be observed in the higher animals, but we will restrict ourselves to their influence in the human psyche. There is no human being in whom they do not exist; they are apparently the same for all men of whatever race or color. However, the symbolic forms in which they express themselves are modified by the cultural background of the particular individual. So, for instance, Joseph Campbell points out that those tribes who derive from a hunting and warring, primitive or archaic people have rituals and myths that differ markedly from those of a people whose ancestors, in the remote past, were pastoral in their mode of life. Yet, even so, the basic patterns are in each case characteristically human.

It appears that when a culture based on certain archetypal symbols grows old not only does the culture eventually die, but the religious symbols on which the culture was based also disappear—fall into the unconscious and are either not remembered at all or persist in secularized form, or possibly the religious ritual survives but in a degenerated and degraded form, as for instance the witch cults and devil worship of the middle ages, where the deity, Dionysus in this case, the god of the very ecstasy of life, had reversed himself and become a destructive devil. Meantime the archetypal image is replaced by a new symbolic form that has the power to engage man's allegiance through its numinous character, and this becomes the center of a new religion or cult, which will grow and flourish for a certain time only to be replaced by a new form when, in its turn, it withers away, having lost its power to attract the devotion of the people. And so we encounter the phenomenon of the "death of God," which has recurred over and over again in the course of history. ("Great Pan is dead!")

The statement that "God is dead" can be used in two entirely different senses. The cross itself signifies that God, in the person of the god-man, Jesus, was killed and suffered a voluntary death followed by a resurrection, so that the death was an experience, an episode, in the continuing life of the god-man. The same idea is expressed in the stories of many of the ancient gods: Dionysus sacrificed and torn to pieces in his form of Zagreus, the bull, Adonis, Tammuz, Osiris, to mention but a few of the gods of antiquity known as the dying and resurrecting gods.

But this is not the sense in which the phrase "the death of God" is being used by a fairly large group of people today. They maintain that God and the very concept of a deity is dead. The subjective value that the conception of God held, however, has not been destroyed. It must be looked for elsewhere than in the heavens.

When anyone feels that God is dead he is naturally thrown back onto himself and will look for his satisfaction in the outer or extraverted world, on the basis of the old saying, "Let us eat and drink, for tomorrow we die." But a life based on such a premise will be utterly barren, banal and boring. Sooner or later one will discover that one has no appetite for eating and drinking—if we may use those activities metaphorically. The fact is that the satisfaction of one's appetites simply cannot satisfy indefinitely, even when appetite is used in its widest sense to include ambition, power, sex, fun or pleasure of all kinds and degrees—these all eventually pall. This is what happens when one views life from the point of view of the ego and evaluates it simply in terms of ego-consciousness.

But if we begin to explore the unconscious in persons who are in distress, even despair, because their lives are so narrow and limited that the whole of life seems to have become meaningless, we find that symbols that carried meaning for earlier people begin to appear in their dreams, symbols of former cultures, perhaps, and as we go deeper and deeper into the unconscious these symbols tend to become more and more archaic, more and more basic, until at length we may actually encounter what van der Post calls "the first man in us"—to whom life was an adventure and was filled to overflowing with meaning. Such a symbolic form may have power to regenerate the individual, on the historic level it may even bring new life to the people. For such a discovery means that one has stumbled upon the "ancient road" of the psyche, and life moves forward again. This is perhaps one meaning of Christ's saying that he came to bring us more abundant life.

The old road, the old way, has been trodden by man and his brothers the animals before him, for ages and ages, and has led this blind creature—man—from the darkness of unconscious functioning safely through all the perils of the way till he has reached his present powers of mind and heart. For such *ways* are archetypal "built in" patterns of instinctual functioning and of psychic experience.

This is the place where psychology encounters the collective problem of the age while still searching for a solution for one individual's suffering. Communities, nations, peoples, the human race itself, are all made up of individuals, and any satisfactory solution of local or world problems must involve a prior solution of individual problems, at least in a few "seed" persons.

From these findings we postulate that the unconscious itself is built up in successive layers representing former ways, earlier cultural forms, corresponding to the successive cultural layers unearthed by archeologists. So that, from one point of view, we can say the unconscious is the same for everybody—and this indeed it is, provided you go back far enough—but at the same time members of different groups, different cultures, will find images characteristic of their own history and the history of their ancestors during an exploration of the unconscious.

Beyond this, obviously, the form the symbolic image takes in a given individual is likely to be something with which he is familiar. For instance, in the dreams of a man of long ago, a threatening hostile force might be represented as a wild beast. A modern dreamer however might find himself being pursued, not by a rhinoceros or a mastodon, but by a truck or some such modern mechanism. One sees the same thing in art, especially in cartoons, where a locomotive may play the part of a dragon.

This will serve to answer the question that is so often asked as to whether Jung postulated a *racial* unconscious or not. In his early writing Jung did use the word *racial*, by which he meant the whole race of man, and it was not until this term began to be misunderstood, some 20 years later, when a new interpretation was put on the word by the Nazis, that any question arose as to its meaning. By that time Jung had replaced the term *racial* by *collective:* and when again the term *collective* came into disrepute through its use by the Communists he started using *objective* to designate that part of the psyche that is outside the personal sphere. Meanwhile his understanding of this extra-personal psychic sphere and his researches in connection with it had enlarged the concept enormously, as can easily be seen by comparing his earlier writings with the later ones in which his early concepts are not contradicted or discarded, but are shown to be more far-reaching and much more profound than he had at all realized in his younger years. For Jung continued to grow psychologically right up to his death at the age of 85.

But it still is not usually realized that what we experience subjectively does not all arise from the personal psyche. There are within us elements that have never been known by us; they are not merely repressed or forgotten contents, but are completely new, so far as our personal lives are concerned. This is one of the things that makes a personal analysis so exciting and so meaningful. But in spite of the fact that most people have experiences, from time to time, of thoughts and feelings and fantasies which have just *happened* to them, they yet tend to feel responsible for all their psychic contents. That there may be elements within their psyche that they did not "make" may even be denied by very rational people. For such persons are convinced that they know what is in their own psyche, even that they know what is or is not in their unconscious—which is obviously a contradiction in terms, to say the least of it. But if instead of repressing his fantasies such a person should begin to allow them to come to consciousness, he might meet with contents he has *not* invented or made up, and sometimes this is a distinctly disturbing experience.

The United States is increasingly torn by disturbances of the orderly, peaceful way of life. The whole population is in grave conflict and uncertainty. It is as though the nation—possibly the whole world—were standing at a crossroads. Is the solution to be found by going to the right or to the left? But this is too simple a statement of the situation. It would perhaps have been a valid description of the similar situation in the 1940s, when the issue seemed to be summed up in the political conflict between regimentation by an authority, ultimately fascism, or on the other hand a move to the left, i.e., a move toward communism. Today the situation is far more crucial. It is not just a matter of politics. We are caught in a profound moral and ethical dilemma, which is often epitomized in the issue of war, or social injustice, or religious terms of a fundamental kind. You notice in speaking of this problem I use such words as *crossroads*, suggesting a choice of one way or another, its opposite. For you cannot go partly to the right while also walking to the left. I also characterize the more fundamental problem as *crucial*, suggesting that a choice must be made between most serious issues, and that this choice would involve suffering and possibly sacrifice. But even these words are not adequate to express the state of indecision and conflict that haunts all thinking people of goodwill. Indeed, now that the issues have become so much clearer, and the far-reaching extent of the problem is being more and more realized, we have to say that we are actually ourselves, as well as the nation as a whole, *impaled on a cross*. For there is no way either to the right or to the left that can release us from our uncertainty, no political or social resolution or enactment that could allow us to go peacefully back to our personal concerns with a clear conscience.

In a sense, happy are those who can salve their consciences by engaging in a crusade through peace marches and protests, or by subscriptions to charitable organizations whose appeal for funds, frequently containing promises of the solution or amelioration of wrongs, clutter up our desks and frequently our wastebaskets. Good as these efforts to tackle one or another facet of the universal problem undoubtedly are, yet they do not, cannot, solve the problem for us. Mass media, mass movements even, can at best do no more than alert the public to the fundamental fact that "the times are out of joint."

We are impaled on a cross. We cannot get free. The problem is too big and we are each so small. Immediately we jump to the conclusion that if only we could get a whole lot of people to take the road which we personally think the most promising, that would at least afford relief in that aspect of the situation we are most deeply concerned with; something could be done about it. And of course each "litter bit helps," as the Sanitation Department of New York City keeps reminding us; but people in the mass do not therefore put their litter in the baskets provided for the purpose. For instance, we recently celebrated Earth Day, to emphasize the need to do something about pollution of the air, the water, the highways, the forests and parks. It was celebrated by a mass holiday, children and adults swarming down all the avenues of New York. I happened to have business on Fifth Avenue. It was one mass of happy holiday crowds—a delightful sight. But the next day we were told it would take practically all the clean-up men of the Sanitation Department two full days to clear up the mess! No! Mass action cannot be counted on to do the job.

Or take the peace movement. A friend of mine asked me if I was going to join one of the marches on Washington. I replied I was not at all sure that immediate withdrawal of troops from Vietnam was the right thing to do. I know so little, really, about the situation and our commitments and moral involvements in East Asia, that I certainly could not embarrass the government by any attempt to coerce them. My friend immediately replied, "Do you then *approve* of war?" Now she is a fine woman of good intelligence. She belongs to that group of people who believe in peace at any price, even if they have to fight for it. Yet they are among the finest, they are moral people. Their action, their stand is taken at considerable personal risk, they are willing to accept even prison for their principles. But I am sorry to say that even those whom one would think would have greater insight often get caught in the pitfall of thinking that their way is the only possible right and moral one. They forget that if we choose only the right and the good the shadow within ourselves will be projected upon the *other*. For no morally sensitive person would claim to be all light, having no darkness at all within him.

There is still another danger of such blindness. For if you depend on the size of any movement you will inevitably find that the moral standard drops proportionately to the size of the group. If one belongs to a large organization one finds oneself obliged to concur in decisions about which one has the gravest doubts. And when a very large mass of people begin to unite or to follow a leader on some course of action, some crusade (again note the use of the word *cross*), the group will degenerate into a crowd, and the crowd into a mass, and if they find, as they usually do, a leader more completely convinced than the majority of the need to do something about it, they will shortly be a mob, with a mob's blind obedience to the leader. This also we see today in the student riots, for instance, where there are a few organized revolutionaries, many truly concerned and disturbed students and many many others who are not concerned particularly with the issues, but come out for the lark.

Certainly mass movements can cause changes, upheavals, and so on; but what guarantee have we that the result will be favorable? You remember Mark Antony's speech at the funeral of Caesar. Now he was an adherent of Caesar and had been attacking his assassins, some of whom were at least, like Brutus, really true and sincere reformers, of the highest moral calibre, who had yet been caught up into a revolutionary movement led by men of whom he could not approve. After his speech Mark Antony too found himself caught in a counterrevolutionary movement and exclaimed, "Now let bloody treason flourish over us." For the symbol of law and order had gone. And indeed in the years that followed Caesar's death, disaster and carnage flourished. Only the extreme revolutionaries want such a thing to happen here, and one cannot but think that the young men who have fallen under the spell of the revolutionary idea do not really want any such outcome either, but they can bring it down upon us, all the same, if they persist in riots and arson and noncooperation. For a city, a university or a country can only function in a democratic society if each works not only for his private well-being but also for the good of the whole.

The crucial question for all of us in the Western world is whether or not the cross as an archetypal symbol offers us a solution of the problem. The cross of Christianity did just that; it gave a solution in terms of Christ's sacrifice, his death and resurrection. But many people are no longer able to avail themselves of a vicarious sacrifice. Today it is we ourselves who are impaled on the cross. We face a modern version of an age-old problem and we need a truly modern solution for it.

Notes

1. Jung, C. G.: *Psychology and Religion* (Collected Works, Vol. 11), Princeton University Press (Bollingen Series XX), 1958, par. 6.
2. *Ibid.*, par. 12.
3. Jung, C. G.: *Mysterium Coniunctionis* (Collected Works, Vol. 14), Princeton University Press (Bollingen Series XX), 1963, par. 42.
4. *Ibid.*, par. 45.

Eugene C. Bianchi

Jungian Psychology
and Religious Experience

The article explores five zones of conflict and promise for Christian theological development in dialogue with Jungian thought. The first conflictual area concerns subjective and objective understandings of religious teachings. Jung's approach to symbolism is examined in order to show ways of linking subjective and objective dimensions. The second point of argument focuses on the problem of human effort and the receptivity of faith. Jung's individuation process is shown to be akin to aspects of the act of faith. In the third section, attention centers on the issue of divine transcendence over against the stress on immanence in Jungian psychology. Similarities and differences between the concepts of God and the Self are discussed. The fourth problem relates to the tension between the authentically religious and the demonic in theology and psychology. The Jungian Shadow is dealt with in the context of suffering and evil. The final section investigates Jung's imaginal methodology as a valuable corrective to rationalism and as an experiential juncture for religion and psychology.

For over half a century, Carl Jung's psychology has been a source of both commentary and controversy in theological circles.[1] The principal appeal of Jung to religious thinkers has been the promise of integrating psychic depths with religious meaning. The Jungian approach addresses the theological quest since Schleiermacher, that is, how intrinsically to relate an ancient religious heritage to individual and social development in an age of scientific consciousness. Yet precisely because analytical or depth psychology borders on the religious domain, it has stimulated intense opposition among theologians. They have accused Jung of many theological "sins" culminating in reductionism, that capital offense which reduces religion to psychology and religious practice to psychotherapy. For these critics, Jung's theory and practice of individuation through the reconciliation of opposites in the psyche takes the place of authentic religion. Theological idiom is decoded into therapeutic language, leaving religion with as much reality as the fading smile on a cosmic Cheshire Cat.

By delving into this disputed terrain, I do not intend to bring about a resolution among contending parties. Rather I proceed on the premise that it is valuable for contested areas to remain in turmoil. For in the ferment between psychology and religion, new perspectives may be shaped and refined. Therefore, I briefly explore five zones of pain and promise for theological development in dialogue with Jungian thought. I presuppose a basic knowledge of both analytical psychology and Christian theology in order to avoid a tedious definition of rudimentary terms. Moreover, I should confess at the outset a bias in favor of the Jungian direction for integrating religion and psychology. The longer I study this field, however, the more cogently do discontinuities and inadequacies come into focus. The division of the essay into five dialectical headings underscores the continuing tensions between Jungian psychology and Christian theology. These polarities overlap; yet they are distinct enough to underline different places of controversy.

I. SUBJECTIVE-OBJECTIVE

In the modern period, shifting understandings of the inner-subjective and outer-historical realms have provided a constant area of controversy between religion and psychology. The epistemological issue of subjective and objective experience is as old as philosophy. With the development of modern psychology, inwardness of mind or soul has been pursued to new depths of conscious and unconscious life. Jung's therapeutic enterprise manifests an intensely subjective emphasis. Moreover, his own temperament, as well as his attempts to resolve personal mental dilemmas, impelled Jung to embrace the subjective approach. In the course of rejecting his pastor father's objectified Christian doctrine, Jung translated religious symbols into a psychological idiom. He claimed to have found that religious symbols well up in humans from the deepest reaches of the unconscious. For Jung the human unconscious constitutes a major means of religious revelation. Jung distinguishes between the psychological aspects of archetypical statements and their objects which may have ontological reality. He asserts that he stays within the limited categories of a psychologist; that he avoids the mantle of a metaphysician. Contrary to his protestations, however, Jung also makes theological claims; it is precisely these areas that form the rich subjective orientation of his psychoreligious thought.

Against this perspective, a long Western tradition stresses the objective and historical aspects of revealed religion. Through the centuries, Christian theology reiterated that saving religious symbols were announced in the life and preaching of Jesus and fostered in a visible church. Of course, it has never been an either/or matter between subjective and objective concerning religious symbols. But these ultimately distinct foci remain as unresolved and controversial points.

An etymological approach to "symbol" and "religion" may help to clarify Jung's subjective orientation. A sign points to an outer, objective reality ordinarily graspable by human reason. A symbol links us to a relatively unknown inward reality.[2] Etymologically, symbol means a throwing together. For Jung, the symbolic images (presented by patients in dreams, fantasies and by other means) were expressions in consciousness of the unconscious, both personal and collective. The symbol, therefore, is an empowering message that bridges conscious and unconscious life. The word "unconscious," although generally accepted among professionals, confuses persons who interpret it as a static faculty. It may help in this regard to speak of the depths of the mind or psyche, those regions not readily accessible to ego consciousness. In contrast to Freud, Jung maintained that this symbolic activity had much more extensive and positive functions than that of merely disguising data repressed from infancy. Symbols have a compensatory and creative function. They assist persons to overcome one-sidedness, and they incline toward a fuller reconciliation of opposites in the psyche. Thus symbolic images arising from the unconscious have the teleological function of aiding a person to pursue goals and meaning in life.

The semantic root of "religion," *religio*, indicates a "tying back" or a rejoining. The symbolic images from the unconscious allow us to encounter within ourselves, to be re-linked to, the numinous depths of our own being. Jung used the term "numinous" in ways similar to Rudolf Otto (as powerfully attractive as well as awe-inspiring); yet Jung also psychologized the numinous much more than Otto. Not that every symbolic image can be classified as numinous or transcendent; but Jung found that certain archetypical images presented by analysands in the course of therapy related closely to the symbolism of ancient and modern religions, east and west, as well as to alchemy and to other philosophical or metaphysical sources. Thus religious dogmas for Jung became symbolic expressions in the consciousness of a given historical epoch of the unconscious depths in the evolutionary march of peoples. Great religious leaders were able to communicate to followers in gripping ways the insights of the founder's symbolic activity in his/her dreams and visions.

Through myth and ritual, religious organizations mediated the original experiences of the founding group for successive generations. On the negative side of the ledger, religious institutions, in order to preserve and control their following, have curtailed the inward spiritual journey for many. But on the positive side, organized religions through scripture, preaching, ritual and pastoral activity, have had beneficial effects. For Jung they protected people from being overwhelmed by psychic symbols of depth. They also provided opportunity for the creative evocation of depth experiences through traditional religious images, doctrines and activities. But in the Jungian perspective, the autonomous dimensions of the collective unconscious or the objective psyche are the revelatory wellsprings of external religion. In this sense the church, as objective religious institution, becomes the handmaid of the psyche.

The direction of the symbolic way is toward an inner religiousness, a quest for inward meaning. The person is called to move beyond the ordered securities, patterned by family and church in childhood, to risk confrontation with the unpredictable numinous of archetypical symbols in the psyche. These archetypical dispositions of the collective unconscious are mediated and shaped in distinctive ways according to the experiences of each individual's personal unconscious. Thus archetypical images such as mother, father, anima and animus, constellate in particular ways in keeping with the biographical conditioning of each person. In more technical

language,   archetypal images of the collective unconscious become nuclei of complexes in the personal unconscious. I do not intend to pursue this specialized therapeutic aspect of the relationship
between collective and personal unconscious. The main point for
our purposes is that the archetypical images of the collective unconscious are filtered through personal and historical conditioning. In
this sense, the symbolic way manifests a secondary but important
historical-objective dimension.

Jungians point out other aspects of the historical rootage of their
inward approach. The presupposition of this psychology is that the
psychically real is eminently historical. Jungian anthropology places
humankind within the long, evolutionary progression of the species.
Jung himself became a lifelong student of primitive folkways, mythologies and religions. He strove to comprehend how, on both an
individual and communal level, the archetypes of the psyche were
evoked and commemorated in myth and ritual. His studies of alchemy and other esoterical systems can be seen as ventures for linking nature, as concrete and historical, with mind. Cross-cultural
exploration of the psyche has led to forms of universalism in dealing
with religious experience. Theologians of strongly particularistic
persuasions have found Jung's pluralistic/universalistic penchant especially challenging to their beliefs. An example of such controversy
has arisen over the Jungian use of the Christ as a symbol of the universal Self. Christianity identified Christ exclusively with Jesus and
thus anchored religion in the historical. But what this heritage
gained in specificity it sacrificed in possibilities for universal exten-
sion.

Jung would maintain that his psychology was not only historical in terms of horizontal progression through time, but that it was
also grounded in the concrete social fabric. Archetypes are a residue
of the experiential heritage of the species. Through these images, individuals are enabled to relate to the group, to become socialized.
This socialization will be modified in countless ways in keeping with
the cultural modalities of basic archetypes such as those of mother,
child, father or God. Yet it is precisely in this cultural shaping of
the archetypes that a serious danger was perceived by Jung. He
feared that persons would become slaves to an external collectivity,
to archetypical images dictated by power-hungry leaders in the in-

terests of their own domination. Jung experienced the collective mind at work in the cataclysms of two world wars. Thus his stress on individual therapy and inner growth was not a denial of the social matrix of archetypical psychology. No doubt, his inclination toward individual renewal was partially dictated by both his own introverted personality and by the style of the therapeutic art of psychiatry as he knew it. But he also believed that society would be better if individuals achieved a stronger appreciation of their own inner needs and promptings. The person who had attained a deeper reconciliation between ego and Self within would be less susceptible to mass ideologies.

Although historical and objective aspects exist in Jungian thought, conservatively orthodox forms of Western religion continue to find it unacceptable. To embrace its subjective approach to revelation calls for a serious reversal of previous tenets. The same would hold for all forms of contemporary neo–orthodoxy as derived from the Barthian movement. While objective dimensions of revelation are not eliminated, the subordination of the latter to subjective revelation is perceived as unnecessary and undesirable. Such subordination is seen as apostasy and as leading to the relativity of all values. Religion appears to be man-made and its promises nugatory in life and after death. Some liberal religious thinkers, on the contrary, see the Jungian perspective as a way of integrating religious symbols into the life of the psyche or soul. For them, institutional preaching, ritual and other ministry continue to possess important but ancillary functions in evoking, shaping and refining religious symbolism stemming from psychic depths.

The Jungian view contains its own peril of moving from subjective understanding to subjectivism. It is not sufficient to assert with Jung that religious symbolism is objective inasmuch as it arises from the collective unconscious with its own autonomous existence. While worthy in some ways, the latter argument suffers from the one-sidedness that Jung wanted to avoid in the process of individuation. Symbolic causation thus appears to proceed almost exclusively from the inward to outward, from the unconscious to myth and ritual. Needed is a more subtle causal explanation which would at once respect the relative autonomy of the unconscious and yet provide wider scope for the influence of external, religious activities of the soul. Archetypal psychology needs to take more seriously the impressive findings of cultural anthropology.

Anthropological literature from Emile Durkheim to Mary Douglas and Victor Turner stresses external, societal causes of religious symbols and beliefs. Some of these schools of anthropology have fallen into their own types of social reductionism concerning religion. Yet the evidence for external and social fashioning of religious symbolism is too extensive to be ignored by either analytical psychology or Christian theology. To say that religious activity simply evokes archetypical material already present in the soul results in a teaching similar to the ancient view of innate ideas. It is closer to the truth to affirm that religious education through worship, study and ministry significantly shapes the archetypes as these rise to consciousness. If external causality is not appreciated, moreover, a Jungian religiousness can lead to a diminishing of community responsibility. Individuation is not intended as a road to individualism; concern for personal uniqueness does not exclude being in tune with others. But the inward preoccupation of therapy can submerge social consciousness and civic responsibility.

II. RECEPTIVE-INITIATORY

A number of popular psychotherapies, influenced in part by the spirit of technology, advocate self-initiative toward human growth. Assertiveness Training and the EST therapy represent such movements. Jungian psychotherapy by contrast promotes a more receptive style that cultivates imaginal listening. In this perspective, important analogies occur between the act of faith as understood by theological traditions in the West and the Jungian experience of dialogue between consciousness and the unconscious. Christian theology as well as Jungian psychology admit self-effort in the process of disposing a person for spiritual growth. Yet theology teaches that what is revealed as an invitation to believe has an autonomous source. Faith is not at its deepest level an act of human will. The thinking-willing person is beckoned by what is seen as a divine initiative. The act of religious faith, therefore, demands the priority of grace; it is a gift to be accepted or rejected. Furthermore, it follows that the act of faith must be a free response, liberated from coercion of all types. Finally, faith is not simply an individual response isolated from community. Rather it is a radically communal happening by which the trusting initiate embraces the vision and ethic of a family of faith. This community of faith in turn assumes a responsibility of care and service toward its members.

These four dimensions of the faith act: autonomy of source, priority of grace, freedom of response, and communal matrix appear in the therapeutic experience. The unconscious is an autonomous zone in the psyche; symbolic activity presents itself to consciousness but is not fully created by the ego. In comparison to other contemporary systems of therapy, the Jungian approach is less ego-directed. In this system, it is said that persons welcome messages from the depths of the psyche as gifts, although not always immediately pleasant ones. The process of individuation proceeds more by serendipity than by striving. Freedom to follow one's inner destiny is also essential. The therapist is not an interpreter of dreams and other phenomena from the unconscious. On the contrary, the analyst is understood as an aide to the dreamer's own interpretation and decision for action. The whole point of therapy is to strengthen a person to choose freely according to profound appeals from one's inner self. In the language of William James, one moves beyond "faith in someone else's faith" to a personally appropriated creed and choice. But this is not a solipsistic endeavor, as if we fashioned a holistic life on a purely individualistic plane. For the images and promptings from within stem from a collective unconscious. We respond, within the mold of our own personal and national culture, to a universal community of images. Moreover, the symbols that rise to challenge us have a fundamentally benevolent purpose, namely, the balancing and deepening of the contending energies of our lives.

The point of this fourfold comparison of Jung's religio-symbolic experience with the act of faith does not imply a perfect correspondence between the two. Analogies can often be misleading. Theologians would emphasize the differences between psychological and religious faith. They would point out that the autonomous source of faith is God not the unconscious. A theologian favorable to the Jungian enterprise might reply that God, as source of faith, is present within the psyche as the Self. Even if this point were granted, however, the content of faith, that which is believed, would seem to differ. For example, a Christian contends that his faith is in the transforming power of Christ to save his soul. But we could ask what prevents such a faith content from being understood symbolically in the inner process of individuation. That is, I am empowered to become the "Christ" that I am called to be. The traditional believer might affirm a stronger assurance for his faith, as it appears to have less admixture of the subjective. Yet Jung himself attested to a powerful assurance from his experience of the numinous within.

The other aspects of the act of faith, unmerited gift and freedom of response, present their own difficulties in analogy with Jungian psychology. How do we know whether the revelation from the unconscious is healing or destructive, a gift or a curse? The Jungian would answer that the revelation is beneficial if it contributes to the wholeness or completion of personality. How free is the client's response in reference to an analyst's suggestions? Was the apparent faith experience induced by the therapist? Similar questions about the freedom of an act of faith could also be put to the traditional believer who is influenced by preaching or other inducements to believe. It would be easier to fault the Jungian perspective concerning the community dimension of the faith experience. Although archetypes represent a communal inheritance, a community of persons becomes less significant in the Jungian outlook; whereas in traditional religion the fellowship of believers engenders a faith-oriented environment through ritual, preaching and good example. Moreover, the accumulated spiritual wisdom of the faith community acts as a guide in distinguishing between authentic and spurious faith.

These similarities and differences on the question of the act of faith open possibilities for fruitful dialogue between theology and psychology. Without recourse to facile harmonizing, we can say that the theology of faith relates more intrinsically to psychic processes than was traditionally thought. The polemic against the Christianity espoused by his father alienated Jung from subtly appreciating traditional theology. Theologians, on the other hand, are excessively fearful of psychologizing away religion. Yet the dialectic between receptivity and initiation in the act of faith pervades both soul and psyche, terms that may, indeed, be synonymous.

III. IMMANENCE-TRANSCENDENCE

The tensions between Jungian psychology and Christian theology focus acutely on the subject of immanence and transcendence. As a therapist, Jung claimed to discover the deepest Self of a patient in veiled symbolic form. His descriptions of the Self sound like those of an indwelling God. He himself spoke of the Self as the God-image within. Jung's thinking, therefore, moved toward an immanent understanding of a God-like force or presence at the center of the human psyche. Theologians, especially those of conservative stamp, underscore the sovereign transcendence of God. To them Jung's doctrine of the Self smacks of pantheism or of an inflated humanism that borders on pride. Without a fuller assessment of both Jung's teaching on the Self and the theology of God, discussants seldom meet on the same plane. What is worse, the discussants become adversaries who choose sides for either immanence or transcendence. Although the topics of immanence and transcendence are vast, a few descriptions and distinctions may uncover ground for a rewarding interplay between psychology and theology.

For Jung, the major religious symbol of the psyche (psyche includes conscious as well as unconscious life) in each individual is the Self. This is the central and deepest point of the unconscious. Since the Self is the heart of the autonomous, objective psyche, it always remains beyond the grasp of reason to define or exhaustively explain. Transcending any such description, it can only be metaphorically expressed as the principle of coordination among opposites, the fire within, or the God image in the soul. The Self is also spoken of with the imagery of wholeness, such as that of the mandala. The Self is the prime symbol of individuation, that process of achieving greater personal wholeness through gradual reconciliation of opposites. The Self acts as a unifying principle which helps us overcome one-sided tendencies in our personalities; the Self also leads us on, sometimes through difficult circumstances, to fuller achievements of our potential. The tension of opposites never disappears in the course of life, but the Self within each person summons toward wholeness in which the polarities can be more creatively unified.

In this process, the Self maintains a dialogical and dialectical relationship with ego consciousness in each individual. For as each

person in the course of life moves away from infancy's union of undifferentiated consciousness (the *participation mystique* of womb life
and early childhood), specific ego identity is fashioned. Here I
would embellish the Jungian theme by saying that the self-conscious
ego soon realizes the precariousness of existence in the face of death
and other threats. Just as the ego incurs existential guilt in the necessary process of alienating itself from identity with its original maternal source, it also ignores or struggles against the promptings of
the Self that call to wholeness. Life on the level of ego-consciousness
thus becomes a single-minded task of attaining safety and satisfaction for the individual or the family. The all-absorbing quest for survival, material comfort and self-valuation through outward acclaim
is especially heightened in technological society. For the technological accomplishments of our culture give a pseudoassurance of protection against threats to human life.

Yet the depths of the Self will not be denied. Jung found that
mental crises in adult life stem frequently from a pervading sense of
meaninglessness. For many, the styles and promises of ego consciousness in contemporary society eventually succumb to a sense of futil-
ity. In extreme cases the alienated ego collapses into serious
depression or identifies with the Self in a dangerous idolatrous inflation. It is not difficult to relate these aberrations to modern forms of
depression and schizophrenia. Yet these very mental problems can
become occasions for alerting individuals to take steps against the de-
feating pursuit of one-sided ego goals. Through such mental crises,
the ego is invited to go inward and establish a hard but healing dia-
logue/dialectic with long-neglected archetypical symbols, centered in
the chief image of the Self. But the ego must learn again to listen to and
approach with humility the indirect messages from the depths. This
therapeutic process of individuation will be distinctive for each person. Individuation through the dialogue between ego and Self has
been described as an intrapsychic manner of translating or interpreting classic religious patterns of alienation and reconciliation.[3]

A key source of difficulty for interpreting religious experience
in a Jungian perspective has arisen from the close association of the
Self symbol with the transcendent deity of religions. The Self has
been referred to as the God-image in the soul of each person. Martin
Buber and other thinkers have severely criticized Jung for appearing

to reduce the transcendent God to the confines of the human psyche, and thus to subordinate religion to psychology. This is seen as the ultimate denial of authentic religion. Jung's written language, at times imprecise, inconsistent and polemical, could lead the reader to conclude that God is fully known and contained in the psyche. But a closer study of the evidence belies such a conclusion. It is particularly difficult, however, for Western religionists to appreciate the Jungian distinction between Self and God because of the fear of psychologizing away the distinctively religious. This anxiety stems from an inability to distinguish and to interrelate history and psyche, external reality and subjective life.

Two considerations may help us appreciate the distinction between God and the psyche in Jungian psychology. First, we do not know directly any of the archetypical images; it is only indirectly through partial yet inexhaustible symbols that the depths are revealed in numinous experience. Secondly, and of even greater consequence, the Self is understood as a God-image (*imago Dei*) or central numinous symbol in the psyche. Jung attempts to avoid identifying the Self with the transcendent God; dealing with the transcendent and "metaphysical" God, according to Jung, is the work of the theologian. Although Jung crosses over into the theological sphere in many writings, he writes as a psychologist about a God-like experience of encounter with the intrapsychic Self. According to his disciple, Aniela Jaffé, Jung as a psychologist does not distinguish the experience from that which is experienced. But this does not deny a possible referent perceptible in psychic experience.[4] The experience of the Self gives a kind of intuitional knowing leading toward psychic wholeness. But beyond this knowledge, Jung claims, is a further realm of faith by which certain theological assertions are made about the transcendent God.[5] His attempts, however, to sidestep the theological issues are particularly disingenuous in *Answer to Job*, where he makes sweeping theological claims.

The presence of the Self as a God-image within the psyche resembles traditional Christian doctrines of God's presence in the soul. Western Christianity has long maintained the teaching of divine indwelling. Copious examples could be cited from the New Testament period onward concerning the divine element within the soul of the believer. Such terms as "Temple of the Holy Ghost,"

Deus Absconditus and "divinization" in the Eastern tradition point to a strong sense of this divine inwardness. Recall that Jung does not make such claims from the theological vantage point. Rather he talks about psychic phenomena which appear to have affinities with the traditional tenets. This is especially true when he refers to the archetype of the Self. The Self functions in the psyche to reconcile opposites; in this way it resembles a God-image. It is indirectly perceived through dreams, fantasy and other imaginal modes; it is fundamentally ungraspable by the logic of the conscious ego. It is not created by ego projection, and it can only be described symbolically. Yet something like a God-image within the psyche functions to bring about psychic healing or wholeness. The Self also preserves an impenetrable zone of mystery and of inexhaustible richness. Jung is not making theological faith assertions about the being of divinity in itself; rather, he indicates psychic functions that bear analogy to theological referents.

Just as it is important to distinguish by analogy the Jungian Self from the transcendent God of theology, so it is also crucial to note Jung's intrapsychic distinction between ego-consciousness and the unconscious realm of archetypes. Another analogy between Western religion and Jungian psychology casts light on this distinction. Theologians have been careful to avoid a univocal pantheism by distinguishing between the divine indwelling and human existence. The mystic tradition with its unitive and individualistic emphasis tends to minimize this distinction and to play down the dualisms attendant on it. The Western theological orientation strives to protect at once the transcendence of God and the uniqueness of each personality. In an analogous way, Jungian psychology stresses an intrapsychic transcendence of the unconscious, archetypical zone. For example, Jung holds that "the Self is not meant to take the place of the one that has always been known as the ego but includes it in a superordinate concept."[6] Nor does the Self dominate the ego: "Inside the field of consciousness it [the ego] has, as we say, free will . . . or rather the subjective feeling of freedom."[7] These psychological and theological analogies do not resolve the problem of an immanent Self and a transcendent God. But the analogies aid us to nuance a mystery. They also incline us to perceive depth psychology and theological reflection as two perspectives of the same phenomenon.

IV. RELIGIOUS-DEMONIC

References to the numinous experience in Jung's psychology tend to be ambiguous. In what sense is the experience creatively religious or demonic, that is, inclining toward evil? How do we determine an authentic religious experience from those of magic, superstition or insanity? In this area of criteria for testing the value of a subjective happening, any test will be relative and partial. The descriptive signs of a religious experience may resemble those of insanity. Moreover, a temporary insanity, as an ego disturbance via encounter with the Self, may be both numinous and healing for an individual. The classic Christian testing of the inner spirits revolved around the doctrine of *agape*. Does the experience in some way contribute to a fuller life of charity, that is, of self-giving love? In the Jungian perspective, the traditional Christian test of experience can be too one-sided, overly stressing self-giving in benevolence to others. The Jungian criterion would ask: does the experience contribute to wholeness in a person's overall life? Does it foster the reconciliation of opposites in the psyche?

The tension between the religious and the demonic focuses especially on the topic of suffering and evil. One of the chief purposes of religion has been to help people deal, theoretically and practically, with the universal problems of suffering, evil and death. Religions have been seen by some to offer both explanation and solace in face of the tragic dimension; others view religious solutions as erroneous opiates for the human condition. Whatever one's position on these issues, the negative aspect of existence impinges on all, usually in barely perceptible ways. It is precisely through these oblique manifestations in clinical practice that Jung unfolds his views. For the therapeutic enterprise itself is a means for both diminishing and utilizing human pain. At the center of the therapeutic encounter is a conflictive, tension-producing experience. Ego consciousness, in its struggle for identity and survival, tends to be one-sidedly alienated from its unconscious depths. The gradual return to wholeness (always a condition of balancing tensions, not one of quiescent, harmonious perfection) necessitates a painful meeting with one's own Shadow. Religious conversion also necessitates an arduous encounter with neglected or even dominant characteristics of the personality.

The Shadow archetype represents that part of a personality whose traits we neither perceive nor wish to perceive. Yet via dream work and "active imagination" the Shadow is encountered as an indispensable guide to deeper experience of the psyche. Thus as portal to the unconscious, the Shadow provokes conflict and suffering. At every further stage of experiencing the symbolic life of the unconscious, there is an aspect of suffering as the alienated ego wrestles with the inward Self. Thus the inner journey or transformative process is an encounter with the numinous as both alluring and wounding. Jacob wrestles a blessing from the angelic figure and suffers pain in the process. This *passio* is intrinsic to the path of individuation. The Self, as God-image within, reflected also in other archetypes is not only *fascinans* but *tremendum*, able to inspire fear and suffering. Jung notes in various places that the journey into the unconscious can be destructively overwhelming unless precautions are taken. But generally the negative aspect of the Self acts as a warning to the ego; this "fear of God" is a call to heed a warning for one's own good. From a slightly different perspective, the inner *passio* can be seen as the prophetic or judgmental dimension traditionally associated with confronting the transcendent deity.

Another facet of inward suffering in confrontation with the Shadow is the recognition and acceptance of evil tendencies. From his boyhood as well as from his professional experiences, Jung felt very strongly that Christianity had developed a destructive attitude toward human evil. The church fostered an ideal of perfection that excluded evil tendencies from both God and the authentic believer. Jung's exaggerations on this point have been sufficiently challenged from historical and speculative points of view. Yet his insight retains value when considered in terms of the propensity to project evil onto other individuals and groups. A religious ideal of saintly goodness with salvation hinging on it could cause the believer to project his own negativities onto others. Coupled with religious motivation for projection is the ego's psychological impulse to seek acceptance from important groups or individuals via projection of unacceptable qualities onto others. The history of our period is replete with examples of such projection. When we encounter and acknowledge negativities, a twofold benefit can accrue from this *passio*. There is a lessening of our penchant to place evil on others. But even more important, we are enabled to channel the energy of our negativities in constructive ways. From an imaginative angle, the strengths of such diabolical figures as Lucifer and Mephistopheles are vital to the transformative polarity of opposites in the psyche.

A core suffering of human existence is death or the threat of death. Whether we reflect on it or not, death is as present to us as the air we breathe. Just as oxygen nourishes vital forces, so death influences in more or less subtle ways our decisions and actions. In the typical curve of life, we come from the unconscious realm of the womb, pass daily through the death rehearsals of sleep and eventually confront the final phases of life. Finitude, therefore, is never far from the experience of dying. In this condition of humanity, ego consciousness is precarious, and consequently it is beset by fear and denial of both the pain of dying and the threat of death. Among humans, the specter of death affects positive accomplishments as well as destructive urges. The attainments of science and culture testify to the universal impulse to enhance the endangered fabric of life. So also, the lust for accumulating material things, for power over others and for self-valuation through external acclaim, is ultimately a desperate attempt to preserve and protect individual ego consciousness at any price. This aspect of "at any price" becomes a root factor of ethical evil on personal and communal levels.

In the religio-symbolic experience, the archetypal images from the unconscious assist ego consciousness to accept and cope creatively with death-oriented finitude. The fear of death is never fully eliminated. But the symbolic activity from one's personal depths teaches an alert and willing consciousness to embrace the cycle of life and to live its phases more creatively. The quest to survive at all costs recedes and the quality of one's remaining years becomes uppermost. As one turns to middle life, the unconscious will usually beckon the ego through symbolic images to pursue a more spiritual and interior journey. By the time of middle life, personal consciousness should have secured its identity in the world, as it moved further from the unconscious matrix of infancy. In mature life the call from the unconscious is to experience the depths with a fully-formed ego identity.

Thus the summons is to accept the circle of life and to enrich it, not by fearful resistance to death as a terror, but to make of death a wise companion, as Hades was to Hermes. The symbolic images from the unconscious not only prepare us for death, but they also intimate the possibility of life after death in some form. When we become attentive to the archetypical dialogue, there arises a feeling of transcending space and time. The symbolic figures themselves relate to human experiences of ages past; they seem to break through from a realm not confined to finitude as we know it. Death will always be suffering in its aspects of pain, separation, loss and surrender to the unknown. But there are powerful symbolic forces within us to help us confront death as part of the fearsome *tremendum* of the numinous God-image.

Yet on the topics of both death and evil, Jung takes a Socratic path, while Christianity embraces the more dire Hebraic position. For the former, death is perceived as a natural happening to be met with calm steadfastness after a life of individuation. Death ideally becomes a return to the unconscious for a person who experienced an enriching reconciliation of opposites during a lifetime. For Christianity death has always maintained a powerful aspect of tragedy; it is seen as a defeat that humans can avoid only with the help of a savior. Death is associated with sin and evil which are ultimately beyond human ability to overcome. For Jung evil derives mainly from ignorance, although its remedy is not formal, intellectual education. Rather, the therapy of analysis, as a process of integrating opposites, e.g., good and evil proclivities in the psyche, constitutes a kind of education. Jung also realizes the power of evil within when it is denied or repressed, but his attitude remains more Greek than Hebraic. Evil can be lessened through *theoria* (right-seeing) of therapy; in the Hebrew perspective, evil stems from a more radical, irrational flaw of the will that calls for constant conversion ("teshuba" or turning—the Greek *metanoia*). It stresses malice of choice and the unpredictable depths of evil over against the balancing of tendencies.

V. IMAGINAL-RATIONAL

Beneath the unfinished dialogue on the above topics lies the issue of method. An important thinker does not choose a method; rather it flows from his cast of mind and emotion. It is shaped by personal style and inclination, as well as by historical accident. Jung, the mystery-oriented introvert, stood against the dual stream

of scientific rationalism and religious objectification. His temperament tended toward the authoritarian and the polemical in dealing
with opponents in both therapeutic and religious communities. At
times this combative penchant skewed his methodology away from
its imaginal-intuitive genius and into special pleading. This takes the
form of textual interpretations that are made to fit a chosen theory.
Examples could be drawn from Jung's use of scriptural and alchemical texts. These writings are open to a variety of interpretations.
There are times when the Jungian explanation is the most compel-
ling, but his perspective could have been enriched by considering
the views of dissenting scholars. Another mode of special pleading
is to distort or diminish unduly the object of criticism. For instance,
Jung judges severely what he sees as a Judeo-Christian distancing of
God from the human psyche in an attempt to preserve divine sov-
ereignty and transcendence. Yet synagogue and church traditions
contain many examples of joining God's transcendence with personal, spiritual interiority.

Jung's methodology is principally influenced on the speculative
level by Kant and on the practical plane by therapeutic technique.
The two are interlinked. Philosophically, the Kantian critique distinguished between transcendentals in the mind and the outward
transcendent that exceeds human intellectual capacity to know.
There is an interesting similarity between Kant's transcendental categories in the mind and Jung's archetypical images in the unconscious. In the realm of religious knowledge and experience, Kant
turned from mind to will, from the inability of discursive reason to
move beyond phenomena to the moral imperative by which the
pious experience the divine. In an analogous way, Jung decried the
religion of his father based on externally-supported church beliefs
with their underpinnings of late Protestant scholasticism. Jung did
not turn to will and the moral imperative of duty to discover the
numinous; Jung found the numinous experience in the encounter of
ego with unconscious depths.

Yet it is precisely this similarity in method to Kant that alienated Jung from the scientists among whom he strongly desired to be
classified. The prevailing mode of science in Jung's time was that of
natural sciences. This style stressed the ability of human reason to
gain knowledge on the level of empirical observation and experimentation, verifiability, repeatability and predictability. In terms of

the objects of natural science, human knowledge can be tested and assured experimentally. Like Freud, but in a different way, Jung wanted to establish a science of the psyche. Yet both objects and the mode of knowing differ from those of natural sciences. Although there is a similarity on the surface between the empiricism of gathering clinical data and the empiricism of the natural sciences, the sameness of method ends on the surface. For the kind of questions that Jung was asking, queries about life's meaning and direction, the relationship between ego consciousness and the numinous unconscious cannot be explored by the scientific method, strictly understood. The canons of the natural sciences falter in the realm of the "wounded cogito."[8]

In contrast to the ways of natural science, Jung's method stresses listening or receptive elements. It relies largely on imagination and intuition; it is Dionysian rather than Apollonian, feminine rather than masculine. I am not employing "feminine" as a gender classification; rather it denotes the receptive and imaginal quality that world literature has attributed to women, although similar traits are found in men. In the deeper realms of religious experience, as seen in the lives of saints and mystics, the feminine and the imaginal are foremost. The writings of John of the Cross and Jacob Boehme, for instance, reveal a constant, listening receptivity to the divine. The works of the mystics also portray a wealth of imagination in describing experiences that transcend reason. Modern psychological therapy was born in the intense period of masculine, rational hegemony. The turn of the last century was marked by heightened confidence in human progress through science and technology. Freud's method consisted largely of casting the light of scientific reason into the murky zone of the unconscious. He wanted to decipher with rational clarity the repressions and subterfuges of subliminal consciousness. Freud was eminently Apollonian; the masculine and the rational predominated, while the feminine and imaginal were to be controlled and decoded.

Hillman has pointed to the basic contradiction in the ensuing method of psychoanalysis.[9] Freud realized that therapy called for a restoration of the feminine dimension, but the method of psychoanalysis, influenced by the prevailing technological mentality, became masculine-rational. The incongruity that has dogged therapy, therefore, is how to achieve the reintegration of the feminine by rational means. The method used defeats the desired goal: to activate the healing potential of listening imagination. The nonanalytic therapies of the contemporary Human Potential Movement cannot be adequately categorized as Apollonian. At first glance, the opposite would seem to be true. Gestalt stresses feelings in the present; Bioenergetics focuses on the physical dimension of emotionality; Psychosynthesis combines a variety of techniques from group work to meditation.

On the whole, however, human potential approaches tend to manipulate imagination and feeling by carefully devised techniques. For all their protestations about "not pushing the river," these movements stress cult heroes rather more than they inspire a willingness to listen to healing depths. Of course, Jung himself has become a cult hero for many, despite his own disclaimers about being a Jungian. Moreover, Jung's desire to be accepted as scientific in his own time inclined him to defend his "science" on the same footing as the natural sciences. Yet it was not strictly scientific according to the canons of verifiability and predictability in the natural sciences. Nor should it be: Jung has developed a hermeneutic of the imagination, a creative way of listening to the healing unconscious that was closed to the modern Apollonian. This attitude, open to the numinous encounter with one's own depths, can also become a way of interiorizing religiousness.

In discussing Jung's method, we easily tend to overlook the metaphorical aspect of his language and its experiential dimension. It would be a serious betrayal of intent to understand words like "ego-consciousness," "collective unconscious," "archetypes" or "Self" as faculties or fixed entities not subject to revision. Rather, we are dealing with provisional language, models and metaphors for psychic activities. James Hillman has underscored better than most Jungians the flexible and "as if" facet of the terminology.[10] Hillman's emphasis on imagination as the creative and healing function of psychology avoids a static understanding of words and opens them to novel, imaginal interpretations. Symbolic language, therefore, is not aimed primarily at clarity of concept but rather at experiential functioning. The concepts themselves are fashioned to facilitate a healing action in the psyche. Thus semantics becomes at once functional for therapy while preserving a form of knowing that transcends ego-consciousness. Religio-symbolic language is inner, "presentational" and experiential as distinct from outer-oriented, logical, discursive terminology. From a somewhat different perspective, however, Jung attempted to bridge these two forms of speech and knowing by stressing the "psychoid" nature of the archetypical language. The psychoid archetype indicates the joining of nature and mind, science and humanism, the I-It and the I-Thou within a flexible, linguistic hermeneutic. In this Jungian attempt to bridge the gap between nature and mind, as well as in the enterprise of linking history and psyche, we perceive the unitive and comprehensive cast of his thought.

Jung's methodology focuses primarily on the therapeutic concerns of patients. His extended analysis of psychic symbols could easily give the impression of a purely theoretical project. Yet as a therapist, his chief concern remained always the cure of mental problems and the general transformation of personality toward integration. I underscore the therapeutic dimension because it helps us see Jung as a psychologist not as a theologian, however much he slips over into theologizing and philosophizing. Moreover, the empirical aspect of symbolic work in Jung emphasizes an experiential juncture where both religion and psychology meet. The theologian may variously distinguish religious experience from psychic event. But these subtle distinctions often cause us to lose sight of a more basic reality: all religious experience takes place in the human psyche. Part of the reluctance of the theologian to translate religious doctrines into psychic events stems from a defensive posture against psychological reductionism. This partially justified defensiveness, however, stunts the theologian's ability to perceive the religious factor intrinsic to psychic development. Exaggerated dualistic splits in theology such as those between nature and grace, matter and spirit resulted from a largely misguided attempt to preserve a religious "turf" clearly delineated from the field of psychic activity. The challenge today is to understand the interweaving of psychology and religion in the zone of the psychically religious.

These reflections on the religio-symbolic experience in Jungian psychology indicate both its dilemmas and promise. In spite of the important work done on the hermeneutics of myth by religious scholars in this century, there continues to be a deep-seated bias among theologians against taking depth psychology seriously. Reductionisms of various kinds have presented major obstacles to religious thinkers. Yet until theologians learn to make creative use of the psychic realm, religious thought will move along on a plane parallel to contemporary experience, but unable to intersect it in lively ways.

Notes

1. James Heisig, "Jung and Theology: A Bibliographical Essay," *Spring* (1973): 204–255.
2. Carl Jung, *Psychological Types*, tr. H. Godwin Baynes (New York: Harcourt, Brace & Co., 1924), p. 601.
3. Edward Edinger, *Ego and Archetype* (New York: G. P. Putnam's Sons, 1972).
4. Aniela Jaffé, *The Myth of Meaning*, tr. R. F. C. Hull (New York: G. P. Putnam's Sons, 1971), pp. 39–40. Jaffé carefully quotes from Jung on this point: "This is certainly not to say that what we call the unconscious is identical with God or is set up in his place. It is simply the medium from which the religious experience seems to flow. As to what the further cause of such experience may be, the answer to this lies beyond the range of human knowledge. Knowledge of God is a transcendental problem."
5. *Answer to Job*, in *Collected Works of C. G. Jung*, Bollingen Series (Princeton: Princeton University Press, 1958), vol. II, p. 555.
6. *Aion*, in *Collected Works of C. G. Jung*, vol. 9, pt. 2, par. I.
7. Ibid., p. 4.
8. Paul Ricoeur, *The Conflict of Interpretations*, tr. Willis Domingo (Evanston: Northwestern University Press, 1974), p. 173.
9. James Hillman, *The Myth of Analysis* (Evanston: Northwestern University Press, 1972).
10. James Hillman, *Re-Visioning Psychology* (New York: Harper & Row, 1975), p. 156.

Ann B. Ulanov

The Self as Other

Recently in my practice as a psychotherapist, I have become deeply concerned with what happens in the later phases of analysis. What does, in fact, happen to persons after their main problem areas have been located, clearly identified, and worked upon, after they have achieved some ease in relating to various elements of their unconscious and have recovered some of the functional reliability of their day-to-day lives?

Many persons continue analysis at this point, at the same rate of intensity, with the same number of sessions and the same arduous work writing up dreams, fantasies, and associations. Others continue analysis on a periodic basis; and still others engage in disciplined exercises of self-analysis. What is happening here? Psychoanalytic literature offers little information and scant guidance for patient or analyst in these later phases of treatment. We must depend here for guidance on our own experience as analysts.

The aim of analysis is greater consciousness, greater contact with the unconscious. The question that presses in upon one as analysis proceeds is: What is the value of greater consciousness? What does it mean to move in the direction of consciousness? What do we then become aware of? I suggest that it is in the later phases of analysis, especially, that we become conscious of values—indeed, we are confronted with *the* question of value—of its abstract importance as a guide to seek for in life, and of its concrete importance as a guide that presents itself to us as an *other*, one with which we must come to terms.

This kind of question sometimes appears in the very first phases of analysis. A new patient asked after a few sessions, "Suppose I am able to get a better sense of my problems and deal with them, then what? How do I go about building up a new sense of myself and find some sense of value in my life?" As treatment goes

38

on, this kind of question assumes a significant psychological function for the questioner; it recurs in many forms, and often becomes the central question achieving a centering effect on the psyche of the questioner. Gradually all the problem areas that have been worked on before, all the day-to-day conflicts and sufferings, all the breakthroughs, tiny and large, seem to be gathered around the central focus of this kind of question: What value do I choose to submit to? What value chooses me?

As this question emerges as the focus of treatment, an unexpected reply seems to emerge with it. Value, one learns, is relational; one cannot get in touch with one's deepest subjective self without also feeling confronted with the self as an objective *other*; one cannot meet this other self without, in fact, meeting many *others*, other persons or figures in one's dreams. Moreover, through these concrete personal relations with others, one is confronted by a phenomenon that can only be called *otherness* itself. One senses the presence of a source of value to which one may pledge oneself and which seems to summon oneself to a tight accounting.

This notion of value, however, even at its most abstract, seems to reveal itself best through intimate personal encounters. The strange reply that seems to respond to the question of value is paradoxical: only through experiencing one's subjective self can one reach others; and finally, only through seeing the self as objectively *other* can one reach the subjective sense of self. Only through relation to others, then, can one have any notion of self at all, and only through concrete personal relationships can one draw near to the sense of value in abstract objective dimensions. Subjective values lead to objective, and objective values give access to subjective. Value comes to one through relation to others, perhaps to ultimate otherness itself. Value comes in and to and through one's relation to others and to otherness through one's relation to self.

A specific example should illuminate and develop these general points.[1] A man in his fifties began analysis at a point of nervous collapse. Driven by a compulsive jealousy, he said that he "ruined every relationship by settling on it like a blanket and smothering the other person." He wanted to "own" others and have them under his control. He felt any meaning in his life or sense of purpose only in terms of getting other persons into his life and keeping them there. What was immediately apparent was his complete lack of recognition of others as *others*—as separate from his needs, desires, and fears, as persons existing in their own right. He also had no sense of himself beyond an immediate compulsion "to go after a relationship." Why he was so desperate, what else he might be feeling, what other aspects of himself he might need to look at and develop, were elements as remote to him as was the independent existence of the other person. And then we discovered that his inability to see the other was linked to an inability to see himself.

He first brought to analysis a number of dreams that featured a bridge motif. In them he was always trying to cross a bridge that spanned great heights. He would always get stuck in the middle of the bridge, frozen with terror at being thus suspended over empty space. In one dream there was a rope bridge over a chasm; in another, an electrically charged wire was strung between skyscrapers; in a third, he was on a large bridge from whose topmost point he viewed a wide river beneath. He described the side of the bridge he was leaving as a "picture post-card world" behind which a barren desert sometimes stretched. The other side he was trying to reach was never shown.

All the dreams focused on him, standing, full of dread, in the middle of the bridge, unable to move forward or back, paralyzed with fear of the yawning space beneath him. On waking, he felt that this kind of dream pictured a panic he felt in his daily life. He knew he was ruining his relationships with others, but he could not go forward or back. He was trying to make connection with others, somehow to reach another side altogether where his perspective and approach might be different. But he felt unable to reach that other side, and in fact had no notion of what it might be like to get there. The image of empty space beneath him elicited the most intense associations. He felt afraid, felt it was an empty "nothing" that somehow spurred him on relentlessly to capture another's affections and allegiance. He was struck by an implied connection between this emptiness and his inability to see the other or himself as amounting to any more than his needs and fears. The whole issue of value was thus presented to him directly from the unconscious. He realized that he had no sense of value, felt committed to nothing, and sensed this inner vacuum only as something to be avoided by grabbing onto someone else and making that person fill up the void. Even that, however, did not work, because if the other consented to this inevitably stifling arrangement, my patient himself soon became bored and did something to end the liaison.

As our work proceeded, he was amazed that three elements seemed inextricably bound up together: his sense of self, his recognition of others as *other*, and the question of value. He was constantly surprised that he did not seem to be able to get a sense of himself without also getting a sense of another person as other than himself. Through this relatedness to himself and to others, he finally felt the possibility of finding whatever held ultimate value for him. He would keep bringing up this question of value. "I know I can't expect another person to be my answer." "I know I've got to find my own roots, but how?" "We've gotten to the bottom of a lot of things that make me miserable. We've torn a lot down; but how do we go about building up now? How do I find a new sense of self, of value?"

When he began asking these questions his dreams shifted. Now he was looking for a new house to settle in, one that would be his home. In all of these dreams, regardless of what kind of city or town, house or apartment building the dreamer looked at as a prospective dwelling place, he was always confronted with the same strange fact: the potential home always had more rooms than he had thought. In one dream, he expected to see a three-room apartment and instead found ten. In another dream, a house that looked small turned out to have endless numbers of rooms. These additional rooms were always dilapidated, badly furnished or neglected, in need of repair, and always, even at their best, cheaply put together. The yawning space of the bridge dreams seemed in these house dreams to present itself in a more contained and relatable form. Now it appeared as forgotten or unexpected space that needed attention and that seemed repeatedly to present itself to be lived in. The dreamer felt this space as an image of his effort to find what sense of value might guide his life. Concurrent with his growing recognition of other persons as separate from himself, with their own motives and thoughts and purposes, was an awareness that his sense of value had to find its own "space" and roots and not just be grafted onto the personality of someone else he was using for his own needs. The process of finding himself, for this man, seemed, as it does so often for all of us, to be bound up with finding his own sense of values, values that objectively presented themselves to him from "the other side," so to speak.

JUNG AND THE AIM OF ANALYSIS

Jung describes the aim and purposes of analysis in two languages: the psychological and the religious. Psychologically, the ego must come into relation with the self-archetype as an *other* that is different from the ego, yet intimately and somehow personally connected to the ego.[2] The center of the personality shifts from the ego to the self. The analysand must recover his religious orientation, Jung says. "Among all my patients in the second half of life, there has not been one whose problem in the last resort was not that of finding a religious outlook on life . . . and none of them has really been healed who did not regain his religious outlook."[3]

To be faced throughout analysis, and especially in the later phases, with the question of value—what value will I commit myself to and what value will demand my allegiance?—means, then, to deal with the self-archetype, which comes to greet ego-identity as an *other*. With it, we recover a religious orientation that connects us to a sense of ultimate otherness. In the concrete and psychological we are suddenly met by the abstract and religious. Yet it is only through the recovery of a sense of mystery that we become able to make contact with our own psychological reality.

The question of value is a distinctly psychological question. We cannot integrate any content unless we are conscious not only of its intellectual meaning but also of its feeling value, the precise difference it makes to us. Even such a crudely phrased question as "What's in it for me?" is a primitive expression of a sense of value. One is asking about the worth, about the personal meaning. To know the feeling value of a psychic content is to know the difference between ineffective and effective knowledge. Ineffective knowledge is to know all about something and still to go ahead without any notion of what difference such knowledge makes in one's life. Effective knowledge changes what you do as a result of having it. To live surrounded by windows on the highest floor of a building, for example, and know that if you go through a window you will fall many stories to your probable death is ineffective knowledge if you go right ahead through a window as if nothing would happen. Effective knowledge changes one's actions. In this case, it makes you cautious around windows. To register the subjective feeling value of a psychic content is to experience its actual and potential effect on the psyche in terms that change one's attitude, motives, and actions.[4] There is more than simply subjective feeling value in these questions. There are also objective values that are "founded on a *consensus omnium*— moral, aesthetic, and religious values, for instance and these are universally recognized ideals or feeling-toned collective ideas. . . . "[5] Jung emphasizes that it is not enough to find one's own center of value, one's own relation to the self-archetype. One must also relate to the world of humanity, to the collective experience of otherness, of God, in a word. This is a religious focus. We ask how our personal private values, our own relations to the self as other, relate to the human experience of otherness.

Fairy tales make the same point. It is not enough in them to reach the treasure after many trials have been endured and many tests have been passed. One must also bring the treasure back to the world, to others. The greatest danger of this venture is precisely at the point where the treasure comes into sight. The lie that is closest to the truth is the most dangerous. In the tales a decisive threat menaces the hero or heroine just when the long-sought treasure is within reach. One may look back and be forever fixed in bitterness over the past just as Lot's wife was turned to salt for looking over her shoulder rather than moving ahead; or one may look back too soon before one finds secure footing in the real world and then find oneself dragged back into unconsciousness as Orpheus and Eurydice were swallowed up by the underworld; or one may fall asleep just when the goal is in sight, threatened as Dorothy of Oz was by the field of poppies when the Emerald City came into view. Unlike Psyche in the tale "Amor and Psyche," who did keep her precious beauty ointment to please her lover rather than give it to the goddess, one may not find the daring to take the treasure for use in the human world.

Our personal private relationship to the self-archetype must somehow be shared and opened to the experiences of others. Unless we do so, our treasure itself will build a wall of isolation between us and our fellowmen. Instead of bringing our glimpses of the light to help illuminate others, we will keep them to ourselves for ourselves and find ourselves dragged back into darkness. Self leads to others or it loses its self. Simply from clinical evidence it seems to be the case that experiences of the ego's encounters with the self are most often felt and described as religious events where the soul meets what religious commitment calls "God":

> It is only through the psyche that we can establish that God acts upon us, but we are unable to distinguish whether these actions emanate from God or from the unconscious. We cannot tell whether God and the unconscious are two different entities. Both are border-line concepts for transcendental contents . . . the God-image does not coincide with the unconscious as such, but with a special content of it, namely the archetype of the Self. It is this archetype from which we can no longer distinguish the God-image empirically.[6]

The mystery of the source of self—the unknown or ultimate otherness of the psyche—overlaps the mystery of the source of God as an objective value, recognized as such by countless persons throughout history. The two unknowns merge. Thus in confronting the question of value that analysis leads us to, we are really asking how are personal experiences of God possible. We want to know what God is to us and how the God within connects or relates to the human experience of the God without, the God of dogma in which so many have asserted belief and which so many have celebrated in prayer and ritual. It is clear that there is no way to the full experience of self without recovery of this orientation to the *other*—the ultimate *otherness* of God, or whatever fundamental value one lives for. It is clear that one lives in relation to value only through being in touch with one's self.

RELIGIOUS AND EMPIRICAL LEVELS OF UNDERSTANDING

Jung talks about relation to God on both a religious and an empirical psychological level. One cannot really become healed without recovering a religious outlook on life. For Jung, religion means its literal interpretation of "binding" to something. We are bound to a direct, personal, numinous experience, an encounter with the self as *other*. Such an experience is both terrifying and awe-inspiring. It produces in us both an attitude of trust and of careful observation. We both take this other into abstract account and sense its concrete presence as a reference point in our day-to-day living. Dogma and creeds are the collective human expression of many such individual experiences. They tell the story of our meetings with the Spirit or the Divine or God—or whatever we choose to call it—inside ourselves and our meetings with other selves. They help explain our responses to this *other's* disclosure of itself to us.

To have a religious outlook is to have such experience and let it change one. Such experience provides value and a language of value. It guides us toward our own special way, *its* way for us. We live with the presence of mystery—with the spirit as objective *fact*, as *there*—not simply as an odd product only of our own psyches. Awareness of this other may occur in rare, blinding moments, when it breaks in upon one. It also comes in the most conventional contexts and tasks of daily life. We know mystery is there. That is what Christian tradition means when it talks about living life *sub specie aeternitatis*. A sense of wonder becomes almost commonplace. A patient's dream offers an example of how a sense of something wondrous can be found in ordinary daily contexts. "I opened my laundry bag and out of it flew a thousand brilliantly blue butterflies."

Jung looked directly at our experiences of God, within and without, from an empirical perspective. This may be a biased perspective that views religious phenomena in relation to the emancipated self. But such a perspective opens religious experience and material to fresh inspection. Jung gives us a way to see and touch the soul. He looks at concepts of God as psychic phenomena. All theology in a way is seen as living witness to an intense, direct experience of God as *otherness* in its most ultimate sense, as otherness that touches us most intimately. For Jung studies religious doctrine and ritual strictly from the psychological point of view to see what they may tell us about the workings of the psyche and of the ways in which God may be experienced.[7] Jung does not treat the issue of the relation of the God within to the traditional notion of the God without. He limits himself to what is observable about the presence of the God-image within the psyche and its effects upon psychic functioning. He sees psychic God-images as indistinguishable from the images of the self-archetype.[8] Experience of the self, he observes, is frequently expressed as a meeting with God, and meetings with the Divine seem effectively to center a person's psyche in ways similar to the effects of the ego establishing relationship to the self-archetype. By observing, classifying, and reporting on the psychic phenomenon of the self, then, Jung studies the empirical effects on the human personality of the notion or feeling or image of God.

In the later phases of Jungian analysis, a patient is led to confront the question of value and of how he might live in relation to it. This confrontation occurs on both an empirical and religious level. The empirical level involves a process of coming to terms with the self-archetype, which aims at emancipating the self from the unconscious so that it can assume its proper place at the center of the whole psyche. This process is itself a kind of celebratory ritual.

THE SELF

In the course of analysis, one can often actually observe the gradual construction or reconstruction of the self and the ego's relation to it. The self makes itself known as a presence or entity that is other than the ego but that has direct far-reaching personal effects upon the ego. By *other* here, I mean that which is felt as sufficiently different from the ego to be experienced as an objective "person" that addresses its purposes, demands, or needs to the ego, and yet that is so similar to the ego and connected with it that the ego feels personally affected by its presence. Symbols of totality such as mandalas, or the uniting of opposites such as the marriage motif, or images of authority such as human figures of wisdom, or god-images are examples of the self-archetype. The appearance of such symbols in patients' dreams or in the development of the imagination often stimulates conscious responses; they often feel blessed or healed or guided or shaken to their foundations or commanded by this presence.

In the course of an analysis, the self is built up and disclosed. It is constructed bit by bit; it is revealed as a given, as a total unity. This sounds like a paradox; it is frequently felt as such by a person experiencing it. It is as if what we should be is already there, given and revealed to us. And yet we are so far from it that our glimpses of it leave us chastened. Christian tradition speaks of man as created in the image of God—as an *imago dei*. This wholeness, this completeness is an image of the divine; it is the way the God who is all seems to live within us. Our spiritual journey is to uncover and recover this likeness to God within, much as our psychological journey is to establish a firm connection between ego and self, with the self firmly at the center of our being.

The self is gradually built up out of successive meetings with other psychic figures within the personality through whom we sense the impact of otherness. In the stages of relating to the self, our egos pass through meetings with what Jung has called the *persona* (our outer, public personality), the *shadow* (our repressed, seemingly inferior, and negative personality), the *contrasexual* element of *anima* or *animus* (if male, our less developed feminine side; if female, the converse) on the way to the self. I would emphasize that in these separate meetings with inner figures, we feel not only their impact upon us, but also that of a larger otherness that touches us through a specific psychic *other*. Equally so, in our meeting with outer others—other people, other ideas, cultural trends, etc.—we increasingly perceive a thread of destiny somehow bound up in the circumstances of our lives. We reach a self that is gradually emancipated from persona compulsion, shadow obsession, or anima or animus possession, but only through successive encounters with inner and outer others.

The experience of the otherness of the self through encounter with an inner other is conveyed in the dream of a man meeting a shadow figure:

> I was sitting on the floor of a bathroom and then G. came in. I was very glad. We talked in a quiet, warm, trusting, smiling way. There was a sudden and very nice realization that we were both males and that it was okay for us to stay in the same bathroom together. He reassured me about my work and we found he was only six years younger than I. I told him about an early humiliation of mine; it was some sort of hierarchy situation about which I was resentful and he was sympathetic to what I had felt. Then I was combing my hair with water. My hair consisted partly of Stagshead ferns. I had a deeply trusting feeling towards G. and put my head on his shoulder. This made a damp spot on his shoulder but he didn't mind. The bathroom was at

a place a party was being given in the city where I grew up.
When we were through I would introduce G. around and I
looked forward to it. I knew I could do it well and it would help
him.

The dream touches many of the dreamer's fears about himself—his sexual and vocational confusion, his suspicion of authority,
and his feeling of never having fitted in with other people, especially
those with whom he had grown up. On hearing the dream one
senses the deep feeling of peace the dreamer felt while dreaming it
and again on waking. He felt accepted by G., who was a man the
dreamer admired and who represented, he thought, all those qualities he wanted for himself. G. was a positive shadow figure for the
dreamer. Through their mutual acceptance in the dream, the
dreamer felt more at ease with his own maleness, his work, his age,
and the society of which he was a part. The dream, however, expresses more than a reconciliation with a shadow figure; there is a
feeling, the dreamer reported, of things having come right, almost
a feeling of having received a blessing, of having drawn near to
wholeness. The image of the dreamer putting his head on G.'s
shoulder recalls the eloquent New Testament image of the beloved
disciple John putting his head on the breast of Jesus. This association of the dreamer and the scriptural figure, both being blessed,
suggests the power of the self in the psychic life of man. It blesses
the ego; it heals the ego; it makes whole.

It is not enough just to have such dreams, report them, and then
forget about them, leaving them behind in the analyst's office. It
always pleases me when an analysand types his dreams and makes
a copy to keep for himself. Not to keep a copy often indicates that
the projection of the self still rests largely with the analyst, the
keeper of the dreams. In fact, the analyst should simply get a carbon
copy of the dream. Just as a patient must not project the self onto
the analyst as if it were the analyst's responsibility and achievement
alone, so he must not underestimate the extent of the self's influence
in his daily life. Having had such a stirring dream as that just cited,
a patient cannot simply depart and let the ego organize the rest of
his day—or week—or life. He must stay with the world of the
other—those others he has met in his dreams—and try to see how
otherness enters the reality of his life.[9]

As one learns to do this, one gradually begins to discern the line of one's life—the underlying direction, the plot. As one discovers this story line one discovers more of oneself; one comes increasingly to feel one's "way." One begins in this way to remythologize one's life.[10] One recognizes a consistent theme in successive encounters with inner and outer people. One sees a repetition of meaning that seems to be circling and centering around value, emerging out of one's own experience and yet seeming to address and shape that experience as well. One feels called out, summoned, addressed. Like fairy tales that tell in hundreds of different ways and in countless repetitions the same psychic facts about the self, our personal facts and repetitious patterns develop into one or two clear tales, a few themes with many variations.[11]

We become acquainted with our inner history and it begins to gather weight and depth as we grow older. Gradually we become conscious receivers of this history and then conscious participators in it. And if we are particularly graced, we become conscious antic-ipators—open, eager, responsive to each new disclosure of being. This is where the mystics differ from the rest of us: they are the eager yea-sayers, always wanting more, seeing their own story as intimately bound up in that *other* who continually discloses itself to them.

JOHN OF THE CROSS

The path the mystics describe has close parallels to certain aspects of analysis. St. John of the Cross describes the pitfalls the "profi-cients," as he calls them, fall into.[12] The proficients are not begin-ners in the exercise of spiritual discipline. They may be thought to parallel persons well into the middle and later phases of analysis. They have already endured the purgation of the sensual part of the soul and have learned how actively to prepare their senses and fac-ulties for union with God through love by denying and purifying themselves. At this point in their development, the proficients are about to embark on the passive night—that dark night of the soul where God will be the initiator in further purifying and preparing those same faculties for union. Before describing the passive night, John reviews the imperfections still found in those about to enter it, in terms of their vulnerability to the seven deadly sins. The central theme of his discourse is the difference between true and false mortification.

True mortification is distinguished from its counterfeit by its goal; it reaches out to the supreme *other*, to God. The soul goes forth from itself and denies itself only in order to "attain to living the sweet and delectable life of love with God." The goal, then, is to love the other. The focus is not on one's own experience, or even one's own efforts, but upon the other, for in the other is the fullness of life that will fill the self.[13] This is not a stingy or cramped view of human existence that enjoins self-denial for its own sake or to win a badge of well-executed self-discipline. This is a view that reaches out toward a vibrant and abundant life of the self that can only be attained by living *toward* and *in* and *through* love for the other. False mortification, in contrast, aims at the self alone, the self's pleasure, the self's esteem. In this nearly meaningless kind of mortification, the self loses the other and loses the very self-enrichment it looks to achieve.

John's discussion of this theme in relation to the so-called "deadly" sins suggests many parallels to a person in analysis. Is one, for example, pursuing spiritual or psychological development for the pleasure such practices bring? If so, John comments—and the analyst may echo him—the soul is still spiritually weak; it is dependent on good feeling for its sustaining power. The *other* is nowhere to be found. So in analysis, if one's only goal is the ego's comfort, then one cannot really move beyond this early point because one has not become sufficiently differentiated from one's feeling to be able really to act, and when necessary, to act in spite of one's mood. One is not emancipated from dependence on feeling, but rather has become its victim because one's actions are governed only by the mood of the moment. Moreover, if feeling "good" replaces the goal of relating to the self as the aim of analysis, the whole analytic process soon degenerates into merely a search for reassurance for the ego at a very low level of affect.

John speaks of the proficient's temptation to fall into pride over what he has accomplished. Such a person speaks of spiritual things to other people as if he had become an expert on the subject. He salutes his own achievements rather than the divine goal and shaping force of his growth. Such a person reduces others in his heart, wanting only to teach them and not to learn from them. Similarly the analysand, especially in the beginning phases of analysis, is full of his new insights and insists on sharing them with everyone, whether they want to hear him or not. He may try to "analyze" his friends, and accuses them of "resistance" or "projection" if they refuse to cooperate.

John says the proficient who is engaged in false mortification wants to be praised for his efforts and agreed with, and will even change spiritual directors to find the "proper" acknowledgment due him. He wants to be his director's special favorite and therefore hides many of his shortcomings for fear of losing standing with the director. Similarly, the analysand may change analysts just when the analytical process has begun to penetrate his façade. Often he makes an initial show of hard work—requests extra sessions, writes out many pages of dreams, gives detailed comments of his reactions to the way the analyst handles the process and so forth. But when the necessity for integrating the work arises, he changes to another analyst or finds some reason for discontinuing treatment.

The person pursuing false mortification makes either too little or too much of his faults; he sees himself as excelling either in virtue or in sin. He feels impatient with his faults, wanting to be rid of them so that he may be more comfortable, rather than learning to bear them for his own or for God's sake. Similarly, the analysand succumbs to psychic inflation or deflation if he takes what his unconscious reveals as the property of his ego rather than relating to it as something other than mere ego-identity.

In contrast to false mortification, John sees true mortification as progressing not by thought of one's progress with envious glances at others' achievements, but rather by thoughts of the other whom one wants to please, to reach, to grow close to. One is too busy with thoughts of how to please God to fall into comparisons. One is eager to be taught by anyone, if only one can constantly enlarge one's love. One does not chatter endlessly about this love, rather one is moved to keep it dark as it grows deep within one. Similarly, the analysand who is truly engaged in the analytical process is so caught by whatever glimmerings of self come to him that he has no time for self-trumpetings. They are empty diversions, he sees, time-wasters that distract him from the intensely absorbing change of heart that is slowly taking place within him. He also knows that to break the confidentiality of his sessions with the analyst reduces the energy available for the work of relating to self.

The temptation of avarice also yields instructive parallels to the analytic process. John comments that the "false mortifier" is not content with the spirituality that God gives him; he always wants more. He piles up more and more relics and images, making up in quantity what he lacks in quality. Similarly, the analysand who focuses more on ego satisfaction than on developing the ego's relation to the self succumbs to a greed for experience. He runs after relationships, indulges in sexual experiments, consults several analysts, and tries for many types of therapeutic experience at once. He is in groups, marathons, sensitivity training, and individual analysis all at once. He is sexually involved with members of both sexes simultaneously. He fails to integrate his experience and instead accumulates a lot of more or less irrelevant information from books, lectures, other people's dreams, psychological jargon. None of that information produces knowledge, because he does not digest what has actually happened to him. He is not content with what life gives him even if it is an abundance; he just searches restlessly for more and more of everything.

In contrast, true mortification, as John defines it, moves a person to desire only what is needed to act well. He sets his "eyes only on being right with God and on pleasing Him . . . "[14] Similarly the analysand who aims to know the self realizes that this is possible only in a concrete personal relationship of ego to self. The limits of his personality and his gifts, therefore, are accepted as part of the structure of a very personal relationship, built step by step, to his unconscious. Hard work and sustained desire leave no room for greedy ambition.

The temptation of gluttony marks still further the distinction between true and false mortification. John says that the gluttonous strive after spiritual sweetness, and this makes them go to extremes. The means has become the end. Bodily penance is put in place of obedience to God, so that one works one's own will and not God's. After such excess, one often loses the desire to perform any penance at all. In the same way, the analysand who puts his own growth before relation to the self often gives way to an all-or-nothing-at-all attitude. "If this doesn't work," a patient once said to me, "then I will kill myself." Another patient said, "I've tried and tried everything I can think of, and if this last effort fails then I'll know I'm hopeless." The patient identifies his ego stance with the self's and thus the ego's conceptions become the starting and ending points of reference. With this approach, one is inevitably exposed to alternating cycles of depression and mania; one appropriates every insight no matter how small, into something positive about oneself, as one's own property and swings up to dizzying heights of self-esteem. Equally, with each encounter with something negative in the psyche, one is dragged down into discouragement or even despair about oneself; one identifies with the negative content rather than seeing it as an inner *other* with whom one must come to terms. Without the notion of otherness, there is no possibility of relationship.

John of the Cross shows us that the key to our deepest, most concrete and personal experience of the self is intimately connected with recognition of the other, in fact is possible only through it. But what exactly does that mean—to recognize the other? What does it mean to say our emancipation from the fetters of the unconscious is possible only through seeing an *other?* Central to any differentiation of the self from the unconscious is an understanding of the phenomenon of projection. Dealing with projections occurs throughout analysis. It is especially important if the self is truly to emerge and to be *seen* to emerge.

PROJECTION

According to Jung, projection "signifies a state of identity that has become noticeable . . . " and leads to "differentiation and separation of subject from object."[15] In projection, one is in a state of identity: "I" and the "other" are one, whoever that other may be, a person such as one's parent or spouse, an idea of teacher or friend, or a psychic content such as an ambition. The other with whom one is in a state of identity may be an inner other such as a shadow figure or an animus symbol. Whoever the other is, the "I" becomes one with it and sees no separation between itself and the other. I may seem virtually to be my ambition to make money, or I may become my resentment of a person or situation. The two are one and often so much of an entity that the "I" is not even aware that this identity exists; it just is. In such a case of projection, to be two separate entities is unimaginable; it is not yet a conscious alternative, because in this state of identity one is not conscious of the "other," let alone related to it.[16]

Projection occurs when such a state of identity becomes a disturbing factor, "when the absence of the projected content is a hindrance to adaptation and its withdrawal into the subject has become desireable."[17] One becomes aware of projection, for example, when one suddenly realizes that he himself is guilty of exactly what he is accusing another person of feeling. A patient of mine once began a session by accusing me of being angry at her. In fact, she was angry at me, but was unaware of it. She saw her anger in my face. Her projection of her anger onto me seriously disturbed our relationship; it was really important that she see that it was she who was angry and that there was an inner "other" whom she had to get to know and to understand to appease that anger.

Another patient, a girl in her late twenties, projected onto me an image of her ideal feminine self. She saw me as a whole, loving woman who could somehow provide her with nurture and endless care. We talked many times about her projection. Though she acknowledged intellectually that I was not an ideal being, or even old enough to be her nurturing mother, unconsciously she continued to relate to me as if I was exactly what her projected image made me. This is an example of ineffectual knowledge. Knowing all about her projection did not change a thing for her. She continued to flare with anger and reproach if I failed to live up to her expectations. What finally made her knowledge effective was a confrontation with reality: I became pregnant, and someone else's real mother, someone else's real fundamental self and source of nurture. Her recognition of the child—of this other's existence—had the effect of moving her far into her own reality. She saw that her images of feminine wholeness and mothering were part of her own psyche. Again it was clear that there was the closest kind of connection between recognizing the existence of another and being able to see oneself more clearly.

The first step, then, in coming to terms with a projection is to realize just what has happened. One must see that as a result of projection one fails to relate to the actual person who receives the projection. One sees him as one would like to see him, not as he is. One has also failed to relate to the content of the projection; one is quite unconscious of it. To go further, in order to dissolve the projection, one must do two things: one must see the other person as he is and one must see the inner content that has been projected as belonging to oneself. In the case of the female patient cited above this meant her trying to relate to me, the analyst, as a human person and not as psychic ideal. She had somehow to relate at the same time to the psychic image of the feminine self that she had projected onto me. Then, gradually, her relationship with me became more realistic and thus capable of genuine growth. Along with that change her relationship to her psychic image of a feminine self became more anchored within herself and thus also became capable of development.

I have learned from experience that in order to build either of these relationships, to another person or to a psychic image, one needs to develop both. Any relationship with an actual person is impeded if unbearably strong projections are flying about. One does not see the other as he is; one either inflates him maddeningly or reproaches him for letting one down. Similarly, to relate to an inner psychic image one needs a clear view of what the image represents and what it does not; otherwise it becomes anything and everything and one cannot grasp it at all. Just as relation to an actual other person leads one deeper into life—one's own, the other's, and the values that one discovers in the relationship—so relation to what might be called the *inner other* of a psychic image leads one more deeply into the self and the values it holds. But to accomplish this a projection must be clearly identified. A dream and the subsequent analysis of the young woman we have been talking about illustrates this process:

> I came to the group therapy session and said, "None of you care about me and I am never never never going to get better better better!" Then I left. I met my analyst and said to her, "You don't care about me and I am never never never going to get better better better!" She said nothing, but stood behind me. Raising my elbows and putting my hands behind my neck, I sensed her presence there, as if parallel to my backbone; somehow that communicated to me that she cared. I felt I would get well.

As we discussed her dream, the dreamer's projections onto me came up again. Her first reaction to the dream was negative. She felt it was just another example of how she wanted her analyst to become her

backbone, to make all well. She overlooked the fact that in the dream
there were two backbones, her own and that of the analyst. Instead,
she identified the figure of the analyst in the dream with her own image of a whole feminine self. Her projection thus blotted out both the
actual person of the analyst in the dream and the image of feminine
wholeness that the analyst symbolized to her. In the dream it is clear
that there are two women present, the analyst and the patient, one behind the other. Thus there are two backbones, not just one, and the
dream seems to emphasize the parallel relation between them. Only
by touching the top of her own backbone in a rather feminine gesture,
lifting her elbows above her head and exposing her face and torso, does
the dreamer receive from the analyst the unverbalized message of caring that supports her confidence that she will indeed get well. Only
through an image of a relationship between herself and another person, then, can the patient's connection to the strength of the self within
her be expressed.

The patient associated to the analyst, as indicated, an image of
feminine wholeness. Instead of seeing wholeness as belonging to the
analyst, the dream depicts the proper way to relate to it. One does
not meet wholeness head on, but rather senses its presence behind
one, backing one up. One co-ordinates one's actions with it, and
even may discover that one can rely upon it. But wholeness is not
the ego's property. The otherness of the self's wholeness is portrayed in the dream through the presence of another person, the analyst. The wholeness is both a part of oneself and of another yet is
experienced as entirely other to oneself. In integrating this dream,
the patient had continually to move back and forth between working
on her relationship to the person of the analyst and the process of
analysis—the outer other, so to speak—and working on her ego's
relationship to her own experience of the feminine self—the inner
other. The dream image of her childish refusal to get well had to
change into her realistic adaptation to her own adult strength.

PROJECTION AND THE REALM OF VALUE

Projections occur just as much in the realm of value as they do in
our personal relationships. In psychological language we speak of
projections of the self-archetype onto authority figures, onto pow-

erful cultural movements, onto places that we feel are holy. When we are in such a state of psychological identity with the object onto which we have projected, we experience the power associated with the self as flowing back into us from the recipient of our projection. Thus we feel that the presence of such authority figures, or the proximity of such holy places, or the deep forces of such cultural movements confer on us a blessed healing effect. We feel reconciled to our enemies; we feel caught up in a surge of growth; we feel we are in the presence of something momentous that is changing our outlook as drastically as a change from darkness to light, from blindness to clear vision. In religious language we speak of projections of our experience of holiness, of personal meetings with the Divine, onto the unknown God as He is in Himself. Somehow we feel our fragmented personal experience is connected to the objective existence of God, so that even though these moments are brief and incomplete, their impact changes our whole life.

Just as in the personal realm, where when we become conscious of our projections we must relate both to the inner "other" of the psychic image and to the outer "other," so in dealing with our projections in the area of religious value we need to become consciously related to the God-within, the psychic image we project onto God— in Jung's language, the archetype of the self—and also consciously to relate to the God-without. We must deal with what traditional systems of value tell us about God in order to gain access to our subjective experience of God; we must deal with our very personal experience of the Divine, to gain access to the God of which organized religions speak. We must deal with the God-within through the self-archetype in order to meet the God-without. In such a way we recover our religious orientation.

In this article I have separated the "God-within" from the "God-without," just as I have separated psychological and religious language. This is only for the purpose of clarity. In reality, these distinctions rarely hold. "Within" and "without" are words that reflect our limited point of view. For a believer, God is everywhere. It is only our limitations that make us see Him as *within* and therefore we must come to see Him as also coming from without; it is only a weakness of language that makes us speak of Him as "above," and therefore we must learn to speak of Him as coming from below as well, and from the left and the right and every other direction.

To withdraw projections in the realm of value and fail to deal with the sense of the outer other—in this case of the God-without—as more than a psychic image is dangerous psychologically. Theologically it corresponds to the sin of idolatry. We take a means for an end, a process for a result, something partial for the whole.

> The withdrawal of metaphysical projections leaves us almost defenceless in the face of this happening [being possessed by psychic factors], for we immediately identify with every impulse instead of giving it the name of "other," which would at least hold it at arm's length and prevent it from storming the citadel of the ego. "Principalities and powers" are always with us. We have no need to create them if we could. It is merely incumbent on us to *choose* the master we wish to serve, so that this service shall be our safeguard against being mastered by the "other" whom we have not chosen. We do not *create* "God," we *choose* him.[18]

We must deal with value as *other* whether it presents itself as God or self-archetype or spirit or whatever, because if we do not, something else that is incomplete and unsatisfying as value imagery will take its place. That is precisely what happened to the analysand who tried to make another person the sole carrier of meaning in his life, an attempt that not only failed, but made relationship to anyone impossible, to himself as well as others. To deal with value as "other" in the religious realm is to acknowledge God as an objective fact. But we can reach that objective otherness of God only by finding what has personal subjective value for us. Conversely, we cannot reach that subjective value except through recognition of the objectivity of the other. As Jung points out, to withdraw all projections from God as objective other and concentrate solely on our own subjective experience is to try to create a god rather than to choose the God that presents Himself to us. To reduce God to a projection of our own inner experience is to expose the ego to endlessly painful deflations and inflations.[19]

Many persons who have been aided by analysis try to make the analytical process into a form of religious orientation, replacing God with the self-archetype as the only true objective other. God is then seen as projection of the self. Our empirical observation of the emergence of the self in analysis, however, does not answer the vital question of value that accompanies it. It may help answer it, but it is not a complete or final answer. To relate to the self-archetype is not and cannot be an end in itself, nor does it provide a system of value. Rather what occurs is a conceptualization of what we observe to happen psychologically when a personality enlarges to include relationship to the unconscious. We may come up with an empirical description of the growth of the human person, of the development of the human spirit.

Jung has given us a valuable tool here: he has shown us a way to explore and record the typical phases that occur as the ego builds a relation to the unconscious. He has shown us a way to reinterpret symbols of value in the human tradition, whatever and wherever that tradition may be—in philosophical, moral, or aesthetic realms—in terms of the psychological meaning of the symbols. The aim of this reinterpretation is to open a way for persons to reconnect to the truth those symbols convey so that they can again participate in that truth.[20]

Analysis, however, is only a tool, not a way of life. Jung himself wrote that psychology's function is to help men see, not to be the light. Psychoanalysis may help men connect to the truth already disclosed in religious dogma and tradition; its aim is not to create new truth.[21] Jung objects to those who make analysis an end in itself as making ends out of means. He objects to those who criticize him for trying to replace religion with his system of analysis, or of trying to create God out of the concept of the self: "How could any man replace God?" he asks; "I cannot even replace a lost button through my imagination, but have to buy myself a new real one."[22]

The very foundation for an emancipated self—the self that operates as life's purpose, as its centering process expressing the utmost of one's individuality and of one's destiny—is based on "an empirical awareness, the incontrovertible experience of an intensely personal, reciprocal relationship between man and an extramundane authority which acts as a counterpoise to the 'world' and its 'reason.' "[23] Thus one cannot even conceive of the notion of a self without also simultaneously developing a sense of an ultimate "other." Similarly, the goal of the emancipation of the self is not discovered in a vacuum. Relating to the self occurs in the context of the world in which one lives, at the very center of one's life.

From the psychological point of view it is not possible for the

ego to build a relation to the self except in the personal context of
one's day-to-day life. Jungians talk about archetypal and personal
layers of the psyche. One can reach archetypal levels only through
concrete personal conditions, those that are in one's family background, physical makeup, cultural context, accidents or illness, all
the networks of relation with others. Christian tradition talks about
this concretization as the Incarnation. One cannot receive or participate in God's truth *in abstracto;* one can only hear it through the
words and presence of the person of Jesus and of the reactions of
countless persons to him throughout history. Only through the human does the divine make itself known.

What this means for the person wrestling with the issue of value
is that it is not enough to know the symbolic meaning of a religious
tradition. One must also live in relation to that tradition. It is not
enough to know about the psychological meaning of one's images of
God; that is ineffective knowledge. One must also let that knowledge change one's being. It is not enough to interpret the psychic
meaning of one's image of the God-within; one must also give oneself to the God-without. To recover one's religious orientation, it is
not enough to deal with the inner other of a psychic content; one
also needs to give oneself over to the outer other, to God.

Beyond projection, then, is relationship in all its fullness. One
cannot participate in, or even really grasp, value without a sustained, committed, personal relationship to one's most subjective
experience of it and to that outer other that reveals value. Through
personal, subjective relationship to the self as other and to the God
who addresses us at the level of self, we touch the mystery of otherness and live our lives in relation to it. We cannot find the kernel
of meaning without also achieving a personal relationship with it.
Thus analysis works to help us uncover the connection between our
subjective experiences of value and the objective presentations of
value that come to us through others. We cannot replace our relationship to others with the tools of analysis. Analysis is only a
method. Relationship is the basic stuff of life. In psychological
terms, to relate to the self we need relationship with others and to
relate to others we need relationship to the self. One does not collapse into the other. In religious terms, then, to relate to the God-
within we need the God-without, and to connect to the God-without we need to relate to the God-within. Thus does the issue of value

in analysis move us to recover our religious orientation. It is even possible to imagine a patient's analysis pushing him out of his chair onto his knees, out of his role as analysand into a concrete relation to Otherness that he not only recognizes but reverences. What professional analysts must provide are exercises that guide the development of this relation to Otherness. For analysands of religious faith, such exercises would have the clearest connection to their beliefs. For those who are not religious, such exercises would at the very least provide specific means to enlarge and direct their gropings toward Otherness.

Without such movement toward Otherness, analysis just goes on and on indefinitely, substituting itself and its endless sessions for commitment to value. The analysand prolongs his treatment by moving from one analyst to another or from one school of analysis to another. Psychological methods replace religion, but they prove much more empty than the religion that some of them criticize. The old-fashioned image of God-as-person has more to show us than modern abstractions. We can talk to God-as-person; we can move ever deeper into personal relationship. Without vital connection to the mysteries of Otherness, we simply drift in a sea of abstractions and methodologies. We lose ourselves as well as Otherness. Jung sums it up movingly:

> The decisive question for man is: Is he related to something infinite or not? That is the telling question of his life. Only if we know that the thing which truly matters is the infinite can we avoid fixing our interest upon futilities, and upon all kinds of goals which are not of real importance. Thus we demand that the world grant us recognition for qualities which we regard as personal possessions: our talent or our beauty. The more a man lays stress on false possessions, and the less sensitivity he has for what is essential, the less satisfying is his life. He feels limited because he has limited aims, and the result is envy and jealousy. If we understand and feel that here in this life we already have a link with the infinite, desires and attitudes change. In the final analysis, we count for something only because of the essential we embody, and if we do not embody that, life is wasted. In our relationships with other men, too, the crucial question is whether an element of boundlessness is expressed in the relationship.

     The feeling for the infinite, however, can be attained only if we are bounded to the utmost. The greatest limitation for man is the "self;" it is manifested in the experience: "I am *only* that!" Only consciousness of our narrow confinement in the self forms the link to the limitlessness of the unconsciousness. In such awareness we experience ourselves concurrently as limited and eternal, as both the one and the other. In knowing ourselves to be unique in our personal combination—that is, ultimately limited—we possess also the capacity for becoming conscious of the infinite. But only then![24]

Notes

1. All references to patients and their material, unless otherwise noted, are taken from my practice as a psychotherapist.
2. By "self-archetype" Jung means the following: "The central archetype; the archetypes of order; the totality of the personality. Symbolized by circle, square, quaternity, child, mandala, etc." Jung, C. G., *Memories, Dreams, Reflections.* Aniela Jaffe, ed.; Richard and Clara Winston, trans. New York, Pantheon, 1961, p. 386. "The self is not only the centre but also the whole circumference which embraces both conscious and unconscious; it is the centre of the totality, just as the ego is the centre of the conscious mind." Jung, *Psychology and Alchemy, Collected Works,* XII, 1967, p. 41.

       (Note: *The Collected Works of C. G. Jung,* translated by R.F.C. Hull, are published by the Bollingen Foundation [Bollingen Series XX], in the United States by the Princeton University Press and in England by Routledge & Kegan Paul. The *Collected Works* will hereafter be referred to as *CW.*)

       Jung also writes that the self-archetype is " . . . The total personality which, though present, cannot be fully known. . . . The ego is, by definition, subordinate to the self and is related to it like a part to a whole." Jung, *Aion, CW,* IX, Part 2, 1959, p. 5. " . . . the self acts upon the ego like an *objective occurrence* which free will can do very little to alter." *Ibid.,* p. 6. The self " . . . is completely outside the personal sphere, and appears, if at all, only as a religious mythologem, and its symbols range from the highest to the lowest." *Ibid.,* p. 30. "As an archetypal concept, the self designates the whole range of psychic phenomena in man. It expresses the unity of the personality as a whole. But in so far as the total personality, on account of its unconscious component, can be only in part conscious, the concept of the self is, in part, only *potentially* empirical and is to that extent a *postulate* . . . it encompasses both the experienceable and the inexperienceable (or the not yet experienced). . . . In so far as psychic totality, consisting of both conscious and unconscious contents is a postulate, it is a *transcendental* concept, for it presupposes the existence of unconscious factors on empirical grounds and thus characterizes an entity that can be described only in part but, for the other part, remains at present unknowable and illimitable." Jung *Psychological Types* (*CW*, VI, 1971), p. 460. "From the intellectual point of view it is only a working hypothesis. Its empirical symbols, on the other hand, very often possess a distinct *numinosity*, i.e., an *a priori* emotional value, as in the case of the mandala, 'Deus est circulus . . . ' It thus proves to be an archetypal idea . . . which differs from other ideas of the kind in that it occupies a central position befitting the significance of its content and its numinosity." *Ibid.*, p. 461.

3. Jung, *Psychology and Religion: East and West* (*CW*, XI, 1958), p. 334. See also Jung, *Memories, Dreams, Reflections, op. cit.*, p. 340; Jung writes there: "Meaninglessness inhibits fullness of life and is therefore equivalent to illness . . . it is not that 'God' is a myth, but that myth is the revelation of a divine life in man. It is not we who invent myth, rather it speaks to us as a Word of God. The Word of God comes to us, and we have no way of distinguishing whether and to what extent it is different from God."

4. Jung writes, " . . . the psychic phenomenon cannot be grasped in its totality by the intellect, for it consists not only of meaning but also of value, and this depends on the intensity of the accompanying feeling tones.

" . . . the feeling-value is a very important criterion which psychology cannot do without, because it determines in large measure the role the content will play in the psychic economy . . . the affective value gives the measure of the intensity of an idea, and the intensity in its turn expresses that idea's energic tension, its effective potential." Jung, *Aion, op. cit.*, pp. 27–28.

5. *Ibid.*, p. 29.

6. Jung, *Memories, Dreams, Reflections, op. cit.*, p. 383.

7. *Ibid.*, p. 350. Jung also writes: "I add to the many symbolical amplifications of the Christ-figure yet another, the psychological one." *Aion*, p. x.

8. Jung writes: "Intellectually the self is no more than a psychological concept, a construct that serves to express an unknowable essence which we cannot grasp as such, since by definition it transcends our powers of comprehension. It might equally well be called the 'God within us.' The beginnings of our whole psychic life seem to be inex-

tricably rooted in this point, and all our highest and ultimate purposes seem to be striving towards it." *Psychology and Religion, op. cit.,* p. 334. Jung also writes: " . . . a term derived from the Church Fathers . . . the *imago Dei* is imprinted on the human soul. When such an image is spontaneously produced in dreams, fantasy, visions, etc., it is from a psychological point of view, a symbol of the self, of psychic wholeness." Jung, *Memories, Dreams, Reflections, op. cit.,* p. 382.

9. Von Franz, Marie Louise, *The Interpretation of Fairy Tales* (New York, Spring Publications, 1970), lecture VI, p. 6.

10. See Ulanov, A. B., *The Feminine.* Evanston, Northwestern University Press, 1971, pp. 128–132.

11. Von Franz, *op. cit.,* lecture I, p. 2.

12. See St. John of the Cross, *The Dark Night of the Soul,* trans. E. A. Peers. New York, Doubleday Image Books, 1959, p. 37.

13. *Ibid.,* p. 36.

14. *Ibid.,* p. 46.

15. Jung, *Psychological Types, op. cit.,* pp. 457–458.

16. Jung, *Aion, op. cit.,* p. 3.

17. Jung, *Psychological Types, op. cit.,* p. 457.

18. Jung, *Psychology and Religion, op. cit.,* p. 87.

19. Jung writes: "The idea of God is an absolutely necessary psychological function of an irrational nature, which has nothing whatever to do with the question of God's existence . . . There is in the psyche some superior power, and if it is not consciously a god, it is the 'belly' at least, in St. Paul's words. I therefore consider it wiser to acknowledge the idea of God consciously; for, if we do not, something else is made God, usually something quite inappropriate and stupid such as only an 'enlightened' intellect could hatch forth." Jung, *Two Essays in Analytical Psychology, CW,* VII, 1953, p. 71.

20. Jung's own way of reconnecting to the Christian myth, I would suggest, is his further development of it in his concept of individuation. He writes: "Our myth has become mute, and gives no answers. The fault lies not in it as it is set down in the Scriptures, but solely in us, who have not developed it further, who rather, have suppressed any such attempts." Jung, *Memories, Dreams, Reflections, op. cit.,* p. 332. Jung continues: "In the experience of the self it is no longer the opposites 'God' and 'man' that are reconciled, as it was before, but rather the opposites within the God-image itself. That is the meaning of divine service, of the service which man can render to God, that light may emerge from the darkness, that the Creator may become conscious of His creation, and man conscious of himself.

"That is the goal, or one goal, which fits meaningfully into the scheme of creation, and at the same time confers meaning upon it. It is an explanatory myth which has slowly taken shape within me in the course of the decades. It is a goal I can acknowledge and esteem, and which therefore satisfies me." *Ibid.*, p. 338.

21. Jung, *Psychology and Alchemy, op. cit.*, p. 13.
22. Quoted from Jung in White, V., *God and the Unconscious.* Cleveland, World Publishing, 1961, p. 257.
23. Jung, *The Undiscovered Self.* R. F. C. Hull, trans. Boston, Little, Brown, 1957, p. 22.
24. Jung, *Memories, Dreams, Reflections, op. cit.*, p. 325.

Robert M. Doran, S.J.

Jungian Psychology and Christian Spirituality: I

CHRISTIAN SPIRITUAL TRANSFORMATION:
SELF-TRANSCENDENCE AND SELF-APPROPRIATION

This is the first of three articles on the subject of Jungian psychology and contemporary Christian spirituality. The present article will focus on the latter of these two items, on Christian spiritual transformation as this is understood at the present moment in the life of the Church. By concentrating on two terms frequently employed in the works of Bernard Lonergan, *self-transcendence* and *self-appropriation*, I hope to provide a context for the next two articles, which will deal more extensively with Jung. This first article will treat, first, Christian spiritual transformation as *self-transcendence;* second, Christian spiritual transformation as growth in self-knowledge or *self-appropriation;* third, the levels of consciousness that can be discovered when one enters on the way of self-appropriation; and fourth, the relation of feelings and symbols to these various levels or dimensions of consciousness. This fourth topic locates that element of our interior lives in regard to which Jung's insights become pertinent for our spiritual self-understanding.

I have discovered that any such treatment of Jung as the present one eventually brings me into that form of discrimination which, in Ignatian spirituality, is called the *discernment of spirits*. Jung is a religiously controversial figure. Not only does my own treatment and evaluation of Jung tend to arouse rather than quell the arguments that surround his person and his work, but, more significantly, my critical response to Jung always carries me to the heart of the Christian exigence to differentiate the true call of God from the subtle attractions of the forces of evil as these two contrary tendencies compete for the allegiance of men and women involved in the renewal of the contemporary Church. Why this is so will hopefully become clear in the subsequent articles, especially in the final one. But perhaps I can offer now some indication of the difficulty.

First, then, Jung *is* a religiously controversial figure. The religious significance of his psychological insights is variously interpreted. John A. Sanford and Morton Kelsey are two well-known authors who have drawn on Jung to promote and understand Christian self-discovery.[1] On the other hand, James Hillman has maintained that Jung's guidelines to "soul-making" are of a completely different order from the well-known paths to spiritual transformation in Christ and from the insights of the other major religious traditions of the world.[2] Martin Buber entered into direct conflict with Jung, claiming that the psychology of individuation and Yahwistic faith are diametrically opposed orientations of the human spirit.[3] Jung himself, as we shall see, gives some indications of his own that the process of individuation will lead the *cognoscentes* to the position of being able to dispense with all forms of traditional religious involvement; but he also attempted to offer his psychology as an aid to the pastoral care of souls.[4]

What is one to make of these differences and ambiguities? Obviously, some framework must be found to enable us to enter on the kind of process that Lonergan calls *dialectic* and *foundations:* the process, namely, in which we not only assemble and review alternative interpretations, but also evaluate and compare them, reduce their affinities and oppositions to their underlying roots, determine which, if any, of these roots stand in dialectical opposition to one another in such wise that only a radical transformation of the basic horizon can achieve reconciliation, and, finally, choose that basic horizon and those resultant positions and interpretations which we will make our own.[5] Such a framework is what I hope to offer in the present article.

Secondly, my own judgments and decisions regarding the potential spiritual fruitfulness of Jung's work are themselves controversial, at least in the sense that they will please neither Jung's detractors nor his enthusiastic followers. For I will sharply differentiate the process of Christian self-transformation from the way to individuation that Jung maps out for us. But I will *also* insist with equal force that there is much that we not only can, but indeed must, learn from him in developing both a theology and an ascesis of spiritual transformation in the context of the contemporary world.

Thirdly, the only final arbiter of the kind of discrimination that I find necessary is what we have come to call the *discernment of spirits.* Jung's theological ambiguities, and the alternative interpretations and evaluations that are offered of his work, are symptomatic of an underlying spiritual conflict that can be mediated only in the context of the dialectic of grace and of sin, of the Standards of Christ and of Satan. David Burrell has indicated correctly that one cannot fail to meet God if one goes on the inner journey to individuation.[6] But one will also meet much that is *not* God, and that is even opposed to God. Not only does Jung not help one to discriminate these forces as they operate in one's psyche, but he also contributes to and even encourages the confusion that can be experienced in such moments that call for discernment, and thus mires one in the conflictual forces that wage an ultimate battle in the depths of one's psyche. Jung's work, if left uncriticized, leads one into a psychological *cul-de-sac* that can assume demonic proportions.

Christian Spiritual Transformation As Self-Transcendence

There are many diverse and quite useful approaches to the understanding of spiritual transformation. I have chosen to focus on two terms that have been developed by Bernard Lonergan. Lonergan's thought has achieved a great deal of notoriety due principally, it would seem, to its difficulty. I have no intention here of repeating the subtle intricacies of his full argumentation. I will rather present in what I hope are quite understandable terms the *results* of that argumentation, and will deal with more subtle points only to the extent that they are necessary to clarify my basic position.[7]

I choose Lonergan's approach to the issue of Christian spiritual transformation for several reasons. First, it is the approach with which I am most familiar and the one that I personally have found most helpful. Secondly, Lonergan explicitly takes his stand in *human interiority*. And, when we are talking about either spiritual transformation or Jungian psychology, we are talking about the realm of interior experience, about the *data of consciousness*, about such events as insights, judgments, decisions, and, as we will see, dreams. All of these happenings are items that we experience. But we experience them interiorly. None of us has ever *seen* an insight or a feeling. But I trust, too, that none of us would claim that he or she had never *experienced* a feeling or an insight, never judged that some proposition was true or false, never made a decision. Moreover, I hope that we all know the experience of *wanting* to understand, wanting to be reasonable in our judgments, wanting to be responsible in our decisions. For it is in the realm of that *desire*, and in being faithful to that desire, that Lonergan locates what it is to be an authentic human person. But our experience of these events and of this desire occurs, not in the realm of outer sense, but in the domain of human interiority. It is in interiority that, through these events of understanding, judging, and deciding, we "process" reality. Sensations come in; language goes out; but between sensations and language there is, as Lonergan has formulated it in some recent lectures, the mysterious "little black box" of our interiority. The workings of that little black box are the domain that we concentrate upon in Christian spiritual theology, in Jungian psychology, and in any attempt such as the present one that would relate spirituality to psychology.

I should mention, in addition, two other advantages that accrue from employing Lonergan's framework for understanding interiority. First, his stress, as I have already indicated, is on human *desire*, and desire is the area of our being that is illuminated by the explorations also of the great depth psychologists, including Jung. Secondly, and most importantly, Lonergan emphasizes that spiritual development is not something that occurs in some realm that is isolated from the insights that we have into the events of our everyday life, from the judgments that we make as to the truth or falsity of the most mundane propositions, from the anxieties we feel and the decisions that we make regarding our orientation and actions as beings-*in*-the-world. God's saving purpose is a will to save the world itself, to redeem the time of our lives, as Eliot would put it. It is not a dimension of reality that is totally extrinsic from the events of understanding, judging, and deciding, that we experience every day. On the other hand, our relation to God is not to be collapsed into a secularistic denial of the supernatural character of grace. Rather, grace is offered *in* its supernatural character within the events of our

everyday lives. So the perspective offered by Lonergan is neither a
fundamentalism or extrinsicism that denies the this-worldly character of our lives, nor a secularism or immanentism that neglects the
absolutely transcendent origin and finality of the relationship to the
divine in which we stand at every moment of our lives.

What, then, is Christian spiritual development? Lonergan's
treatment of this question is provided at the end of a lengthy analysis
of human cognitional and moral development that concludes with
the realization that the flowering of human potential, the sustained
development of the human person, the solution of such social ills as
injustice, alienation, and the dominance of totalitarian aspirations in
both the West and East today, are impossible on the basis of human
resources alone. We are confronted with a *problem of evil* in our development as human persons and in the social organization of human
affairs. This problem is rooted in our very constitution as human
subjects, in our finitude, in the tension between our always limited
possibilities and our aspirations to transcend these limitations.

I will not go into the intricacies of Lonergan's analysis of the
roots of moral impotence. Suffice it to say that he argues persuasively that we are faced with a problem of evil that we are powerless
to resolve. If there is going to be a solution to the problem of evil,
it must come in the form of redemption. Either there is a divinely
originated solution to the problem of evil, or there is no solution at
all. If God exists, if God knows of our plight, and if God is good,
then there is a divinely originated solution that is offered to our freedom, one that we can accept or reject, and that, if we accept it, will
involve us in a whole new area of growth and transformation, an area
which we would not even know in any explicit way if God had not
come to meet us. This distinct area of development is related to our
cognitional and moral development. It is not the product of our
knowing and our choosing. It is not something that we vainly imagine, or that we produce by wishful thinking. Rather, it is offered to
our knowledge and our freedom as a *gift*. And, if we accept it, it
transforms our values, and provides a new context for our knowing,
a new atmosphere or environment that enables us to be truly intelligent in our questioning and genuinely reasonable in our judgments. This new context is *faith*, which Lonergan defines as "the eye
of love," the eye of the love that is ours, that is the atmosphere in

which we live, when we know ourselves as unconditionally loved by, and rooted in, the love that is God's alone.[8]

The divine solution to the problem of evil, then, is God's gift of his love that is poured forth into our hearts by the Holy Spirit who has been given to us.[9] Our desire for this love is a natural desire: with Thomas Aquinas, Lonergan insists that we have a *natural* desire for the vision and love of God.[10] He insists, too, that our subjectivity is mutilated or abolished, unless we are stretching forth towards God:

> There lies within [our] horizon a region for the divine, a shrine for ultimate holiness. It cannot be ignored. The atheist may pronounce it empty. The agnostic may urge that he finds his investigation has been inconclusive. The contemporary humanist will refuse to allow the question [of God] to arise. But their negations presuppose the spark in our clod, our native orientation to the divine.[11]

Being in love with God, then, is for Lonergan the basic fulfilment of the deepest human desire, that desire that he calls "conscious intentionality."

> That fulfillment brings a deep-set joy that can remain despite humiliation, failure, privation, pain, betrayal, desertion. That fulfillment brings a radical peace, the peace that the world cannot give. That fulfillment bears fruit in a love of one's neighbor that strives mightily to bring about the kingdom of God on this earth. On the other hand, the absence of that fulfillment opens the way to the trivialization of human life in the pursuit of fun, to the harshness of human life arising from the ruthless exercise of power, to despair about human welfare springing from the conviction that the universe is absurd.[12]

God's love is offered to all men and women at every time and place. This universality of God's self-communication (a notion that he has in common with Karl Rahner) Lonergan speaks of in terms of God's *inner word*, the word that God speaks in the solitude of our hearts, drawing us to himself. But this love is also embodied, incarnate, revealed for all to see, in the *outer word* of the life, preaching, death, and resurrection of Jesus.[13] "And I, if I be lifted up from the earth, shall draw all men to myself."[14] The disciples of Jesus through the centuries constitute that community whose task it will be until the end of time to give *explicit witness* in external words and deeds to the offer of divine love as the only resolution of the otherwise hopeless human dilemma of personal incapacity to grow, of social injustice and alienation. As another superb contemporary thinker, Eric Voegelin, has labored for thirty years to argue, no social order that is not permeated with the love of the unseen measure that Christians call God can be just or humanly fulfilling.[15] In language current among those who have followed recent deliberations within the Church, faith and justice are inextricably linked in the mission of the disciples of Jesus in the world.[16]

Christian spiritual transformation, in this context, is thus a matter, first, of a process of conversion that involves a growing intimacy with the source and fountain of redemptive love, an intimacy that takes the form of being ever more patterned after the example of Christ; and, second, of a growing commitment and ability to participate in the mission of Christ, which is also the mission of that community whose task it is to render explicit to the whole world the fact that, in Jesus the Christ, God has definitively revealed the saving action that he is always working in the world. To be in love with God is also to be *sent* by God. To grow in the love of God is also to grow in participation in the mission—the saving and revealing mission—of Jesus.

Christian spiritual growth thus involves a number of elements:

a) One comes to a developing familiarity with God, so that one is able ever more readily and ever more easily to find him and to participate with him in his redemptive work after the pattern of Christ, the suffering servant of God.

b) One grows in the ability to discern precisely what it is that God wants of oneself and of one's community, and in the willingness to do what it is that God asks, confident that what one is doing is not one's own work but God's.

c) Summing up all of what this development involves, one grows in *self-transcendence*. This is the first key term that I take from Lonergan. One grows in self-transcendence, until, in the saint, there is reached a point of the union of one's own understanding, reason, and desire with the knowledge and love of God, a union that can only be broadened and heightened, deepened and enriched, but not gone beyond; and a point of self-abnegation and humility that rejoices in sharing the lot of the poor, despised, and humiliated Son of God himself, in his mission of establishing the kingdom of God on earth. Christian spiritual transformation is a matter of continual conversion to self-transcendence, within the community of the disciples of the Lord that is the Church, until there is reached the point where one's understanding, one's judgments of fact and of value, one's desires, and one's choices, while not ceasing to be one's own, are a participation in the understanding, the judgments, the desires, the choices of God himself, working in and through oneself and one's community, to continue and to spread the redemption of the world that only God can effect.

If, then, we are talking about Christian spiritual development as a transformation of our insights, our judgments, our desires, and our choices, we are speaking of it as fundamentally a transformation of our *interiority*, of our basic horizon. The difference that God's solution to the problem of evil makes in the social world, in the world of economics and politics, in the world of institutions and organizations, is a *function* of the difference it makes in persons, in the unity of personal consciousness, in people's vision and choices. Christian spiritual development, considered most radically, is a transformation of one's understanding and of one's willingness, so that these two are brought into harmony and cooperation with God's redemptive purpose in Christ Jesus and through the community of his disciples. The transformation, once again, is in the direction of *self-transcendence*, so that, by accepting God's offer of both salvation and vocation, one becomes ever more God-centered and Christ-centered in one's apprehensions of value and in one's decisions, in one's pursuit of meaning and truth, and in one's affective engagement with other persons in the dramatic situations that constitute the stuff, the setting, the stage, of one's own personal story and of history itself.

Christian Spiritual Transformation as Self-Appropriation

Now, besides self-transcendence, there is another term that Lonergan uses when he speaks of development. That term is *self-*

appropriation. Self-appropriation is a matter of self-knowledge, of self-discovery, of self-understanding. One can be quite self-transcendent, quite loving and generous, quite genuine in one's relations with others, quite sincere about wanting to understand things correctly, without being very adept at *intricate and precise* self-knowledge.[17] One can be, in Lonergan's terms, quite religiously and morally converted without being *intellectually converted*.[18] Intellectual conversion is a matter of knowing *precisely* what one is doing when one is pursuing understanding, reaching for truth, trying to decide in responsible fashion. Many people genuinely try to understand, and succeed in doing so, without being able to say *precisely* what they are doing when they understand, how their insights are related to their sensations, their questions, their beliefs, their images, their concepts, their feelings. One can *also* be quite religiously and morally converted without being what I have called "psychically converted."[19] *Psychic conversion* is a matter of knowing what one is feeling, of being able to tell one's story, and to tell it as it is. One can have a quite genuine and even beautiful life of feeling without being able to tell what he or she is feeling, how *this* feeling is related to *that*, how both feelings are related to the objects they intend, how one's feelings are related to one's images and symbols, to one's questions and insights, to one's beliefs and ideas. In other words, one can have a quite profound and genuinely self-transcendent interiority without being able to articulate one's inner life with any notable clarity and precision. We all know wonderful and holy people who are quite unsophisticated when it comes to self-knowledge, or who will put their self-knowledge in very common sense terms—people who make at times heroic decisions, but who, when asked *why* they made this or that decision, or what went on in their minds and hearts which led them so to decide, can answer only, "I don't know; it just seemed to be the right thing to do."

Such genuine self-transcendence without self-appropriation is by no means to be disparaged. It is the condition of most good and holy men and women down through the ages, the source of most that is good in human history. But there are factors at work, especially in our age, that seem to indicate that self-appropriation, in addition to self-transcendence, is becoming ever more necessary if one wishes to choose responsibly, to judge reasonably, to inquire intelligently, or just if one wishes to know what God wants and does not want.

Perhaps there was a time when common sense wisdom and homespun practicality were enough for most people. Perhaps, too, there was a time when the only addition to common sense that some people needed was a good dose of theoretical understanding that was basically in harmony with the Gospel. But there are a number of indications that would seem to argue persuasively that we are now living in a world where self-transcendence, backed up by a common sense framework, or even by a cogent and brilliant theory, is simply not enough; where religious and moral conversion must be complemented by intellectual and psychic conversion; where self-transcendence must be aided and helped, complemented and augmented, by self-appropriation, by precise and even technical self-knowledge, by an ability to articulate just what is going on in one's "little black box." If this be the case, then spiritual transformation today is a matter not only of growing self-transcendence, but also of ever more precise and technical self-knowledge.

What are some of the indications that would back up this conviction that I share with Lonergan? Let me talk first about the insufficiency of common sense, and then about the ambiguity of theory. And let me do so within the context of the Church's recent pronounced recognition that the *promotion of justice* is a constitutive element in the preaching of the Gospel.

The paper that issued from the 1971 Synod of Bishops, "Justice in the World," and the statement of Pope Paul VI, *Octagesima Adveniens*, mark the beginnings, I believe, of a substantial leap forward in the Church's social, political, and economic insight and praxis. One of the few public statements that Pope John Paul I had a chance to make was to the effect that we need a new and worldwide economic order. The achievement of that order, I believe, is going to demand that we take our stand, and that we enable others to take *their* stand, not on practical common sense, and not on theory, but on the *self-appropriation* of our interiority and especially of our orientation to value.

Why do I say this? Well, let us treat common sense first, however briefly. One of the characteristics of practical common sense is that it not only is incapable of treating complex, long-range, and ultimate issues and results, but also that it resentfully brushes aside and ignores any attempts to raise questions that are concerned with such issues. It has the world's work to do, and it cannot be bothered by questions that would take time away from doing that work.[20] The person exclusively operating from practical common sense is concerned only with "getting the job done." Everything else—motivation, rationale, social organization, interpersonal communication—is oriented to that end. The question of whether the job is worth doing at all, or whether the most expedient way of doing it is also the most authentic way, is a bother, yes, but more than that: it is a threat, a subversive question that could overturn the entire project. Rejection precisely of such kinds of questions is what is responsible for the fact that our objective world-situation today can be characterized in terms of opposed totalitarianisms: the totalitarianism of the multinational corporation, predicated on the assumption of the need of automatic progress and expansion; and the totalitarianism of the communist state, rooted in the assumption that class conflict can bring the social order into harmony with what is right.[21] Both myths neglect the fact that there are religious, personal, and cultural values that must be pursued in an integral fashion if there is to be a *just* social order that *really* provides for the basic needs of all the members of a society. In both systems, however much theory may be involved in their establishment, we see operative the bias of practical common sense against the kinds of questions that must be asked if the job is to be done, not only expediently, but also humanely, genuinely, authentically. The question of *integrity* is, not just overlooked, but actively repudiated and repressed.

Nor is *theory* sufficient to reestablish the significance of that question. For there are theories that support the question, but there are other theories that discredit it. The theories of B. F. Skinner or of orthodox Freudian psychoanalysis are just as coherent, just as thorough, just as all-encompassing, and, for many, just as convincing, as are the theories of a Christian philosophy and theology.

The Church's reliance on theory as the ground of praxis arose in the Middle Ages, more specifically with scholastic philosophy. One of the interesting things about that period, though, is that there were not many theories from which to choose, and there was not all that much to be learned in order to piece together a convincing theory. Even the disputes in the world of theory did not touch, as they do today, on the really basic issues, such as the existence of God, the fact of revelation, the ethical end of the human person, the value of a virtuous life, and so on. Right down into the Renaissance, there was so little to be learned that it was possible for one person to be at once an artist, a natural scientist, and a man of practical affairs—and we have Leonardo da Vinci to prove it.

The need for specialization to master one tiny dimension of reality is a distinctly modern phenomenon. And while one is spending most of one's time specializing in one's own area, one's contemporaries are adding theory upon theory in *their* specialized domains. And these theories sometimes contradict one another on the most fundamental issues, on issues that *every* developing adult must confront. But how is one to take a stand, if one has to devote all of one's energies to his specialization? There are issues on which we *must* judge and on which we *must* decide if we are to live a human life. Yet there is simply too much to be learned before we can judge and decide.[22] Unless we find a ground *beyond* theory—for it will not do just to fall back on common sense—our situation becomes one of hopeless relativism. It is my contention that this ground-beyond-theory lies in the self-appropriation of human interiority.

This point about the need for a quite technical self-appropriation can be developed at great length; we do not have space to do that here. The point I wish to make in the present context is that *only* through such self-appropriation can one discover the precise relation that obtains between religious, personal, and cultural values on the one hand, and the social value of a just economic and political order on the other hand. And one needs to discover these relations, not simply in the abstract, as through some theory of value, but in the concrete order in which one is called upon to judge, to decide, and to act. And so I return to my general statement: *Christian spiritual transformation is a matter of self-transcendence that, at a certain point, calls for a movement to self-appropriation.* Christian spiritual development is a matter of ongoing conversion, and ongoing conversion means today not only religious and moral, but also intellectual and psychic conversion.

The Levels of Consciousness

There are five levels of operations that one discovers when one enters upon the project of the self-appropriation of interiority.[23] Inner and outer sensations, memories, and images constitute the level of empirical presentations. These empirical presentations are organized by understanding, which is a second level of consciousness. For example, if you are reading without any understanding of what I am saying, you are operating at the first, empirical level of operations. If you are reading *and* understanding what I am saying, your understanding is organizing the empirical presentations into some kind of intelligible whole. You are processing what you hear by the operations that go on in your "little black box." You are operating not only at the first, but also at the second level of operations. If, moreover, you not only *understand* what I am saying but are also trying to *judge* whether it is correct or not, you have added a third level of operations, where we either assent to, or disagree with, something we have understood.

These three levels of operations are what make us to be human knowers. Lonergan calls these levels *experience*, *understanding*, and *judgment*.

But we are not just *knowers*. There are times in our lives when, after we have made a judgment, "This is true," a further question arises, "What am I going to do about it?" Then we have to *decide*. And decision constitutes a fourth level of operations.

Finally, there is another whole dimension of interior reality that is not dealt with by speaking of the empirical, intelligent, rational, and decisional levels of consciousness. There is a fifth level of consciousness that is a matter of being addressed by and in relation to God. There is the experience of mystery. There is the reality of falling in love with God. There is prayer, worship, mystical experience, the dark night of the soul, the living flame of love, the search for and discovery of the holy, the gift of the divinely originated solution to the problem of evil.

Religious self-appropriation, obviously, is a matter of articulating what is going on at that fifth level of consciousness. The means of discovering oneself in one's relation to God are many: there are spiritual direction, retreats, various methods of keeping a journal, and so on. But what is important for us also to appropriate is the manner in which experience at that fifth level of consciousness has an effect on other levels. The influence of God's grace moves downward in our consciousness. It changes our values (fourth level), so that it provides us with entirely new orientations for our decisions, and enables them to be more self-transcendent. It changes our view of the world, our vision, the way we understand and judge things (second and third levels), and provides us with a determination to understand thoroughly and to judge reasonably; and it brings about a harmony and peace at the level of inner sensation, a peace that "the world cannot give," so that our inner being and our bodies rest securely in the love of God.

Symbols, Feelings, and Drama

Such is the pattern of interiority that is discovered when one enters upon the way of self-appropriation: five levels of consciousness, each related to the other, whether we move from below upwards, or from above downwards.

And now, finally, we are able to locate with precision the region where Jung's discoveries become significant for spiritual development, especially for self-appropriation. For all of the operations that we are talking about—sensing, imaging, remembering (first level), inquiring, understanding, putting our understanding into words (second level), reflecting, weighing the evidence, judging (third level), deliberating, deciding, acting (fourth level), praying, worshiping (fifth level)—all of these operations are permeated by *feelings*. We have feelings about the objects of all of these operations. The operations themselves are always dramatic. When you try to understand, it is because you are confused. When you succeed in understanding, the confusion ceases and you experience satisfaction, maybe even excitement. When you want to know whether you understand correctly, it is because you are not satisfied with just a set of bright ideas; you want to get things right and not just go about spouting opinions. When you have to make a decision, the drama of the situation stands out clearly. Some decisions can be agonizing. *All* decisions have a great deal of affectivity accompanying them, for we are dealing in decisions with questions of value. And value is something we feel before ever we judge about it or act on it.[24] Finally, fifth-level religious experience has those peculiar sets of feelings that we call "consolations" and "desolations." In sum, we are not just structured conscious operators. We are also the subjects of a drama, precisely in and through these operations. There is a *story* to our operating, because there are feelings that permeate all of those operations.

Let us focus a bit more on this drama, because it is more complicated than I have so far indicated. In addition to the desire to understand, there is also a *flight* from understanding (second level). I can flee insight just as passionately as I can pursue it. Moreover, I can resist the truth just as strongly as I can intend it (third level). I can try to escape responsible decision and live a life of ease or of drifting or of hiding my talents, just as persistently as I can conscientiously examine every situation to find the best course of action (fourth level). I can flee contact with God just as passionately as I can seek to find him and do his will (fifth level).

There are feelings that permeate not only genuine performance at each of the five levels, but also *inauthentic* actions at each step of the way. The ultimate drama of my life, in fact, is this drama of *authenticity* and *inauthenticity*. The authentic person is the person who pursues understanding, who seeks truth, who responds to what is really worthwhile, and who searches for God and his will. The inauthentic person is the person who flees understanding, who runs from the truth, who resists further questions about his or her decisions, and who tries to escape God. And those feelings never go away. They are present in the entire drama. They are precisely what make it so dramatic.

What, then, are feelings? Feelings are *energy*-become-conscious. Feelings are a matter of psychic energy. Feelings are the basic sensitive component of every human operation. Feelings make of spirituality a *story*. To know one's feeling is to begin to tell one's own story. Feelings are the drive and momentum of the life of the human spirit. Feelings join the spirit to the body in a conscious unity.

There is one further aspect to this matter. Feelings always enter consciousness through being connected with *some* representation. Now, the most basic form of representation lies in symbols. A *sym-*

bol, Lonergan says, is an image of a real or imaginary object that evokes a feeling or is evoked by a feeling[25]; what this means is that there is never a feeling without a symbolic meaning; never a symbol without a feeling. To *name* one's feelings is to discover the dynamic images, the symbols, that are associated with them. To have *insight* into one's feelings is to understand the symbolic association. To *tell one's story* is to narrate the course of one's elemental symbolizing. And where does one's elemental symbolizing occur in its purest form, untainted by the biases that, in waking life, can lead us to distort our story? The place of elemental symbolizing is in our dreams. It is in the dream that we first are conscious, and it is in the dream that we find a "story" going forward that we cannot distort without being aware that we are doing so.[26] If we want to know our "story"—the story of insight, the story of judgment, the story of decision, and the story of prayer—we can find it in our dreams. There is a psychic conversion that puts us into contact with that story. It affects us deeply once it has occurred. For it enables us to judge ourselves in our waking life as authentic or inauthentic in our pursuit of understanding, in our seeking of truth, in our decisions, and in our search for God.

In the next article I will situate Jung's psychology of individuation within this context of the discussion of self-transcendence, and, especially, of self-appropriation. In the third article, though, I will use this same framework to criticize Jung's psychology. For Jung did *not* have an accurate understanding of the structure of our operations as human subjects—our understanding, our judgments, our decisions, and our search for God. His basic philosophical and theological standpoint did not take its stand on a notion of authenticity as self-transcendence. And this basic flaw renders his contributions to Christian spiritual development very ambiguous until these contributions are transposed into some such context as I have tried to indicate in the present article.

Notes

1. See, for example, John A. Sanford, *Dreams: God's Forgotten Language* (Philadelphia and New York: Lippincott, 1968); *Healing and Wholeness* (New York: Paulist Press, 1977); Morton Kelsey, *Dreams: The Dark*

Speech of the Spirit, A Christian Interpretation (New York: Doubleday, 1968); *Encounter with God: A Theology of Christian Experience* (Minneapolis: Bethany, 1972).

2. See James Hillman, *The Myth of Analysis: Three Essays in Archetypal Psychology* (Evanston: Northwestern University Press, 1972). I quote from p. 21: "The spiritual-director models of *guru*, rabbi, of Ignatius or Fenelon, of Zen master, are only substitutions on which we lean for want of surety about the true model for psychology."

3. See Edward C. Whitmont, "Prefatory Remarks to Jung's 'Reply to Buber,' " in *Spring: An Annual of Archetypal Psychology and Jungian Thought* (1973), pp. 188–195; and C. G. Jung, "Religion and Psychology: A Reply to Martin Buber," *ibid.*, pp. 196–203.

4. Compare C. G. Jung, "Is Analytical Psychology a Religion?" (notes on a talk given by Jung, in *Spring*, 1972, pp. 144–148) with Jung's "Psychotherapists or the Clergy," in C. G. Jung, *Modern Man in Search of a Soul* (New York: Harcourt, Brace, and World, 1933), pp. 221–244.

5. Bernard Lonergan, *Method in Theology* (New York: Herder and Herder, 1972), Chapters Ten and Eleven.

6. David Burrell, *Exercises in Religious Understanding* (South Bend: University of Notre Dame Press, 1974), p. 221.

7. There are, of course, dangers in such a procedure, for the reader can easily take the results of Lonergan's explorations as a series of concepts that could dispense one from the task of insight into oneself. There are no short-cuts to the self-appropriation to which Lonergan invites one. But precisely because there are no short-cuts, I can only ask the reader interested in pursuing the process to go to Lonergan's works themselves.

8. See Lonergan, *Insight: A Study of Human Understanding* (paperback edition, New York: Harper and Row, 1978), Chapters Eighteen and Twenty; *Method in Theology*, Chapter Four.

9. Rm 5:5.

10. See Lonergan, "The Natural Desire to See God," in *Collection: Papers by Bernard Lonergan* (New York: Herder and Herder, 1967), pp. 84–95.

11. Lonergan, *Method in Theology*, p. 103.

12. *Ibid.*, p. 105.

13. *Ibid.*, pp. 112–115.

14. Jn 12:32.

15. See Eric Voegelin, *Order and History*, four volumes to date (Louisiana State University Press, 1956–1974).

16. See the document of the 1971 Synod of Bishops, *Justice in the World*. See also the Documents of the 32nd General Congregation of the Society of Jesus, and especially Decree 4, "Our Mission Today."

17. See Lonergan, *Insight*, p. 475.
18. On intellectual conversion as self-appropriation, see Lonergan, *Method in Theology*, pp. 238–240.
19. See Robert Doran, *Subject and Psyche: Ricoeur, Jung, and the Search for Foundations* (Washington, D. C.: University Press of America, 1977), especially pp. 240–246.
20. See Lonergan, *Insight*, pp. 225–242.
21. *Ibid.*
22. Lonergan, "Dimensions of Meaning," in *Collection*, pp. 252–267.
23. On the levels of consciousness, see Lonergan, *Method in Theology*, Chapters One and Four.
24. *Ibid.*, pp. 31–33.
25. *Ibid.*, p. 64.
26. See Doran, "Dramatic Artistry in the Third Stage of Meaning," in *Lonergan Workshop II*, edited by Frederick Lawrence (Missoula: Scholars Press, 1979).

Robert M. Doran, S.J.

Jungian Psychology and Christian Spirituality: II

THE JUNGIAN PSYCHOLOGY OF INDIVIDUATION

The significance of Jungian psychology for spiritual theology lies in the fact that Jung is concerned with understanding and promoting a development in the realm of human interiority. The interest in Jung on the part of Christians concerned about their own spiritual transformation is thus not surprising.

In the previous section, I argued that Christian spiritual development is a growth, first, in self-transcendence, but, secondly, also a development in self-knowledge or self-appropriation. I located the area where Jung's discoveries aid this development. Permeating the whole range of the operations of human interiority, which Bernard Lonergan has shown to unfold on five levels, there is the dramatic life of feeling, which makes of our inner lives as human subjects a story. Getting in touch with one's story is a matter primarily of identifying the affective component of all our human operations. This task can be greatly aided if we learn the art of *symbolic identification.* The privileged place of symbols in human consciousness occurs precisely in those domains that Jung explored so fully: our dreams, our spontaneous waking fantasies, and our engagement in the techniques of what Jung called active imagination.[1]

To the material included in the previous article, I wish now to add the caution that it is easy to get *stuck* in the symbols and images that emerge elementally in our dreams. Let me recall a dream of my own that occurred precisely at the time when I was engaged in writing a doctoral dissertation whose whole point it was to explore the

relations between the conscious intentionality so thoroughly elucidated by Lonergan and the depths of the psyche studied by Jung.

At the time of this dream, I was in Zurich, Switzerland, where
I had gone to complete work on my dissertation. I had been there
better than a month, had attended lectures at the C. G. Jung Institute, had immersed myself as much as possible in the atmosphere
breathed by Jungians, and had reached a point of rather complete
frustration with my efforts to articulate a series of relationships that
I already knew obtained in the domain of human interiority, but
whose intelligible, connecting link I had not yet discovered. In the
dream, I am descending a flight of stairs, and am clearly intending
to go down into the basement of a very large house. The house, in-
cidentally, resembled the building in which I was living in Zurich.
I have almost reached the ground floor of the building, when I meet
none other than Bernard Lonergan coming up the same flight of
stairs. He stops me in my descent, looks at me very intently, and
says, "If you really want to see some images, come with me." He
takes me *up* the flight of stairs, to what appears to be the top floor
of the house, and leads me into a large auditorium. We select a pair
of seats next to one another, with Lonergan sitting to my right. Immediately a movie begins to be shown on a screen in the front of the
room, and we begin to watch it.

The images that were provided me in this dream were precisely
the material that I needed for the insight into the connecting link
between intentional consciousness and the psyche for which I had
been searching. The point of the dream is, at least in part, that the
images of the psyche are not to be negotiated down in the basement,
i.e., in the lower reaches from which they emerge. Rather these images are to be allowed to be processed by the levels of consciousness;
and their ultimate significance lies in their relevance for the uppermost level (the top floor) of human subjectivity, i.e., for the operations of that existential level of consciousness whose task it is to
evaluate, deliberate, discern, decide, and act. The images that
emerge from the depths of the psyche are materials for insight, judgment, and decision. Thus they must be interpreted; the interpretation must be judged to be sound; and the self-knowledge thus
gained is to be employed as one moves to existential self-determi-
nation in free decision. The dream contains, too, a warning regarding the need for an existential and aesthetic distance from the images

themselves if one is going to be able to negotiate freely these elemental symbols. The detached and disinterested desire to know and the self-transcendence of existential deliberation are prerequisites for the proper negotiation of the psyche's elemental symbols. To attempt to negotiate the symbols from the inappropriate proximity of the lower reaches from which they emerge is, in fact, the stuff of madness: the overwhelming by psychic processes of the human spirit's capacities for intelligent inquiry, critical reflection, and responsible deliberation.

One further introductory point may prove helpful. I find it significant that the dimensions of intelligent, rational, and existential consciousness, on the one hand, and of elemental symbolism on the other hand are two quite distinct, though not separate factors in the processes of human interiority. I find it both convenient and ontologically correct to refer to the first set of determinants of interiority as *spirit*,[2] and to the second as *psyche*. And I add to this pair a third constituent of the self, the organism, whose processes, precisely as organic, constitute what depth psychologists have been calling *the unconscious*. The metaphysical implications of this notion of the human compound that is the self or the subject are too complicated for us to investigate here,[3] but the distinctions thus established will prove helpful in our subsequent remarks.

I now wish to proceed in the present article to outline in heuristic fashion the Jungian understanding of the inner journey that one ventures on when one begins to appreciate the immense significance that accrues to one's spontaneous, elemental symbolizing.

The Individual and the Collective

Jung's term for this inner journey is "the process of individuation." In one of his writings he calls individuation "the process of becoming one's own self." I quote Jung more thoroughly: "Individuation means becoming an 'individual,' and, insofar as 'individuality' embraces our innermost, last, and incomparable uniqueness, it also implies becoming one's own self. We could therefore translate individuation as 'coming to selfhood' or 'self-realization.' "[4] The Jungian stress, of course, is on that dimension of the self that I have referred to as the psyche, i.e., on the complexes of feelings and symbols that permeate all our operations as human subjects. Individuation is a process of discovering, exploring, attending to that dimension of our being that is properly called psychic. Through this exploration, one comes to, one becomes, oneself, and one does so precisely by discovering a superabundance of meaning, beyond rational comprehension, that enables one to live what Jung called the "just-so" life.[5]

The implications of this notion of individuation are important. If one must explore and successfully negotiate the psychic dimension of one's being in order to become one's own self, this must mean that the same psychic dimension of one's being can also alienate one from one's self. There must be tendencies in the psyche that would lead one astray, away from the path that leads to oneself. These tendencies must be confronted head-on and be overcome. This is the point of speaking of a *process* of individuation, of insisting, too, that such a process is incumbent on more and more people in our age if they are to come to a satisfactory sense of meaning in their lives, and if civilization and its values are to be preserved from destruction. And so it is that Jung speaks of two tendencies in the psyche that can lead us astray, that can, in the terms established in the previous paper, encourage the surrender of our own desire for accumulating insight, for the unconditioned, and for dedication to what is really worthwhile. One can identify with *collective consciousness*, or one can surrender to or be inflated by the *collective unconscious*. In either case, one is not assuming responsibility for self- and world-constitution, is not fulfilling one's unique vocation within the universe.

a. The Ego and the Persona.

The dimension of the psyche that must find its way to the self, Jung calls the *ego*. The ego is the set of psychic complexes—constellations of images, ideas, feelings, and capacities—that constitute what in Lonergan's terminology would be called differentiated consciousness. The ego is constituted by the range of performance in which we feel at home as conscious operators, that is, in which we know ourselves to be competent to understand, pass judgment, and make decisions. The individuation process depends on the establishment of a relatively well-developed ego, that is, on a realistic sense of one's own areas of competence in the social and professional world, in the life of the family, in the world of the "other." The ego will develop further and will be transformed in the process of individuation, but for that process to begin, there must be a solid base in a relatively self-esteeming ego. The development of this base is the task of the first half of life.[6]

Even a well-developed ego, however, does not constitute an individuated personality. The journey to individuation, as an explicit and consciously assumed responsibility, remains a task for the afternoon of life. Closely connected with the ego, and in some respects undifferentiated from it in the course of its normal development in the first half of life, is another aspect of psychic experience that Jung calls the *persona*. The *persona* is the face that we turn outwards in the process of the socialization of the ego, the outer mask that we wear before others. Its development depends for its integrity on the kind of social recognition that we have received from others from very early on in life, on what we have had to do to secure the esteem of others, and consequently our own self-esteem. It is very easy for the ego to identify with the *persona*, particularly if the parents have not communicated to the child the inner sustenance to enable him to be relatively well-centered in his sense of his capacities. The differentiation of the ego from the *persona* is a first, and often a lengthy, task to be accomplished in the process of individuation. One's social role, the network of his external relations with others, the recognition granted one by the significant others in his life, may have been very important in the formation of one's ego. But one is *not* one's role in society, nor is it appropriate that one receive his identity as a person—as a subject of intelligent, rational, and moral operations, and as a carrier of affective intentionality—from one's social role. The differentiation of ego from *persona* means, however, not that one is to abandon one's social role or position, but that one is to cease receiving his identity from it. "Who I am" is a far more extensive and rich story of experiences, feelings, insights, judgments, decisions, and religious commitments than "what I do."

Ego-*persona* identifications can take many forms, and their resistance to differentiation depends on the extent to which one was forced to turn outwards in one's development for a source of self-esteem. Moreover, one does not need to be what we call a task-oriented person (as opposed to a person-oriented task?) in order to stand in need of serious work at differentiating ego from *persona*. The common element in all forms of ego-*persona* identification is that one tends to identify oneself in terms of *who one is for others*, whether functionally or interpersonally. Ernest Becker's well-known book, *The Denial of Death*, though reliant more on Otto Rank than on Jung, is in part a helpful treatment of the inveterate human tendency to seek self-esteem from one or other form of collective identification, even if only one other person.[7]

Breaking ego-*persona* identifications can be very difficult. Jung's experience of the process of individuation in his own life-story involved, for instance, an extremely painful course of events that led him to dissolve the false identity he had assumed from his associations with the Freudian circle and from Freud's projections upon Jung, which, if maintained, would have prevented Jung from developing in his own way and would have locked him into an amalgamation of social and professional relationships that would have blocked the emergence of his distinct perspectives on psychological reality. To bring the issue closer to home, the problem of ego-*persona* differentiation can be very acute in religious life, and in fact wherever community living is pursued as a desirable goal. True community is based on shared meanings and values.[8] But in religious life it involves also living and working together for the same apostolic ends. The complexities of common life and of corporate apostolic work are such that the temptation is ever present to identify too exclusively with one's job or function or with the opinion held of oneself by others—an opinion that in many cases may have been formed in a previous stage of one's development as a person or as an apostolic religious, and that does not take into account one's subsequent growth and cumulative discovery of the Lord's unique call upon one's talents and resources. There is a fine line to be drawn between the self-alienation that can develop from such identification and the kind of self-assertion or individualism that is clearly contrary to the union of minds and hearts to which one commits oneself by religious vows. Only the gift of discernment in a context of obedience and mission can resolve such difficulties. The full reciprocity of genuine community involves keeping channels of communication open on all sides when a decision is being made concerning the disposition of a man's or woman's apostolic energies. Religious who are too caught up in functional or interpersonal ego-*persona* identifications can all too easily introduce into their decision-making processes a variety of "shuttle diplomacy" that is destructive of community life and apostolate.

Ego-*persona* identification is a relatively minimal instance of identification with collective consciousness. The latter can assume far more distorted and bizarre forms, as in the hypnotic surrender of an educated nation to a Hitler or of the masses to a Mao, or in the mass hysteria by which the residents of Jonestown submitted unto self-destruction to a religious madman who already had successfully persuaded them to abdicate whatever capacities for insight, judgment, and moral decision they still possessed before coming under his demonic spell.

b. The Ego and the Collective Unconscious.

Let us employ further the last-mentioned example, and add that the madman, Jim Jones, was identified in his ego-consciousness, not with collective consciousness, but with what Jung would call "an archetype of the collective unconscious"—with, it would seem, the very image of God.

Jung's term, the collective unconscious, is perhaps unfortunate. For it makes us think of an "already down there now" real thing, a kind of Platonic world of Ideas, but now located in the depths rather than the heights. Spatial imagery is deceptive when we are speaking of psychic reality, and yet we *do* need some imagery to get us started on the road to insight, and the imagery of mysterious depths does seem, in fact, to be that employed by dreams themselves to indicate the unconscious. In fact, though, what Jung means by the collective unconscious is the innate or inherited tendency of human neurophysiology to achieve conscious representation at times in the form of powerful images that are invested with a primal force that is not personally or even culturally determined but that seems to convey a significance that is cross-cultural or universally human. The images released from these depths have a universally meaningful appeal, because they seem to express themes that characterize the human drama wherever and whenever it occurs.

The experience of archetypal images, which has its own time in the natural course of the process of individuation, and which is not to be hastened or artificially induced, is an event fraught with significance. It brings with it an integrating, healing sense of the transpersonal meaning of one's existence within the context of the immense universe of being. And yet the power of archetypal images is also their danger. For one can begin to identify with an archetype, either by the submergence of one's ego in the imaginal undertow of conscious existence, or by the inflation of the ego through the conscious appropriation, rather than negotiation, of an archetypal image.

The natural time for the negotiation of the archetypal world in the process of individuation occurs, in general, *after* not only the dissolving of ego-*persona* identifications, but also the withdrawal of the projections of the shadow and the encounter with the contrasexual opposite, i.e., with the *anima* or *animus*. The shadow represents the dimensions of one's own being that are awkward, undifferentiated, and even downright malicious or evil, the dimensions that ego-consciousness chooses not to admit to belong to oneself. The shadow is projected onto another person or onto a group, who then become scapegoats upon whose shoulders the sins of the ego-centered subject are laid. The encounter with and negotiation of the shadow marks the beginning or coming to terms with the unconscious, but still in its personal dimensions. The withdrawal of the shadow-projections leads in the natural rhythm of things to the discovery of the contrasexual opposite, whose successful negotiation is the gateway to the discovery and experience of the archetypal images.

If the archetypal images are *appropriated* by the ego, rather than being negotiated as irretrievably other, and if one succeeds in convincing others of his suprahuman significance, he has started a movement of mass hysteria. Thus, for example, Jung's psychology provides a way of understanding the events that occurred in Germany's succumbing to the influence of Hitler. Germany had been defeated in the First World War. Her economic life after the war was in shambles, her cultural heritage in a state of confusion, her moral values in disarray, effective political leadership lacking. There appears on the scene a man held in the grip of a myth and proclaiming himself and his myth as the solution. The myth is the result of Hitler's identification with forces released into his conscious life from the neural depths. He is the savior, proclaiming a myth of racial superiority. To identify with an archetype is to distort not only one's ego, but the archetype itself. Moreover, the German people were in search precisely of a way out of their individual and national malaise. And they shared our common propensity to find the solution "out there," instead of taking the journey to a heightening and expansion of consciousness. So they projected what can be authentically found only in interiority onto an external figure who has identified himself with what in itself is rather a symbol of an inner reality. The projection gives rise to a collective consciousness, with which they identify their own ego-consciousness, under the dominance of a figure who has appropriated for himself the power of a primordial energic constellation and, in the process, distorted that constellation itself. The people then projected onto a scapegoat, the Jews, the source of their own frustration, i.e., the collapse of their own meanings and values. The inner source of their collective confusion, waywardness, frustration, powerlessness, despair—the enemy within—is projected onto a group that is different, that represents a set of experiences, meanings, and values that they find alien, mysterious, threatening. The external group, in this case the Jewish race, is "mythicized," by being identified with the inner source of confusion, the shadow.

A leader, then, creates a cult by identifying with an archetypal image and by persuading others to project onto himself the same image, thus surrendering to the power with which they have invested the leader the use of their own intelligence, rationality, and moral responsibility. The same process lies behind the formation of the various cults springing up in the United States today. The conditions are ripe: economic anxiety, loss of national purpose, breakdown of long-cherished meanings and values, and so forth. Jung saw our country as a potential scene of the same kind of aberration that occurred in Germany; for our materialism and practical denial of ultimates leaves us empty, ready to be victimized by inflated personalities held in the grip of some demonic power.

From this perspective, too, it is possible to interpret one of the strangest facts recorded in the Gospel; namely, the fact that Jesus "strictly charged the disciples to tell no one that he was the Christ" (Mt 16:20; see Mk 8:30, and Lk 9:21). The experience of Jesus at his baptism by John marks the beginning, let us assume, of his personal coming to terms with an extraordinary identity and mission. And what he wrestled with in the desert experience is the temptation to identify in an inflated fashion with the energic power represented in the title, Son of God, and so to distort the meaning of this elemental symbolic constellation. Such temptation is precisely demonic. Is it any wonder, then, that he forbids the disciples to proclaim him as the Messiah, i.e., to project upon him an energic symbolic constellation that belongs to their own religious interiority, and so to distort the meaning of the constellation by converting it into a mass movement? Walter Kasper conjectures that it is likely that, at his trial before the Sanhedrin, Jesus *did* admit to being the Messiah, but only when it was no longer possible for that admission to be distorted by projection and converted into the instrument of a demonic and violent quest for political power on the part of his followers.[9] In order to *be* in reality what he is, he has to *resist* identifying himself with the energic force of that reality and to *forbid* his disciples from engaging in the distortion that would result were they to project upon him their own interior image of the Christ.

Primordial or archetypal images, then, are invested with immense power. It is crucial that they be negotiated from a distance, as other, if one is not to lose one's way on the journey to individuation. And it is equally crucial that they not be projected onto an external other or a group. Perhaps some more mundane examples of the latter necessity will help to clarify its meaning and importance.

As we have seen, Jung insists that we all bear in our psychic repertoire an image of the opposite sex, who is at the same time the carrier of our own contrasexuality. The image is built up, in its concrete details, as a result of one's own experience of the opposite sex. Thus it takes different forms in different people. For some men, the *anima* is determined too exclusively by their own mothers. For others, the *anima* is a plaything, or a vessel of hidden wisdom, or an emasculating power whose influence they must resist with all their force. We tend to project the *anima* or *animus* onto real people and to relate to these persons as embodiments of the image. The *anima* is an inner reality, and, when she is discovered and negotiated as such, she can be a source of guidance on the journey to the self. But her reality as inner is dissipated by projection onto a real woman, whose own reality is itself distorted by becoming the bearer of one's idealization.

Perhaps the most complicated and painful human relationships are those in which one party is the carrier of the projections of the primordial images of the other, and *vice versa*. People who have accomplished a great deal in a long lifetime, who have taught others important truths, have frequently to suffer being the recipients of the projection of the archetypal images of the Wise Old Man or the Wise Old Woman. The fact that they may even appear as such in our dreams does not entitle us to treat them in that way in our external relations with them. Nor, for that matter, does it entitle *them* to be so treated!

People in the helping professions—in psychiatry, medicine, pastoral ministry, education—are often the recipients of archetypal projections. A transference relationship develops, in which the dependent person overinvests in the helper. What is worse, a counter-transference can develop, in which the helper invites the projection, needs it, wants it, and is in turn projecting this need or desire upon the person being helped. Then what Hegel referred to as a master-slave dialectic develops, a network of intersubjective events that is extraordinarily painful for both parties, who more often than not have very few clues as to what is really going on.

The Reconciliation of Opposites

A notion that became ever more important in Jung's mature thought about the process of individuation involves the progressive reconciliation of the opposites in one's being. The steps we have seen thus far come to be interpreted in accord with this notion. Thus, the first reconciliation is between the ego and the complexes that constitute the personal unconscious. In the course of the development that occurs in the first half of life, one's psyche tends to become more or less one-sided in its differentiation. One's development occurs along the line of least resistance, which itself is a matter of one's superior function. That is, one finds success and social approval by differentiating his consciousness in one of the four functions: thinking, feeling, sensation and intuition. If thinking constitutes one's superior function, feeling will be his inferior function, and *vice versa*. So too, if sensation is one's superior function, intuition will be his inferior function, and *vice versa*. The shadow is constellated around one's inferior function. The other two functions will be more or less differentiated, and so will function either as auxiliary to the superior function or as contributing to the shadow, or as allied with both the inferior and the superior function. The first step toward the reconciliation of the opposites involves the relativization by the ego of the supremacy of the differentiated function, so as to grant to the other functions more of a prominent place, or at least more recognition, in one's conscious life.

Next, there is required the reconciliation of one's ego with its contrasexual counterpart. Meeting the opposite here and successfully negotiating it, without identification or appropriation, leads to a psychological androgyny that moves one along the way to wholeness. The contrasexual element is also the key to the journey through the world of the archetypes, where one finds the transpersonal meaning of his life and story: both the myth that one has been leading and the myth that is one's own to lead. The inner journey through this transpersonal source of significance leads one eventually to the reconciliation of ego and self. The self is the deeper center of the psyche, and also the totality of the entire psyche. Its symbols are symbols of centering and of wholeness: the mandala, the quaternity, the cross in the circle, and so forth.[10] Once again, the important procedure is not that the ego identify with the self, but that it negotiate the self's higher authority, that it receive from the self, that it recognize that the ego is not the center of the psyche and yet that the ego is responsible for the restrictive shaping of psychic possibilities contained in the totality of the psyche, in the self.

There is one other area of reconciliation treated by Jung: the reconciliation of *good and evil*. Jung starts from the correct position that the ego tends to regard as evil whatever it finds strange, and thus despises many of the complexes of the unconscious that are not evil at all, but that can and should be negotiated and attended to on the path to individuation. He proceeds from that assumption, however, to a relativization of the issue of the struggle between good and evil, to a position that good and evil can be reconciled in the same manner as ego and unconscious, or masculine and feminine, or ego and self. Evil becomes in Jung's thought a substantive reality; it becomes as real as the complexes themselves. And in this way it becomes relativized as evil. The upshot of this position, as we will see in the final paper, involves the formulation of positions on God and Christ that are unacceptable from a Christian standpoint. But let me suggest in concluding this paper where the principal difficulty lies.

The reconciliation of opposites for Jung is located too exclusively within the psyche. It is more accurate to say that the basic set

of opposites in the constitution of the human person is that of spirit
and matter. These opposites are reconciled by negotiating the psyche, which shares in both. But the problem of evil remains: it is a
spiritual problem, not a psychological one. It is resolved, as I suggested in the first paper, only by the reception of the gift of God's
love, which transforms the human spirit in a movement that extends
downwards into the psyche. But the basic transformation is at the
level of decision, where one's values are transformed in such a way
that one chooses and wants to choose the good, one opts for self-
transcendence. The option has effects on the psyche. But it is an
option that one makes, not down in the basement of the psyche and
its complexes, but at the level of spiritual intentionality in the existential mode as the latter is transformed by God's grace, so that it
comes more and more to opt for, to choose, the good that carries one
beyond oneself.

Notes

1. On active imagination, see Rix Weaver, *The Old Wise Woman* (New
   York: C. G. Jung Foundation, 1973).
2. On the spiritual, see Bernard Lonergan, *Insight: A Study of Human Understanding* (London: Darton, Longman, and Todd, 1957; paperback
   edition, New York: Harper and Row, 1978), pp. 517–520.
3. See *ibid.*, pp. 467–479, 514–520.
4. C. G. Jung, "The Relations between the Ego and the Unconscious," in
   Collected Works, Volume 7: Two Essays on Analytical Psychology, translated
   by R. F. C. Hull (Princeton, Princeton University Press, 1966), p. 173.
5. See C. G. Jung, *Memories, Dreams, Reflections*, translated by Richard
   and Clara Winston (New York: Vintage Books, 1963), p. 325, for a
   description of the experience leading to this awareness.
6. See C. G. Jung, "The Stages of Life," in *Collected Works, Volume 8: The
   Structure and Dynamics of the Psyche* (Princeton: Princeton University
   Press, 1969), pp. 387–403.
7. Ernest Becker, *The Denial of Death* (New York: The Free Press, 1973),
   especially Chapters Seven and Eight.
8. Bernard Lonergan, "Dimensions of Meaning," in *Collection: Papers by
   Bernard Lonergan* (New York: Herder and Herder, 1967), p. 254.
9. Walter Kaspar, *Jesus the Christ* (New York: Paulist Press, 1980), p. 106.
10. C. G. Jung, "Concerning Mandala Symbolism," in *Collected Works,
    Volume 9: The Archetypes and the Collective Unconscious* (Princeton:
    Princeton University Press, 1969), pp. 355–390.

Robert M. Doran, S.J.

Jungian Psychology and Christian Spirituality: III

The previous section gives us some indication of the potential overlapping or correlation of Jungian psychology and Christian spirituality. The withdrawal of projections mentioned previously correlates well with the Ignatian notion of removing inordinate affections and attachments from one's life, so as to be able to give oneself in spiritual freedom to God and to his will for oneself. Jung's talk of the withdrawal of projections onto people, things, and situations is a contemporary and psychological way of expressing both this Ignatian insight and the *via negativa* which the great mystics such as St. John of the Cross emphasize as so central to the spiritual life.

A psychological understanding of the development and flowering of human affectivity, then, *is* pertinent to our spiritual self-understanding. There are, in general, two extreme positions on the relation of psychology and spirituality that must be avoided.

The first extreme is a reduction of spirituality to psychology, so that religion is "nothing but" a more or less complex psychological mechanism. Such an understanding is to be found in the works of Freud, who is prevented from properly understanding even the sensitive psyche itself because he does not admit the spiritual dimension of the human person, to which the psyche is oriented. The rational affirmation of spiritual reality is, of course, quite a sophisticated philosophical achievement. But one alternative to such an affirmation is to conceive the human person as consisting only of psyche and organism, and to explain psyche by moving backwards to the organism. Then spirituality is reduced to psychology, and psychology to organic instinct.

The second, and opposite, extreme is one of divorcing spiri-

97

tuality from psychology so completely that discernment itself becomes impossible. Spirituality becomes a separate realm of human
activity that is not integrated with psychological reality. This tendency, once, perhaps, pronounced in Christian spirituality, is still to
be found; there still are spiritual theologians for whom the relationship of spirituality to the life of affectivity is negligible. Such an orientation, when put into practice, leads to a split consciousness and
a compartmentalized life. The orientation itself is perhaps often
rooted in both a fear of the complexities of affective self-knowledge,
and in an epistemological conceptualism that finds little relation between the concepts of spirituality—grace, the supernatural, self-denial, the following of Christ—and the concepts of psychology. But
it is the task of spiritual theology to mediate these two conceptual
worlds, the one with the other, by taking its stand in interior experience, which is the dimension to which both sets of concepts refer if they are talking about anything real.

It may well be that Jung will prove more helpful for spirituality
and spiritual theology in the negative way suggested in the previous
paper, that is, in helping us to recognize inordinate projections and
disoriented affections, than in orienting us positively to the God of
Christian faith and to Christ. On the issues of the psychological orientation to God and the psychological meaning of the Christ of
Faith, Jung, I find, is quite deficient, and his thought derails him
from the appropriate orientation to the reality of God. I propose to
treat these problems in the present paper.

One of the insights of scriptural spirituality and of the major
theologies of the Christian tradition concerns the incomprehensibility of God. His ways are not ours.[1] "Where were you when I laid
the foundation of the earth?"[2] "I will be who I will be."[3] "How un-
searchable are his ways."[4] According to St. Thomas Aquinas, even
in the direct vision of God, God will remain for us an incomprehensible mystery.[5] The denial of God's ultimate incomprehensibility involves one in some form of what has been called *gnosis*. The
incomprehensibility of God comes to its sharpest focus in our own
experience of the mystery of inevitable and uncontrollable suffering, the only response to which, as Karl Rahner says, is to "let ourselves fall into the incomprehensibility of God as into our true
fulfillment and happiness,"[6] precisely as Christ himself surrendered
in the hour of his most intense darkness. Nothing is more difficult

than this surrender to what we cannot understand. And one of the ways of resisting this surrender—the way, I suggest, that Jung manifests in some of his very late works—is to deny that God is all good, to think of God as a unity of good and evil, to see Christ as the representative only of God's goodness, and Satan, as the symbol of the evil in God. From such an understanding, it is only a short step to the affirmation of oneself as superior to God and to assigning to oneself the task of reconciling the good and evil in God by reconciling the good and evil in the self which is the image of God. Such seem to have been Jung's final conclusions on the ultimate religious problematic, and any treatment of the relation of Jungian psychology to Christian spirituality must face these issues head-on.

The Integration of Spirit and Matter

In our previous section we summarized the Jungian understanding of the process of individuation as a matter of reversing false identifications of the ego with collective consciousness and with the collective unconscious; of withdrawing projections, whether they be in the realms of the shadow, of the *anima* or *animus*, or of archetypal symbols; and of ceasing to allow oneself to be swayed and derailed by the projections others may have placed on oneself. As the process of individuation goes forward, then, what happens is that the individual emerges as a conscious unity in his or her own right, with a self-possession in the realm of affectivity that enables one to live the "just-so" life, the life of simple giving and receiving, of real reciprocity, of self-transcendent individuality, without ulterior motives, available for the performance of his own tasks in the world without losing himself in the psychic resonances that non-individuated relationships always entail. The culmination of the process lies, ideally, in what Jung calls the experience of the self. For me, this is an experience of oneself as a self-possessed, integrated totality, whose very integration enables one to operate simultaneously as a self-transcending subject of the operations of insight, judgment, decision, communication, collaboration, love, and prayer. The self-possessed person is not a self-enclosed person, but is an independent agent of self-transcending action in the world.

Such a state of integration is hard to describe. Jung himself probably comes closest to succeeding in his work, *A Commentary on the Secret of the Golden Flower.*[7] But may it not be the case that the best descriptions are still found in the great religious documents of world history? In the Bible, for instance, St. Paul says: "I have learned, in whatever state I am, to be content, I know how to be abased, and I know how to abound; in any and all circumstances I have learned the secret of facing plenty and hunger, abundance and want. I can do all things in him who strengthens me."[8] In the Sermon on the Mount, Jesus says: "Do not be anxious about your life. . . . Seek first his kingdom and his righteousness, and all these things will be yours as well. Do not be anxious about tomorrow, for tomorrow will be anxious for itself. Let the day's own trouble be sufficient for the day."[9] In other religious traditions we find other ways of expressing similar states of being. The *Bhagavad Gita* speaks of acting, but renouncing the fruits of one's action;[10] the *I Ching* says: "If one does not count on the harvest while plowing or on the ground while clearing it, it furthers one to undertake something."[11] Mystics of various traditions speak of a state of detachment from inner states and outer objects, where detachment is not unrelatedness but free, non-demanding relatedness, where one is no longer preoccupied with compulsive plans or with the images of things, because one lives from that deeper center where the soul is at one with God, that shrine for ultimate holiness which is the innermost mansion of the soul. "I live, now not I, but Christ lives in me." Thus Jung can speak of a higher and deeper authority than the ego. The ego is not identified with this authority, but receives from it, so that a person is enabled to forge his life and his work with all the energy at his disposal, and at the same time to give his life and his work over to God to let God do with it whatever he chooses, making no demands at all. So, too, Lonergan can speak of a condition of universal willingness, where one's whole way of life is dominated by a detachment and disinterestedness that comes from a vision of reality in which one's ego is no longer the center of reference, but is rather subordinated to some universal destiny governed by the Providence of God.[12] And T. S. Eliot's *Four Quartets* concludes by speaking of:

> A condition of complete simplicity
> (Costing not less than everything)
> And all shall be well and
> All manner of thing shall be well

When the tongues of flame are infolded
Into the crowned knot of fire
And the fire and the rose are one.[13]

The fire of spirit and the rose of the earth are one; the opposites of spirit and matter are joined, at peace and harmony with one another. The culmination of the process of individuation is a reconciliation of the opposites in the human person. In what is perhaps his most important scientific paper, Jung comes very close to identifying the ultimate opposites in human personality with spirit and matter, to be joined by negotiating the psyche, which shares in both.[14] And as long as his thought is interpreted in this way, it can prove very helpful in the development of a spirituality that leads one to the point of union with God, of dependence on God alone, that is the fruit of the mystical journey. Thus, finally, William Johnston, one of the finest spiritual writers of our time, can make good use of Jung in his excellent book, *The Still Point*.[15]

The Still Point

But what is that "still point" of the turning world, that place where the deeper center is found, from which the ego receives its strength to do all things in him who strengthens it? Is that "still point" myself, or is it in the place of the indwelling of God in my soul? Is it ultimately self or God? *Is it nature* or *is it grace?* Is it *in* human interiority or beyond interiority? What is that supraordinate authority that Jung calls the self? Does Jung predetermine the answer to that question by calling it the self? Christian tradition does not call it the self. It declares emphatically that the "still point" is not just me, but is rather the region where God dwells in my innermost being. "And I will pray the Father, and he will give you another Counselor, to be with you forever, even the Spirit of truth, whom the world cannot receive, because it neither sees him nor knows him; you know him, for he dwells with you, and will be in you."[16] "If a man loves me, he will keep my word, and my Father will love him, and we will come to him and make our home with him."[17] The innermost region of our interiority is, in the Christian mystical tradition, no longer ourselves, but the place of grace, where the gift of God's love is poured forth into our hearts by the Holy

Spirit who has been given to us.[18] It is what Lonergan calls the region for the divine.

The last works of Jung, and surely too the writings of some of his closest disciples,[19] are reluctant to accept such an interpretation of the innermost center of our being. They evince a desire to reduce the scriptural and traditional Christian terminology about this innermost center to merely figurative language. They want to explain the "still point" in terms, not of grace, but of nature. Christ, in St. Paul's "I live, now not I, but Christ lives in me," becomes merely a symbol of the self. What St. Paul really means would be something like, "The ego is no longer the center of my being, for I have found the self." Edward Edinger, in his book *Ego and Archetype*, explicitly speaks of St. Paul's conversion as an example of the encounter with the self.[20] The relation of the human person to God is immanentized, so that it becomes a relation of ego to self. Prayer, then, is literally reduced to talking to one's self. It is not to be ridiculed for that reason, for it is psychologically important for the ego to be in relation to the self.

I propose to examine a dream of Jung's shortly before he wrote his most controversial work, *Answer to Job*, where these problems come to explicit formulation. I will offer of this dream a Christian theological interpretation, one with which orthodox Jungians will most likely not be happy, but one that at least establishes the issue on which, I believe, a Christian adaptation of Jung centers.

In the portion of this dream that is most relevant to our consideration, Jung is in a large hall with his father. The hall is a high, circular room with a gallery running along the wall, from which four bridges lead to a basin-shaped center. The basin rests on a huge column, and forms the round seat of a Moslem sultan, who from this round seat speaks to his councilors and philosophers, who themselves sit along the wall in the gallery. The scene is, as Jung says, "a gigantic mandala," i.e., a symbol of the self. To quote Jung:

> In the dream I suddenly saw that from the center a steep flight of stairs ascended to a spot high up on the wall—which no longer corresponded to reality. At the top of the stairs was a small door, and my father said, "Now I will lead you into the highest presence." Then he knelt down and touched his forehead to the floor. I imitated him, likewise kneeling, with great emotion. For

some reason I could not bring my forehead quite down to the floor—there was perhaps a millimeter to spare. But at least I had made the gesture with him. Suddenly I knew—perhaps my father had told me—that that upper door led to a solitary chamber where lived Uriah, King David's general, whom David had shamefully betrayed for the sake of his wife Bathsheba, by commanding his soldiers to abandon Uriah in the face of the enemy.[21]

And what Jung says about this portion of the dream is the following:

When I was in India, the mandala structure of the *divan-i-kaas* (council hall) had in actual fact powerfully impressed me as the representation of a content related to the center. The center is the seat of Akbar the Great, who rules over a subcontinent, who is a "lord of this world," like David. But even higher than David stands his guiltless victim, his loyal general Uriah, whom he abandoned to the enemy. Uriah is a prefiguration of Christ.[22]

In what follows it is important to remember that this dream prefigures Jung's writing of his *Answer to Job*,[23] which vividly portrays his conviction that God is ambivalent, that God is not the highest good, as Christianity would have it. But let me first say how I interpret this dream, and then we will examine Jung's understanding of it.

Jung was always fascinated by the mandala as a symbol of wholeness. When he saw the council hall of the sultan in India, it had to make a deep impression on him, and this impression remained in his memory, ready to be released into consciousness once again as a way of portraying the wholeness that, he believed, was the goal of the process of individuation. The mandala, then, symbolizes the integrated self, which is both center and totality of the personality. As center, it is the sultan, the higher authority, the king in the middle of the round room, giving out his orders to his ministers who surround him, and who together with him constitute the totality. But this higher authority is in itself nature; it is this-worldly. The sultan is a "lord of this world." This higher authority is the "greater personality, the inner man," which has an impact "upon the life of every individual."[24] Jung's father, who himself had been a clergyman and whose faith had always dissatisfied Jung, tells

him that there is a still higher authority, the highest presence, beyond the door at the top of the flight of stairs, at a spot high up on
the wall "which no longer corresponded to reality," i.e., which was
other-worldly. The relation to this highest authority, this highest
presence, is embodied in the innocent suffering of the Just One, here
Uriah, whom Jung sees as a prefigurement of Christ. The mystery
of the suffering of the innocent points beyond nature and calls one
to the response that Jung's father shows in the dream, the response
of touching one's forehead to the floor, the response of letting oneself fall into the incomprehensibility of God as into true fulfillment
and happiness, a response similar to Job's at the end of the book to
which Jung tried to compose a response. In this voluntary acceptance of innocent suffering—what in Christ we call the law of the
cross—evil loses its power, and we are elevated into a relationship
that transcends the dimensions of nature, a relationship beyond the
perfect symmetry of nature's finest achievements. Jung's father is
telling him that there is an other-worldly, supernatural authority, a
highest presence, revealed in the mystery of the Christ, and before
whose dominion the self has to be stretched to the point of adoration, submission, and ultimate silence. *That* is the real answer to
Job, the answer that Job himself came to, the answer *of* Job when
God questioned him: "Where were you when I laid the foundations
of the earth?" Interestingly, earlier in the dream, Jung's father had
been reading from Genesis, and expounding eloquently on it, but
Jung found his father's words incomprehensible, even though he
marveled at them. And what is it that Job answers when confronted
with the incomprehensibility of God? "I have uttered what I did not
understand, things too wonderful for me, which I did not
know. . . . I had heard of you by the hearing of the ear, but now
my eyes see you. Therefore I despise myself, and I repent in dust
and ashes"[25]—I touch my forehead to the floor in adoration.

The dream reflects, I believe, Jung's ambivalent attitude to that
final step in coming to the point, the condition, of complete simplicity. There is a fascination with the wholeness of the mandala, of
the self, of nature, that prevents him from granting that the mandala
is *not* self-enclosed, that there is a small door that opens from the
center of the self, through the mystery of suffering, onto the incomprehensibility of a God in relation to whom we have to adopt the

final posture of Job himself. But, "Something in me," says Jung, "was defiant and determined not to be a dumb fish."[26]

The Mystery of Evil and the Incomprehensibility of God

What that defiance, that millimeter to spare, meant in terms of Jung's final religious testament is not difficult to discover. There is an option made to limit our understanding of the deepest dimensions of our selves to the contours of the mandala-shaped council-hall; there is expressed in Jung's defiance a desire *not* to transcend the realm of nature in order to come to the end of our journey to individuation, *not* to acknowledge the small door that leads beyond the self and its wholeness and into the dimension of the other-worldly and incomprehensible, a desire *not* to surrender *gnosis* to faith, since the aspect of reality that beckons us to this opening of the self-beyond-itself is the mystery of suffering; the inclination not to be opened beyond oneself, not to fall into the incomprehensibility of God, is an inclination to resent the fact that the final step in the journey is not our own doing, not even the doing of the deeper center of the self, but the activity of God, an activity that is not fully comprehensible in natural terms. This God who opens us through suffering to his own incomprehensibility as to our happiness and fulfillment is then viewed as evil as well as good. The attitude adopted toward him is one of anger. This means for Jung that Christ cannot be the full embodiment and revelation of this God, for Christ is only good. Satan, too, must be viewed as a revelation of God, as the fourth person in the Godhead. In his late book, *Aion*,[27] Jung reverts to astrological speculation in order to explain where the history of the image of God is heading. We are, Jung says, at the end of the astrological age, Pisces, an age symbolized by the warring fishes, and we stand at the beginning of a new age of Aquarius, whose symbol is the *Anthropos*, the human being in whom the opposites are reconciled. Christ and Satan are the warring fishes, and in the age of Aquarius they will be reconciled, through the emergence of Anthropos, the realization of the individuated self. This means that human beings are helping God to find himself, to get beyond his own inner contradictions. We have to redeem God from his own unconsciousness. The overcoming of evil, then, is reduced to a matter of achieving greater consciousness; through this process evil and good come to be relativized, and so capable of being integrated with one another. We are encouraged to adopt a different attitude to evil: not to reject it, but to give it a place in our lives. Then the final opposition, that of good and evil, will be overcome, and the image of God will lose its fearsome aspect of incomprehensibility precisely in the process through which the self comes to integration.

Christian theology would offer an alternative interpretation of the same issues. Most radically, it would suggest that we must make the option not to limit the deepest dimensions of the reaches of our intentionality to the contours of the closed mandala, but must acknowledge the small door that leads beyond the self and onto the other-worldly dimension of the incomprehensibility of God. It *is* in the limit-situations of suffering, loss, and ultimately death that we are beckoned to this opening of the self. And *not* to open oneself to the mystery of God in these situations is evil, a denial of our creaturehood, what Ernest Becker would call a *causa sui* project,[28] a desire to be God. It is faith, not *gnosis*, that enables us to fall into the incomprehensibility of God as into our true happiness and fulfillment. The mystery of evil is rooted, not in God's incomprehensibility, but in the radical depotentiation of moral agency that Christian tradition has called original sin, and even more radically in that whole dimension of reality that St. Paul was struggling to articulate when he spoke of "principalities and powers." Christ is the incarnation of God's saving purpose in our regard, the full and explicit sacrament of the divinely originated solution to the problem of evil. Satan is the expression of all the enmity of God in the world that will not surrender to God's incomprehensible purpose, and that wants the control that comes from being the cause of oneself, the control that refuses faith and chooses *gnosis*. Christ and Satan are irreconcilable enemies, in the same way as is expressed in the fact that one cannot both surrender and not surrender at the same time, cannot both touch one's forehead to the floor and still leave a millimeter to spare. The astrological speculations about the age of Aquarius are themselves pure myth posing as science, and so *gnosis*. For a scientist such as Jung to turn to such speculations represents a disreputable neglect of the evidence. And the evidence found in the conditions of the contemporary world hardly inspires us to believe that, by some natural course of events, all contradictions and enmities are about to come to an end, and the human race about to achieve a harmony with itself and with nature through a natural reconciliation of good and evil. The requirement for peace and justice in our world is still the same as it always has been; accepting the divinely originated solution to the problem of evil that comes to us in Christ Jesus; allowing God to transform us into agents of love and justice and reconciliation; and *bearing the suffering* that the powers of evil will unleash on us because of our option. The age of martyrs is anything but over. The overcoming of evil, then, is not a matter only of coming to greater consciousness, even if self-aspiration is a moral demand of our time. And achieving greater consciousness will not relativize good and evil, but rather will sharpen our ability to differentiate what is worthwhile from what is worthless, seductive, malicious. The process of coming to greater consciousness is a process of *conversion*. It involves a more discerning rejection of what is evil, not a compromise with evil in our lives. Good and evil remain contradictories. They cannot be integrated, as can spirit and matter, or the masculine and feminine dimensions of the personality, which are not *contradictories*, but *contraries*.

The ground of the individuation process, then, must be the gift of God's love, and the eye of that love which is faith. And the goal of the process is not properly symbolized in the utterly closed mandala with no opening onto the absolutely transcendent. The symbolic significance of Christ is clear: in the moment when the powers of darkness are unleashed against him *because* he is from God, he surrenders to the incomprehensible reality that lies beyond that small door at the furthest dimensions of the self, and he comes in victory through that door into the highest presence, to the right hand of that good God who in Christ has proposed once and for all his redemptive solution to the problem of evil.

Notes

1. Is 55:8.
2. Jb 38:4.
3. Ex 3:14.
4. Rm 11:33.
5. See Karl Rahner, "Thomas Aquinas on the Incomprehensibility of God," in *Celebrating the Medieval Heritage: A Colloquy on the Thought of*

Aquinas and Bonaventure; Journal of Religion (58: Supplement, 1978), ed. David Tracy, especially p. S114.

6. *Ibid., passim.*
7. C. G. Jung, "Commentary on 'The Secret of the Golden Flower,' " in *Collected Works, Volume 13: Alchemical Studies* (Princeton: Princeton University Press, 1967), pp. 1–56.
8. Ph 4:11–12.
9. Mt 6:25–34.
10. *The Bhagavad Gita*, translated from the Sanskrit with an introduction by Juan Mascaro (Baltimore: Penguin Books, 1962).
11. The I Ching or Book of Changes, the Richard Wilhelm translation rendered into English by Cary F. Baynes (Princeton: Princeton University Press, 1967), p. 102.
12. Bernard Lonergan, *Insight: A Study of Human Understanding* (New York: Harper and Row, 1978), pp. 623–624.
13. T. S. Eliot, *Four Quartets* (New York: Harcourt, Brace, and World, 1971), p. 59.
14. C. G. Jung, "On the Nature of the Psyche," in *Collected Works, Volume 8: The Structure and Dynamics of the Psyche* (Princeton; Princeton University Press, 1969), pp. 159–234.
15. William Johnston, *The Still Point: Reflections on Zen and Christian Mysticism* (New York: Harper and Row, 1971).
16. Jn 14:16–17.
17. Jn 14:23.
18. Rm 5:5.
19. See Marie-Louise von Franz, *C. G. Jung: His Myth in Our Time* (New York: C. G. Jung Foundation, 1975).
20. Edward Edinger, *Ego and Archetype* (New York: C. G. Jung Foundation, 1972), p. 76.
21. C. G. Jung, *Memories, Dreams, Reflections* (New York: Vintage Press, 1963), pp. 218–219.
22. *Ibid.*, p. 219.
23. C. G. Jung, "Answer to Job," in *Collected Works, Volume II: Psychology and Religion: East and West* (Princeton: Princeton University Press, 1969), pp. 355–470.
24. C. G. Jung, *Memories, Dreams, Reflections*, p. 221.
25. Jb 42:3–6.
26. C. G. Jung, *Memories, Dreams, Reflections*, p. 220.
27. C. G. Jung, *Collected Works, Volume 9ii: Aion* (Princeton: Princeton University Press, 1973).
28. Ernest Becker, *The Denial of Death* (New York: The Free Press, 1973), pp. 115–123.

John A. Sanford

The Problem of Evil
in Christianity and
Analytical Psychology

The problem of evil loomed large in Jung's life and thought. It was a problem that affected him emotionally, and not simply philosophically, and a number of his emotionally most powerful writings are concerned with it, including the problematical *Answer to Job*. So deeply was Jung affected by the question of evil and its relationship to individuation and to God, that his longstanding friendship with Fr. Victor White almost came to grief because of their different standpoints. It is also this issue, more than any other, that has separated Jung from many persons in the Judaeo-Christian tradition who otherwise find his psychological insights so helpful. In this article I make no pretense at having "solved" the problem of evil, but I offer some thoughts about evil as seen from the Christian and the Jungian perspective that I hope may clear up more misunderstandings than they create, and that will be a contribution to resolving the issue that Jung's work so ably explored.

THE PROBLEM OF EVIL IN EARLY CHRISTIANITY

The problem of evil is unresolved in Christian theology. In the early, formative centuries of Christianity the thinkers of the Church were too involved in matters of Christology to come up with a theology of evil as well. This is the major reason why to this day there is no official Christian theological statement regarding evil in Roman Catholicism, Protestantism or Orthodoxy.

However, this does not mean that the early Christians were

unconcerned with evil. To the contrary, evil was an ever-present reality for the early Christian world. Evidence of the powers of evil were all around and were personified in the figure of Satan and his host of demonic powers, and the practice of exorcism was widespread. In fact, so important was evil in early Christian thinking that the first doctrines of the Atonement were couched in terms of it. How was it that Christ on the Cross enabled man to become at-one again with God? The early Christian answer gave two explanations. The first theory, called the *ransom theory*, argued that because of Adam's sin mankind had fallen under the power of Satan. Christ on the Cross offered himself as a ransom to the Evil One. In exchange for Christ, the devil let mankind go, but then, because Christ was blameless, the devil could not hold him either. So the victory over evil was complete. The second theory, which we might call the *victory theory*, said that on the Cross a sort of cosmic struggle took place between Christ and Satan and the victor was Christ who vanquished Satan and broke the power of the forces of darkness. To this day, when we "knock on wood" after making some positive, happy statement, we hark back to this theory of the Atonement. For the wood on which we knock is the wood of the Cross which has the power to nullify the power of the Evil One who hovers about everywhere ready to destroy human happiness and good fortune.

I mention this early Christian emphasis upon evil because one of Jung's main concerns is that Christianity does not take evil seriously. In the first centuries of Christianity this was certainly not the case. In fact, the later theory of the Atonement, commonly called the "satisfaction theory," came into existence in the early 12th century because it was believed that the Church had emphasized the role of evil *too much*. For if God had to resort to a ruse to win mankind back from the power of evil, does that not make Satan almost on a par with God?

But of course none of this explained the origin of evil nor the nature of evil. If there was only one God, and if God was just and good and loved mankind and created a good world, then why was there so much evil in the world? And did God simply allow this evil to exist, or had He created it deliberately? What was the ultimate place of evil in the divine scheme of things? These were unresolved questions in the thinking of the early Church.

There were those, however, who wrestled with the problem. Irenaeus, Bishop of Lyon, for instance, argued that God deliberately allowed evil in His creation in order to create a universe in which man's moral powers could be exercised and man's soul purged, cleansed and developed. According to his view, without evil there would not be a world in which man's nature could be perfected. Irenaeus regarded even the original fall of mankind (Adam's and Eve's sin) as a blessing in disguise that was intended for man's ultimate good, arguing that the original destiny of man was not abrogated by the fall, the truth being that the fall was planned by God from the beginning as a way to lead humankind to the ultimate perfection of being for which they were destined.

A second Christian thinker of importance with regard to the problem of evil was Origen. He agreed with Irenaeus that without evil in the world man could not properly develop in a moral and spiritual sense. He went a step farther, however, by asserting that in the very end the devil himself would be saved. The devil, Origen said, was allowed by God to bring evil into the world because it was necessary. But when every creature was finally completed, the devil himself would be redeemed and evil would be destroyed. The devil, having finished his proper task on the earth would be, as it were, freed from his evil role, and evil, no longer necessary to God's plan, would be abolished.

Others, such as Lactantius and the early Christian author of the document known as the *Recognitions of Clement*, (to which Jung often alludes) argued along similar lines. God, they said, has a right and a left hand, and both are necessary if His Will is to be carried out; the left hand of God is the origin of evil, and the right hand of God executes the good, and both hands are necessary. For how can there be virtue if there is not vice? And how can anyone attain a holy state of being if there is not the evil power tempting a person to a life of evil? And what can the praise of God of the faithful mean if there is not an Evil Power that wants to turn us away from God?

To the best of my knowledge, Jung had no quarrel with these early Christian attitudes toward evil, unless it might be an objection to Origen's thesis that after the devil is saved evil ceases to exist. But he did quarrel bitterly with another Christian answer to the problem of evil, and it is to this that we now turn.

THE DOCTRINE OF THE *PRIVATIO BONI*

The early Christian thinkers I have mentioned deal mainly with the question of the purpose that evil serves in God's creation. The doctrine of the *privatio boni*, however, deals with the question of the substance or being of evil. What *kind* of existence does evil have? Is it an absolute? Is it relative? Can it exist on its own? Essentially the answer given by the doctrine of the *privatio boni* is that evil owes its existence to the diminution of the good. The basic idea of the doctrine is that the good alone has substance (substantial existence on its own), and that evil has no substance and cannot exist on its own, but derives its existence from a privation of the good. Stated more simply, when anything falls away from the perfected state of being for which God intended it, then evil is created.

The doctrine of the *privatio boni* actually first originated with Aristotle who suggested in his *Metaphysics* that evil was untruth and existed only insofar as it departed from the truth; the truth alone had being, and untruth could not exist in itself. Early Christian thinkers, however, soon picked up and expanded on the idea, and the doctrine of the *privatio boni* finds representation among a great number of the major early Christian philosophers in both the East and the West, up to and including Thomas Aquinas.

However, it was St. Augustine who elaborated the doctrine of the *privatio boni* more than any other Christian thinker. He did so in reaction to Mani, the Persian religious philosopher who attempted to solve the problem of evil by an out-and-out dualism. Evil, Mani said in the best Persian tradition, exists because there are two deities, one responsible for the good and one for the evil. Augustine objected vehemently to this dualism and sought to preserve the monotheism of Judaism and Christianity which it so threatened, but in order to do this he had to account for the nature and existence of evil. To do this he turned to the doctrine of the *privatio boni*, and argued that there could not be two deities, because evil had no substantial existence on its own since it existed only by virtue of the good. In his *Confessions* he said, "As yet I knew not that evil was naught but a privation of good, until in the end it ceases to be altogether." By "in the end" he means that when ultimately the whole creation is in its perfected state, with every creature as God intended it to be, evil will then cease to exist. For, if evil derives its existence from the lack of this perfection and fulfillment, it follows by definition that it will cease to exist when this perfection and fulfillment has been accomplished.

JUNG'S CRITICISM OF THE *PRIVATIO BONI*

The doctrine of the *privatio boni* has been attacked by Jung, who has subjected it to searching criticism. As we have seen, the doctrine of the *privatio boni* is not an official Christian teaching about evil and is only one of several approaches to the problem that can be found among Christian thinkers. Therefore Jung is not quite correct when he says that, according to the thinking of the Church, evil is simply the accidental lack of perfection since there is no single teaching of the Church in this regard. Nevertheless, Jung's criticisms of the doctrine are important and deserve careful scrutiny. They can be summarized as follows:

1. Because the doctrine of the *privatio boni* regards evil as insubstantial, it splits off evil from any integral relationship with the Godhead and therefore creates a one-sidedly light representation of Wholeness. Specifically, the figure of Christ as presented in the tradition of the Church is one-sidedly light. Christ is only goodness, love, justice and mercy; there is no hint of darkness in him. As a result of this one-sidedness, the dark side appears in the figure of the Antichrist who compensates for the one-sidedness of Christ. Just because the dogmatic figure of Christ is sublime and spotless everything else turns dark beside it, and this creates, out of psychological necessity, a psychic complement to restore the balance. This results in a split in the image of wholeness and creates the irreconcilable separation of the kingdom of heaven from the world of the damned.

Jung contrasts the one-sidedly light figure of Christ with the nature of the empirical Self as it appears in dreams, visions and other symbols from the unconscious. It is in the nature of the Self, he notes, to unite the opposites, even the opposites of good and evil. "For in the Self good and evil are indeed closer than identical twins." And, "in the empirical Self, light and shadow form a paradoxical unity." Because this unity is essential to the Self, the dark side, when it is excluded as it is in the Christian symbol, must necessarily turn up elsewhere.

For Jung this is not an academic, philosophical problem but is a contributing cause of the present unresolved world problem. Where the prevailing symbol of wholeness is incomplete, lacking its dark side, there must necessarily come about a state of conflict, and this psychic conflict is expressed in the world situation of today in which the Communist world and the Western world are split in two. (I do not know what Jung would make of the current situation in which, in addition to the Communist world and the Western world, there is now the so-called Third World.)

Jung feels Christianity got into this problem because it could not think in terms of paradoxes. He notes, however, that the Self is absolutely paradoxical "in that it represents in every respect thesis and antithesis, and at the same time synthesis."

Thus Jung objects to the doctrine of the *privatio boni* because it seemingly disregards or underestimates the power of evil and evokes a one-sidedly light image of wholeness. This has, he feels, contributed to a world problem and, in addition, is contradicted by the empirical facts. And while Jung has no inclination to delve into metaphysics he must, he says, object when "metaphysics encroaches on experience and interprets it in a way that is not justified empirically."

2. It is because Jung believes that the doctrine of the *privatio boni* has practical, deleterious results for humankind that he becomes heated in his attack upon it. Evil, left to operate on its own, with no relationship to wholeness, is left to victimize mankind with disastrous results. One could say that at this point Jung has a feeling reaction to the doctrine of the *privatio boni* because, in his view, it works against human values.

Now if it were true that evil is "nothing but the privation of good" it might not be so bad that it is left to operate on its own with no relationship to a symbol of wholeness, for one would not expect a principle that has no substance in itself to have the power to do much damage. But, in fact, this is not the case. To the contrary, evil is exceedingly real, Jung says, and a doctrine like that of the *privatio boni*, which tends to diminish its reality, does humankind a disservice. Therefore human feeling is against the doctrine of the *privatio boni* or any such doctrine that overlooks humankind's sufferings and weakens the psychological preparedness of people to recognize and deal with evil.

3. Finally, Jung finds a logical objection to the doctrine. He notes that man is compelled to think in terms of good and evil, even though what is good and what is evil is a human judgment, and we do not know what they are in themselves. He argues that we cannot think good without thinking evil, for they are "a logically equivalent pair of opposites." There is no white without black, no right without left, no above without below, no warmth without cold, no truth without error, no light without darkness, and neither can there be any good without evil. Therefore, the existence of evil cannot derive from the good but both must exist together. So if evil is an illusion, he asserts, good is necessarily an illusion too. For this reason he holds that the *privatio boni* is "illogical, irrational, and even a nonsense."

Because of all this Jung feels wholeness is best represented by the number four, not by the number three, and argues that the Christian symbol of the Trinity is not as adequate a representation of wholeness as the symbols of the quaternity which the unconscious often produces to represent the Self. Specifically, one must add to the three-ness of consciousness the fourth, which is the unconscious and which is personified sometimes as the devil, sometimes as the seemingly sinister inferior function and sometimes as the missing feminine. Theologically speaking, one must add the devil to the Father, Son and Holy Ghost, and then the symbol for wholeness is complete.

To summarize: Jung's argument against the *privatio boni* has three major points to it: (1) That the one-sidedly light image of Christ is contradicted by the empirical facts that the Self is a combination of opposites which includes dark as well as light. (2) That the splitting off of evil from the image of God has given evil too much autonomy with disastrous results for mankind. (3) That the doctrine is illogical, since we cannot posit good without also positing evil, and thus the one cannot derive its existence from the other.

A CRITIQUE OF JUNG'S VIEW OF THE *PRIVATIO BONI*

Jung's position with regard to the relationship of evil to God has not received the attention among Christian and other thinkers that it deserves. Nevertheless, it has not gone entirely unnoticed and has received a careful review by at least one religious philosopher, H. L. Philp, who, in his book *Jung and the Problem of Evil*, pays Jung the compliment of taking him seriously. Some of Philp's arguments are worth noting.

Philp rejects the idea that the Quaternity, as Jung understands it, can be taken as a symbolic representation of God, because it "enthrones evil forever." This, in his view, creates an amoral God, for if the Godhead itself is both good and evil, then "Evil is inevitable and eternal and amorality is enthroned forever, for if goodness comes then evil cannot be far behind, and so the circle turns—for eternity."

He also points out that if, as Jung says, human feeling revolts against the idea that evil is insubstantial, it revolts even more against the idea that the Ultimate Source of Life, God, is inherently evil. In short, Philp finds Jung's idea that God contains good and evil repugnant from the human feeling point of view, just as Jung finds the doctrine of the *privatio boni* repugnant from the feeling point of view because it seemingly declares that evil is unreal, thus making, as it were, a mockery of human suffering.

Philp also tries to defeat Jung's argument that the doctrine of the *privatio boni* is illogical since good and evil are logical equivalents so that to assert the existence of one is necessarily to posit the existence of the other. Not so, Philp argues, for not all qualities have their logical opposite. To be sure, outside implies inside, and up implies down, but the sun would be hot even if nothing were known about a colder condition. So too, he feels, we can posit the good without necessarily having to think of the evil.

Allan Anderson, Professor of Religious Studies at San Diego State University, supports Philp's position in this regard. Good and evil, he points out, are not logically equivalent opposites because they are to be understood not in terms of each other, but in terms of a norm. In this case, we decide what is good and what is evil when observing how the meaning of evil depends on the meaning of good.

The norm by which we determine what is good and what is evil, we can say, is the higher good of wholeness. Whatever detracts from or destroys wholeness we call evil, and whatever supports, furthers or maintains wholeness we call good. We can think wholeness without having to think its opposite. According to this view, Jung errs in failing to see that both good and evil, as perceived from our human point of view, are to be defined in terms of a norm that is beyond them both.

In at least one place Jung himself seems to recognize that good and evil are to be defined in terms of some other norm. In *Aion* he writes, " 'Good' is what seems suitable, acceptable, or valuable from a *certain point of view;* evil is its opposite." (Italics mine). Here we can see that good and evil are determined from a "certain point of view," and this viewpoint suggests there is a norm which determines what is good and what is evil. From the egocentric human point of view this "norm" is, no doubt, what suits our pleasure, convenience or plans. For instance, the Puritan settlers in this country said it was good that a plague had rid the country of the Indians, but the Indians surely deemed that plague an evil, each judging what was good and evil in terms of the norm of personal desires. But from a larger point of view that norm could be a wholeness that lies beyond relative good and evil.

Jung also, at least occasionally, speaks of a goal toward which all life strives, in terms of which good and evil may be judged. This teleological view of good and evil is reflected in *Aion* where Jung says, "To strive after *teleios*—completion— . . . is not only legitimate but is inborn in man as a peculiarity which provides civilization with one of its strongest roots. This striving is so powerful, even, that it can turn into a passion that draws everything into its service." But elsewhere, where Jung equates good and evil as a pair of opposites to be united in the Self, rather than as judgments devised by mankind in terms of the norm of wholeness, he departs from his teleological attitude.

Dr. Anderson also argues that the doctrine of the *privatio boni* does not deny the reality of evil but defines its nature. Jung, as we have seen, finds the doctrine repugnant because it "nullifies the reality of evil," and declares that evil is "something that does not exist." This is not so, says Anderson, for the doctrine of the *privatio boni* does not deny the reality of evil but states what evil is. It says that while evil exists it can only exist by living off the good and cannot exist on its own.

Now if the highest Good (with a capital "G") is wholeness, and if we say that the good is what promotes wholeness and the evil is that which seeks to destroy wholeness, then we can see in what sense it is true that evil cannot exist on its own, even though it is real. For suppose that wholeness were perfectly established. There would then be no basis for the existence of evil since there would no longer be anything destructive, everything being included in the whole. Or, suppose that wholeness were completely destroyed. Once again evil could not exist, for if there were no longer anything to destroy, evil would cease to be.

We can use here the analogy of illness and health. We can argue that illness is a diminution (privation) of health and that illness, while very real to human life, cannot exist on its own, but that does not deny its existence. If all living creatures were perfectly healthy, there would be no illness. And if an illness has succeeded in completely destroying a healthy organism, that illness also ceases to exist. If, for instance, a person succumbs to a disease such as cholera, once the health of that person's body has been totally destroyed the illness of cholera also ceases to exist (at least in that person), for how can there be an illness except in a relatively healthy host? (The cholera bacteria, of course, might continue to exist, but cholera bacteria are not an illness until they are activated in a healthy body. They do no harm until they are destroying an organism.)

In one of his letters to Fr. Victor White, Jung anticipated this argument in a debate with his friend over what constitutes a "bad egg." White had evidently written him a letter arguing that an egg is bad insofar as it lacks what an egg should have— which is analogous to the doctrine of the *privatio boni*. Jung responds that a bad egg is not characterized by a mere decrease in goodness since it develops its own qualities, among other things H_2S, which produces an unpleasant smell. The response, however, would be that H_2S is not evil in itself, in spite of its unpleasant smell, but can only be regarded as evil insofar as it represents the state of being of an egg which is not what it should be. In short, the argument is that the only bad thing about an egg is when it is not what an egg should be. The chemical elements of a "bad egg" are not bad in themselves, and their "badness" is only derived from the fact that they represent the failure of the egg to be a whole egg.

A REFORMULATION OF THE PROBLEM OF EVIL

In the light of these considerations, let us see if we can reformulate the problem of evil in a way that takes into account both Jung's criticisms and the arguments against these criticisms.

But first we must clarify some terms. One thing that makes it difficult to come to grips with Jung's arguments regarding evil is that he does not define terms. This gives to the whole issue a certain slipperiness; we think we are catching hold of something, and it suddenly eludes us. For instance, Jung uses the terms "dark" and "evil" seemingly interchangeably and without regard for precise definitions of these terms. For instance, he speaks of "the opposition between light and good on the one hand and darkness and evil on the other." The dark and the light certainly seem to go together in order to make a whole, just as night and day belong together to complete a whole cycle, but this does not mean that evil and good coexist together in some eternal arrangement of wholeness. What is dark is not necessarily evil, but may be the necessary complement to the light. In fact, we instinctively sense that dark and light *do* belong together, and that a world that was all light and all day, with no darkness and no night, would be intolerable. This sort of seduces us, then, into accepting the idea that evil belongs eternally with the good, but this is not necessarily so. "Shadow" is another word Jung uses without precise meaning. A shadow is not necessarily evil, but Jung uses this word in a way that implies that it is. Neither, for that matter, is black necessarily evil, even though it is to be contrasted with white.

Even more important is the fact that Jung does not make clear distinctions among the different experiences of evil. The word "evil" appears in Jung's writings as though it always had a single meaning, but in fact there are different experiences of what we call evil.

1. There is, for instance, what we can call "the dark side" of God or the Self. When we go counter to the Self we can expect to be confronted by it as an adversary, much as the prophet Balaam was confronted by the angel of Yahweh in the story we find in the 22nd chapter of the Book of Numbers. If we persist in going against the Self we may well be destroyed by it. Hence the term, "the dark

side of the Self." However, we cannot call this dark side of the Self something that is intrinsically evil because it has a certain positive purpose, namely, to bring about wholeness. And even when destruction results from the dark side of the Self it can be said that what has been destroyed was found not fit to exist.

2. There is evil as we find it personified in the figure of the devil in mythology and folklore. In this case, the devil is a personification of those aspects of the Self which have been split off and repressed. When these repressed contents seek to return they trouble consciousness and produce disturbing effects, including the danger of possession. Such a state of being is an evil condition, but the evil is relative, for if the repressed and denied psychic contents are integrated they are then redeemed from their evil condition by becoming a part of the whole. In short, the evil in such a case is the condition of alienation, and when the state of alienation ceases, so does the evil.

3. There is evil as an intrinsically evil force, which we will examine shortly.

The point here is that a discussion of evil will become garbled unless such distinctions are kept clearly in mind.

Furthermore, when Jung does make distinctions between different experiences of evil they are not clear or helpful. He does occasionally, for instance, use the term "relative" and "absolute" evil. In *Aion* for instance, he says that "it is quite within the bounds of possibility for a man to recognize the relative evil of his nature, but it is a rare and shattering experience for him to gaze into the face of absolute evil." And in one of his letters to Fr. White he also refers to an "absolute evil," contrasting it with "absolute good." Unfortunately, Jung does not elaborate on what he regards as the distinction between relative and absolute evil and elsewhere in his writings ignores such distinctions entirely. But since something that is absolute exists entirely on its own, we must suppose that Jung means that there is an evil that is unconditioned by anything else. However, that would nullify the existence of good, since, in philosophical parlance, there can be only one absolute. Thus the existence of an absolute evil nullifies the possibility of an absolute good. To speak of absolute evil is to state a doctrine of *privatio boni* in reverse. One would then have to say that evil is absolute, and good is whatever diminished the evil, but that the good cannot exist on its own apart from the evil, for something is not absolute if its opposite has an equal existence.

However, we can regard Jung's statement above as having emotional meaning. That is, that in some cases we feel we are looking at something that is only relatively evil and therefore might be redeemed, and in some cases we are looking at something that is intrinsically evil and thus has a more horrifying effect. In terms of the idea of the *privatio boni* an entity exhibits the qualities of intrinsic evil the more dissociated it is from the whole, yet intrinsic evil cannot exist apart from that which it seeks to destroy. In terms of the *privatio boni* only Wholeness (the Good) is absolute, and evil, while it may exist in either a relative or a more intrinsic form, cannot exist apart from the wholeness it seeks to destroy.

Jung himself speaks of saving the world and man's soul through the assimilation and transformation of evil. For instance, in an interview with Mircea Eliade, held at the 1952 Eranos Conference, Jung states, "The great problem in psychology is the integration of opposites. One finds this everywhere and at every level. In *Psychology and Alchemy* I had occasion to interest myself in the integration of Satan. For, as long as Satan is not integrated, the world is not healed and man is not saved. But Satan represents evil, and how can evil be integrated? There is only one possibility: to assimilate it, that is to say, raise it to the level of consciousness. This is done by means of a very complicated symbolic process which is more or less identical with the psychological process of individuation." Now, if evil can be assimilated and integrated and thereby the world is healed, then clearly it cannot be an absolute, since one cannot change the nature of an absolute. Thus Jung here seems to be saying that evil is not absolute, but is relative, and that the relativity of evil is to be judged in terms of the norm of wholeness. This is exactly what the doctrine of the *privatio boni* is saying in slightly different language.

Jung justly criticizes the Church for neglecting the task of dealing with evil. Because the Church declined the task, it fell to alchemy and, in our time, to psychology to complete the work. Jung notes in one of his letters, "Historical Christian psychology thinks rather of suppression of evil than of a *complexio boni et mali*. Thus alchemy tried the idea of a certain transformation of evil with a view to its future integration. In this way it was rather a contribution of Origen's thought that even the devil may be ultimately redeemed."

As mentioned previously, the idea of the transformation of evil suggests that there is indeed something called wholeness in terms of which evil is to be defined. In the case of Origen, however, it was not evil that was to be redeemed, but the devil, which is to say that the figure of the devil would be saved but not the evil within him. Thus the destructive effects of the devil would be nullified, but the devil, as a creature of God, in whom evil at one time resided, would be won back.

Let us now attempt to reformulate the situation with regard to evil. We can say that intrinsic evil is a force of destructiveness that destroys wholeness. However, that which is evil can be redeemed by being freed from a dissociated, destructive condition and won back to the whole. The process of psychological integration aims at this. We can say that something that is dissociated is relatively evil because its evil varies with its state of dissociation. We cannot, however, speak of an absolute evil unless we wish to subordinate the good to the evil.

It was because Jung seemed to assert that evil has an absolute existence that many people reject his ideas, like Philp, who rebels at what he regards as the enthronement of evil. Actually, I do not think that is what Jung means. Jung means that there is a genuinely evil condition that can be altered when that condition is transformed and its legitimate contents integrated into the whole. But since Jung is not very clear about this and insists on speaking of evil as though it were an absolute, one can understand how the impression is given that Jung intended to enthrone an absolute evil as part of the Godhead.

That Jung did not believe God to be a combination of good and an absolute evil is shown, I believe, in his autobiography where he discusses God as love. Like many others before him, Jung is unable to explain the mystery of love, but says that the realm of Eros escapes our rational understanding and rational modes of representation. He feels that St. Paul's words in 1 Corinthians 13 "say all there is to be said; nothing can be added to them." Jung states that "we are in the deepest sense the victims and the instruments of cosmogonic 'love' " and that in "the sentence 'God is love,' the words affirm the *complexio oppositorum* of the Godhead." This is, after all, not so very different from the Christian position expressed in the *privatio boni*. To say that God is a *Summum Bonum* or that God is a cosmogonic love is saying much the same thing. Nor does Jung feel that in affirming that God is love one must also affirm the opposite, that God must be hate as well. Evidently in this case Jung has no difficulty thinking love without at the same time positing hate as a logical opposite that must have an equally substantial existence.

The fact is that Jung is sometimes frustratingly inconsistent in his arguments regarding evil and God. His inconsistency would not be so difficult if it were not that at each point of his inconsistency he is quite adamant about his position.

JUNG'S OBJECTIONS REVIEWED

Now let us look again at Jung's objections to the doctrine of the *privatio boni* in light of this reformulation. Jung's objections lay in three areas. First, Jung felt that the doctrine declared that evil was insubstantial, therefore had no reality, and that this was an offense to human sensibilities since evil is experienced as all too real. We can now see that the doctrine of the *privatio boni*, properly understood, does not deny the reality of evil, but declares what evil is and under what conditions it exists. It does say, however, that evil cannot exist on its own. If, for instance, the power of evil were to triumph completely, all wholeness would be destroyed. But this would result in the destruction of evil as well, since, as a power of destruction, evil can only exist by virtue of something to destroy.

This conclusion agrees with the *I Ching*. Consider Hexagram 36, *Ming I—Darkening of the Light*, which depicts a situation in which the sun has sunk under the earth and so has been darkened, that is, a state in which the dark or evil power is in the ascendancy. The sixth line reads:

Not light but darkness.
First he climbed up to heaven,
Then he plunged into the depths of the earth.

Richard Wilhelm, in his commentary on this line, says: "Here the climax of the darkening is reached. The dark power at first held so high a place that it would wound all who were on the side of good and of the light. But in the end it perishes of its own darkness, *for evil must itself fall at the very moment when it has wholly overcome the good, and thus consumed the energy to which it owed its duration.*" (Italics mine).

We find a similar philosophy of evil in Hexagram 23, *Po—Splitting Apart.* In this hexagram an evil situation is developing as the dark lines are mounting upward to overthrow the last of the light lines by means of a disintegrating influence. The sixth line of this hexagram says:

> There is a large fruit still uneaten.
> The Superior man received a carriage.
> The house of the inferior man is split apart.

Richard Wilhelm says of this line: "Here the splitting apart reaches its end. When misfortune has spent itself, better times return. The seed of the good remains, and it is just when the fruit falls to the ground that good sprouts anew from its seed. The superior man again attains influence and effectiveness. He is supported by public opinion as if in a carriage. But the inferior man's wickedness is visited upon himself. His house is split apart. A law of nature is at work here. *Evil is not destructive to the good alone but inevitably destroys itself as well. For evil, which lives solely by negation, cannot continue to exist on its own strength alone.*" (Italics mine).

It is interesting to compare these quotations from the *I Ching* with a statement from St. Augustine: "Evil . . . can have no existence anywhere except in some good thing. . . . So there can be things which are good without any evil in them, such as God himself, and the higher-celestial beings; but there can be no evil things without good. For if evils cause no damage to anything, they are not evils; if they do damage something, they diminish its goodness; and if they damage it still more, it is because it still has some goodness which they diminish; and if they swallow it up altogether, nothing of its nature is left to be damaged. And so there will be no evil by which it can be damaged, since there is then no nature left whose goodness any damage can diminish."

A second objection Jung has to the doctrine of the *privatio boni* is that it contradicts the psychological facts. That is, symbols of the Self include the dark as well as the light; they combine good and evil into a paradoxical whole. The Self is not light, but dark and light; not good, but good and evil all at once. This holds true as long as we recognize that what is dark is not necessarily evil, and that it is not evil that is included in the wholeness of the Self since evil is, by definition, destructive to the wholeness. That which is relatively evil performs in a destructive way as long as it is not included in the wholeness of things, but when wholeness is operative, then all things are united and destruction ceases. The Self, in other words, does include "the devil" as the personification for what has hitherto been rejected but can ultimately belong to the whole. Jung is correct in saying that the missing "fourth" is necessary if wholeness is to occur. But this is not to say that the power of evil is at the heart of the Self or of the Divine Order that presumably lies beyond the empirical Self. For by its very nature the Self, as the archetype of wholeness, must exclude and negate the power of evil, which is a principle of destruction. Nor is there any empirical evidence that the Self has any of the attributes of evil. To the contrary, where the Self is manifested we find something of supreme value, a true *Summum Bonum*, and the power of evil is nullified.

Finally there is Jung's logical objection that to think good requires us also to think evil. We can now see that this is not necessarily the case, when by "good" we mean not the human judgment of what is good and evil, but the ultimate norm by which we evaluate what is good and what is evil. This norm can be called the Good (with a capital "G") or Wholeness. It is clear that to think "Wholeness" we do not have to think its opposite, just as we can feel, experience and think health without thinking illness.

As we have seen, Jung has no inclination to involve himself in metaphysics, but feels impelled to do so because in the case of the *privatio boni* he feels that metaphysics is encroaching upon experience in a way that is not justified empirically. But I think we can now see that the doctrine of the *privatio boni* does not conflict with the empirical facts. Indeed, the *Summum Bonum* of the doctrine of the *privatio boni* looks very much like Jung's *Self* since the "Good" of the *privatio boni* refers to the perfect fulfillment of a purpose or function. Nevertheless, the doctrine does remain metaphysical. To say it is possible that there is a God Who is a *Summum Bonum* is not to prove that this is actually so. For no one can say they know what the Ultimate is. For all we know, perhaps all that exists is a world in which one force works for wholeness, and another force works against wholeness, and there is nothing beyond this. This is a point we must examine more carefully, but first let us look again at the Christian position with regard to evil in the light of what we have said, and then at certain corrections in the Christian attitude that Jung's position on evil makes imperative.

ANOTHER LOOK AT THE CHRISTIAN POSITION

I have tried to show that the doctrine of the *privatio boni* is a defendable philosophical idea. Interestingly enough, this does not detract from the other early Christian attitudes toward evil that we have mentioned. For instance, the *privatio boni* does not in any way detract from the reality of evil. As we have seen, the original Christian position found in the Gospels and early Church was so cognizant of its reality that its theory of the Atonement was couched in terms of the problem of evil.

Nor does the doctrine of the *privatio boni*, understood in the correct way, contradict the position taken up by Clement and others that evil is allowed by God in order to accomplish His purpose. If wholeness is the highest Good, and if this is to be accomplished, then everything that is created must perform its proper function. The proper function of the ego is to achieve consciousness. This would not seem to be possible without the activity of evil. It is only when we come up against evil that consciousness is raised to a certain height. So it may be, paradoxically, that God allows evil because, even though it seeks to destroy wholeness, wholeness in the spiritual sense would be impossible without it.

This position has already been summarized in statements referred to earlier. If this be so, it may even be that Origen is correct, and that at the end of history evil, too, will cease to exist, its proper function having been played out in the cosmic drama and therefore no longer necessary. We are left with the seemingly paradoxical statement by the Russian philosopher Nicholas Berdyaev: "It is equally true that a dark source of evil exists in the world and that in the final sense of the word there is no evil."

Jung says very much the same thing. In "A Psychological Approach to the Dogma of the Trinity" he discusses the role of the devil. He writes:

The question we are confronted with here is the independent position of a creature endowed with autonomy and eternality: the fallen angel. He is the fourth, "recalcitrant" figure in our symbolical series. . . . Just as, in the *Timaeus*, the adversary is the second half of the second pair of opposites, without whom the world-soul would not be whole and complete, so, too, the devil must be added to the *trias* (the One as the Fourth), in order to make it a totality. . . . Through the intervention of the Holy Ghost, however, man is included in the divine process, and this means that the principle of separateness and autonomy over against God—which is personified in Lucifer as the God-opposing will—is included in it too. But for this will there would have been no creation and no work of salvation either. The shadow and the opposing will are the necessary conditions for all actualization. An object that has no will of its own, capable, if need be, of opposing its creator, and with no qualities other than its creator's, such an object has no independent existence and is incapable of ethical decision. At best it is just a piece of clockwork which the Creator has to wind up to make it function. Therefore Lucifer was perhaps the one who best understood the divine will struggling to create a world and who carried out that will most faithfully. For, by rebelling against God, he became the active principle of a creation which opposed to God a counterwill of its own. Because God willed this, we are told in Genesis 3 that he gave man the power to will otherwise. Had he not done so, he would have created nothing but a machine, and then the incarnation and the redemption would never have come about.

I have quoted Jung at length because it shows that he is actually very close to the original Christian thought regarding evil. It would be hard, for instance, to tell the difference between what Jung says here and what Irenaeus said about the blessedness of the fall of man, since because of it Christ's redemption could take place.

There remains, however, a basic optimism in the Christian attitude toward evil that we do not often hear in Jung. Without denying the reality of evil nor overlooking the destructive power of evil and its dangers to mankind, the Christian symbol of the Crucifixion and Resurrection points to an ultimately optimistic conclusion to the Divine Drama. For the Resurrection symbolizes the ultimate indestructibility of wholeness. It is a way of saying that in the final analysis, no matter what the forces of evil do, the integrity of wholeness cannot be destroyed. That is why Christ rises again victoriously even after having been seemingly destroyed by the evil forces.

On the psychological level this would correspond to the indestructibility of the Self. It would be a way of saying that when the Self is realized, there is an invulnerability to the powers of evil; the destructive powers cannot destroy the realized Self. On the human level it means that if a human being is centered and related to the Self, there is a certain protection against evil; that when the center of the personality is established, such a person is supported by a more-than-human strength to resist and overcome the evil powers.

This Christian optimism toward evil, however, is not based on an optimistic view of either human nature or of this world. Evil will not be overcome because people are good nor because the world is or can ever be a good place. It can only be overcome by virtue of the superior power of God. Human nature remains all too vulnerable to influences of evil, and Jung is correct that we should not be too sanguine about it. And the world, insofar as we can foresee, will always remain an imperfect cauldron full of turmoil and trouble, but a world in which some individual persons might nevertheless achieve consciousness.

Again, we are talking the language of metaphysics. We cannot know scientifically what the Ultimate Plan of life is, or even if there is such an Ultimate Plan. At a certain point knowledge comes to an end, and faith must take over. The only empirical knowledge of these things we have is the psychological fact that *if* a person's life is grounded in the wholeness of the Self, then there does seem to be a certain permanence and indestructibility about it that keeps that person's soul from succumbing to evil. And, who knows, such a soul may endure in a life beyond death as well.

Our argument now comes full circle, and paradox builds upon paradox. We have noted that evil may be necessary if wholeness is to come about, since wholeness can only occur when all creatures perform their proper function, and it would seem that human moral and psychological consciousness can only develop in the face of evil. It may be, therefore, that even evil is part of God's plan. We are back, in other words, to Clement's idea that God has a right and left hand with which to carry out His Will. Yet at the same time we say this, we also say that wholeness does not include evil, and that when wholeness is established, or when it is destroyed, either one, evil also ceases to be.

Yet it is correct that in this study of the ontology of evil we should find that the loose ends do not all come together and that the final answer escapes us. The worst thing in the world might be to suppose that the problem of evil had been solved on either an intellectual or emotional level. It is better for us to be left wondering, with a hint, to be sure, about the relationship between evil and God, but with no final answer. For we are more apt to discover the truth as we contemplate God as the Great Mystery, instead of supposing that we have reduced God to a final truth we can understand in human terms.

I have tried to argue that the position of the *privatio boni* with regard to evil is possible and not inconsistent with the psychological facts. Nonetheless, Jung's work has made it imperative that the typical conventional stance toward evil evidenced by most Christians must be significantly altered.

For instance, when Jung says that our image of totality must shift from three to four he is psychologically correct insofar as this means there must be a shift away from an attitude based on a purely conscious position to an attitude that includes the unconscious as well. This means the recognition and inclusion of the devil. As we have seen, this does not mean that intrinsic evil is accepted or "enthroned," as Philp would put it, but that the necessity for evil is accepted, and an attempt made to transform it. On the operational level, this means there must be an attempt to include and integrate into our conscious attitude all that belongs to our essential wholeness that has been rejected, split-off and repressed into the unconscious.

This process of integration cannot take place if the conscious attitude remains rigid, one-sided and insistent on only the light side of things. Only if the dark side of life and the dark side of the Self are accepted, is this process possible. And its ultimate success can only come about if consciousness is willing to accept a paradoxical view of wholeness and is willing to work out an individual, rather than collective solution to the problems of life and personality. In short, we can never be "perfect," that is, without spot, blemish or imperfection, but we can move toward wholeness which is, as Jung says, a highly paradoxical state.

The traditional Christian attitude as it has been mediated

through the Church has rejected too much. It has refused to accept the shadow side of the personality and has rejected the dark side of the Self. It has insisted upon an impossible standard of perfection and has not acknowledged the necessity, even the value, of a wholeness that comes about through imperfection, not through perfection. In refusing to accept the paradoxical nature of totality it has specifically excluded the feminine aspect of life and personality. This has not brought about a state of light and perfection, but has increased evil by driving parts of the personality into a split-off state. The conventional Christian attitude must therefore turn itself about and see the necessity for the redemption of that which has fallen into the hands of evil, even though this involves a descent into the dangerous realm of the unconscious.

References

Berdyaev, Nicholas. *Meaning of the Creative Act*. New York, 1962.
The I Ching. Trans. Richard Wilhelm. New York, 1955.
Jung, C. G. *Aion. Col. Wks.*, Vol. 9,2. New York, 1959.
———. "Eliade's Interview for 'Combat' ". In *C. G. Jung Speaking*, ed. William McGuire and R.F.C. Hull. Princeton, N.J., 1977.
———. *Letters 2*. Princeton, N.J., 1975.
———. *Memories, Dreams, Reflections*. New York, 1955.
———. *Mysterium Coniunctionis. Col. Wks.*, Vol. 14. Princeton, N.J., 1963.
———. *Psychology and Alchemy. Col. Wks.*, Vol. 12. New York, 1953.
———. "A Psychological Approach to the Dogma of the Trinity." In *Psychology and Religion. Col. Wks.* Vol. 11. New York, 1963.
Philp, H. L. *Jung and the Problem of Evil*. London, 1958.

Part Two

Morton Kelsey

Rediscovering the Priesthood through the Unconscious

In the past twenty years my conception of the priesthood has undergone a drastic change. Starting from a warmed-over intellectual approach, I have come to the deep conviction that this profession is urgently needed by men today, and that the priesthood and religion can be rediscovered in modern life through an understanding of the unconscious, as this part of man's psyche has been discovered and described by one particular branch of psychological thought. The change has occurred, in fact, as I have worked with the findings of Dr. C. G. Jung and his associates, first in my own pastoral ministry in the Episcopal Church, then with clergy of several denominations, and finally at present with educators in the Catholic Church at the University of Notre Dame.

Others, of course, have investigated the unconscious, but they have considered mostly aspects exposed by some special point of view. It is no wonder the church has felt that psychology offered little to religious understanding. Most schools of psychological thought have either shunned religion and the priesthood or dismissed them as simply unimportant to the mature life.

This is certainly not true of Dr. Jung and his followers. On the contrary, the school of analytical or Jungian psychology has come to see that religion is an essential part of mature living. The priesthood, which is the profession concerned with religion and its mediation, thus is seen as necessary to men and their development. In fact Jung's understanding of the individual psyche, finding its way among a vast complex of unconscious realities, gives the priesthood a unique importance. It is the only profession committed to helping men deal religiously with these primary realities and is needed by them even when they would like to deny it.

This has not always been my understanding. A discovery took place in my own life, and since then I have talked with other priests who have had similar experiences and who found other lives touched once this had happened. This paper is an attempt to summarize some thoughts about this discovery and to consider the value that can be received by the priesthood today from an investigation of the unconscious. I shall first suggest the change that took place in my own life and how it occurred, and then discuss the implications of Dr. Jung's thought for the priesthood and religion. The subject is a complex one, and there is much that we shall leave to be investigated by the individual.

A CHANGING ATTITUDE

When I first became active in the church, my view of the priesthood was greatly influenced by the humanistic point of view. Looked at from this position, the priest is the leader of the religious activities of the community. He stands for moral order and is responsible for moral teaching. He is the community service expert. He deals with people in trouble. He is also the authority on religious ideas and the philosophy of meaning, and he organizes and runs the religious institution and its public and private services.

Such a role is a valuable one, as anyone would agree, except certain people who view any religious influence as destructive. But even so, the priesthood is not indispensable, or even central to the social structure. Priests are nice to have around, but doctors and lawyers and dentists, even scientists and school teachers, are more important. The priest adds a sweet savor to society (and sometimes feelings of a different kind), but he is far from being at the heart of things.

This point of view has become far more pervasive than we ordinarily realize. It is widely held inside the church as well as out of it. Although few priests would agree intellectually with such a formulation, nonetheless this is precisely the way many of us have acted. For instance, when it comes to valuing oneself, most of us have avoided the real needs of our being like a plague. We have tried instead to put the individual into a socially accepted straightjacket. Yet how are people to value the priesthood, these human beings who are the carriers of the church's message, if the priest does not value himself?

I now view this profession in a very different light. I have come to see that the role of the priest is the most essential in society. Unless he regains his position in the very heart and center of society, I question whether this civilization of ours can hold together and not collapse. The priest is the one who is, or should be, mediator of a vast realm of reality which relates to the spirit of things, rather than to the outer physical world, and thus exerts the final and most significant influence for good or evil on man's life and his destiny. It is this realm which some psychologists have called the unconscious.

Unless men consciously relate to this part of reality, usually only the negative aspects, the demonic element of spiritual reality, can break out. What happened in Nazi Germany, in Russia, at places like My Lai, and increasingly on our own streets, is only a foretaste of things to come unless men can once again come to a serious consideration of non-physical reality. The priest is most urgently needed. He is the one who can become the expert in this realm, the mediator of it to mankind, just as the scientist becomes the expert who mediates the physical world to men.

This change of attitude began in an attempt to solve some of my own problems, as I thus became deeply concerned with the psychology of Dr. Jung. There was a time when I was quite hesitant about mentioning the fact that I had become interested because I had personal problems. But as I have come to know more people well, I find that most people have inner problems just about as difficult as my own. The important consideration is not that a person has problems, but what he is doing about them.

At any rate, my real interest in Jung's thought came as the problems began to disappear. This was not brought about by rational means. Instead, it is accomplished by an honest sharing of one's life with another person, by allowing this relationship to become very real, by an attempt to understand one's dreams, by a use of imagination and introspection under guidance and direction, and then by using one's best rational powers to make some sense of what has happened. Through this experience in analysis I came into contact with parts of my being, with levels and layers within myself which I had never known existed.

I found, first of all, layers of darkness and ugliness from which

I had been hiding. But more important, I also found elements wiser than I coming into this self of mine, impinging upon the depth of my being; and these were elements that seemed bent on bringing me to a less one-sided and less neurotic adjustment. In other words, by looking deeply and directly within, I came into contact with positive as well as negative elements of *the unconscious*. Although they were found within, these elements can by no means be described as "only psychological." The term unconscious is applied to them simply because they are elements that one has not been aware of. But this, of which we shall say more later, does not limit the kind of element that may be perceived, or where it may come from.

As I came into contact with this vast realm of the unconscious which had been troubling me, learned a little about it and adjusted my life to it, I was amazed and delighted to find problems disappearing. While certainly I became no paragon of maturity, yet there has been a real change. Not only did my inner difficulties grow far less intense, but I found myself functioning better than I ever had before. At the same time there were two very specific results that had a profound effect on my outlook and ministry.

SPECIFIC RESULTS

First of all, once I had begun to handle my own problems, I found that people began knocking at my door with their problems. I hung out no shingle; the way I had come to my new-found knowledge was still an embarrassment. But people can tell when one of us is trying to deal with the depths of himself. When people begin to seek us out because we understand, it is hard to resist the temptation to move primarily into a counseling ministry. So much of our effort as priests seems to have little effect in changing lives; the preaching, teaching, even our sacramental actions appear to touch people so little, and yet one can see individuals changed in intensive, long-range counseling. The priest who has any flair for it can find his time almost totally absorbed in this work.

In taking a rather extensive detour on this counseling road, I became certain of one thing. It is not wise for the clergy, unless they are in a special situation, to become too deeply involved in long-range counseling. It is not that the clergy are incapable of doing the job, but that they are needed as priests. If they abandon this role and its function, for whatever reason, then the priestly role is not expressed, and a function of the greatest importance is left unfulfilled in our society. And there was another, far more important result from my encounter with the unconscious which added conviction to this understanding.

This came as I returned to a consideration of the New Testament, and discovered that everything one learned in analysis was to be found there if one took it seriously. In order to give some talks on the healing ministry of Jesus and the early church, I began to study the New Testament intensively. I was dumbfounded to realize the depth of insight in it which had escaped me when I studied or read it formerly. And I was not the only blind one; the understanding found in Jesus and Paul of the nature of man, their view of the depth and complexity of man and his universe, were rarely discussed.

It was clear what had happened. In the process of getting rid of my problems, I had had to put away the rationalistic point of view and the essentially materialistic philosophy which had been very much a part of me. In order to get well, I had had to lay these prejudices aside, and once they were at least partially gone, I could listen to the New Testament and hear what it had to say. And this was quite different from what most of contemporary Christianity said about man and the universe.

All of the realities experienced in the analytical situation—the same realities Jung had written of from a scientific point of view—were discussed and dealt with there. In fact, the very parts of the New Testament which the rationalistic church had avoided or even denied, for fear of making Jesus look silly, were the interest and concern of Jungian psychologists as they attempted to make sick people well.

Listening seriously to Jesus and Paul, one realizes that they were speaking of a realm of reality which they had experienced when they spoke of God, demons, the devil, angels, the law, dominions, principalities, and powers. These things were just as real as the physical world—more real, in fact, for they could influence physical reality. They could affect the lives of men, corrupting them in sin and sickness, or breaking through in revelations, in visions, dreams, ecstatic utterances and experiences, and in physical and mental healings. Far from considering these things silly, Jung and his followers, with no special religious interest, but with the passion to heal which allowed them to look in any area for help, had discovered experiences that were a large part of what the New Testament writers were describing. Although Jung called them by other names, the realities were clearly the same. Yet the church and its priesthood, as I knew them, had avoided the function of coming to know this realm of reality and helping men deal with it.

One of the most important areas the church has avoided is the whole matter of the healing ministry, which plays such a significant part in the New Testament. This ministry forces us to realize that our minds and bodies can be influenced by another realm of reality; and this means that the spiritual can influence the material, that the nonmaterial is real and can play upon our lives. The healing ministry forces us to take spiritual reality seriously, and men are afraid to deal with this reality, often for good reason. But if Jung is right, this is the real function of the priesthood and is needed today as never before. Let us look at some of his basic understanding.

THE THINKING OF DR. JUNG

Jung's basic premise is that man cannot be studied adequately by using the ordinary scientific method. The most important part of man, according to Jung, cannot be objectively verified. Consciousness cannot be directly observed. It can be studied only by listening to what men say goes on in it. But this fact has been ignored by most scientific psychologies. They start by ruling out the most important data about men, and so they come up with the most distorted views about men, views which either ignore his religious life entirely or are actively hostile to it.

Jung's view and his method were quite different from this. He started with the idea that man is somewhat more complex than other things. He observed what men said about their conscious lives, listened to what they expressed about themselves and their actions, and then studied these data scientifically. This has been termed a method of "non-experimental empiricism."[1] What is more than a little surprising is the fact that so few intelligent thinking men today have realized the need to observe themselves and other individuals in this way. This failure of most people, church people included, is one indication of how deeply the materialistic ideas of our time have cut into our ability to think about certain things.

Applying this method, Jung learned to free himself to listen objectively, without "scientific" prejudices. He was able to consider empirically what men said about themselves, their dreams and subliminal experiences. As these data accumulated, he came to the conclusion that man has not only a conscious mind (which is even dismissed by some psychologies), but also a *personal unconscious* in which are deposited forgotten or repressed memories that can be called forth under the right circumstances. In addition he found experiences of another sort that seemed to cross space and time, and appeared to come from what he called the *collective unconscious*—from an inexhaustible reservoir of psychic reality which impinges upon the human psyche and has a very real influence on it. Freud, in one of his last published papers, came close to the same formulation.

Because this is known through the inner activity of our minds, it is easy to assume that it is just mental activity, a final spinning-out of cerebration. But this, Jung found, is anything but true. On the contrary, just as our physical senses bring us into contact with a real, but imperfectly known, external world of matter, so one's inner, psychological faculties bring him into touch with a real, but imperfectly known, non-material, non-physical world. It is called "unconscious" because we are unconscious of it for the most part. Most of the time we are aware only of bits and pieces that often seem foolish to us, unless a larger experience of this world comes through to show that it is far from being our own creation.

While Jung became aware of such experiences early in his practice, he did not investigate this realm out of curiosity, but because he had to in order to help certain neurotically sick people get well. Most often, he found those who became sick were the very ones who had no way to deal with this part of reality, and they did not recover until they had dealt with it in a satisfactory way. Once a person had encountered this deep level of reality with the help of the therapist as intermediary, there was often a dramatic experience from the collective unconscious which offered new meaning in his life, and his health improved, often physically as well as mentally. It was clear that the non-material, the non-physical has a very real effect on the physical world in man.

Jung recognized that historically it was the priesthood who helped men deal with such non-material realities, and he also saw that people had begun to pay a price for trying to live by the material and the rational alone. They needed a religious approach to this other reality of spirit. As early as 1928 he made a plea for clergy equipped to help meet "the urgent psychic needs of our age," adding, "It is indeed high time for the clergyman and the psychotherapist to join forces to meet this great spiritual task."[2]

Jung did not come by this view just "naturally." Starting practice at the turn of the century, he accepted as axiomatic the rational materialism of the medical school. Like most of us, he seriously doubted that any other reality existed. But unlike most of us in the church, he looked carefully at his own experiences—particularly his dreams—as well as those of his patients, and noted their effect on one's outer, conscious life. These experiences forced him to take very seriously communications coming into the psyche at some deep level of men's being. Among them were certain profound spiritual experiences that had a tremendous effect on his own life.

He also found that such things sometimes happened among his mental patients—experiences which they were not able to integrate into their lives, but which, because they were deficient in control, they could not shut out and were not ashamed to talk about. Certain of these, as Jung said, "bit him," in particular one vision which a psychotic patient in the mental hospital in Zurich described and tried to show him. The man pointed to the sun and, in awed tones, told him to watch the tube swinging from it, for this was the origin of the wind, the breath of God. A little later, in a journal completely inaccessible to the patient, indeed in a language he did not know, Jung came across a description of the same vision in practically identical phrases, translated from a mystical Greek papyrus unearthed from the sands of Egypt.

It is no wonder Jung's eyes were opened. He broadened his studies to include religion and mythology, and also fairy tales and folklore, finding the same basic images and ideas running through the stories of diverse peoples who had had no communication with each other. As patients began coming to him from all over the world, he found that similar imaginings and dreams and visions occurred to many of these individuals, widely separated by distance and culture and race. There were also much the same hints in his own dreams.

This variety of experience convinced Jung that when men withdraw their attention from exclusive preoccupation with the outer material world, they come into contact with a real world found within. Ordinarily a person discovered this other world in his dreams, but it could also be encountered in visions, and Jung helped many of his patients to experience it through a process very similar to religious meditation.[3] Thus, although he had started with a definitely negative view of religious reality, his medical and scientific work forced him to see the existence of this part of reality.

He discovered further that individuals, particularly in the second half of life, run the risk of neurosis when they become cut off from this realm of the unconscious, of non-physical, non-rational being. In other words, neurosis—which may be caused by many different things—can also result simply from a lack of religious roots, a failure to find adjustment to the whole of reality. A person may have been adequately reared, may learn and be very successful, without sexual hang-ups, and still find his life falling to pieces if he has not taken this realm of spiritual being into account. The results in physical as well as mental illness can be just as disastrous as if one had developed a brain tumor. Yet, as Jung found in case after case, such illness is really healed only as the person relates to the realm of spirit and gains a religious outlook on life.

By investigating this world of spirit, Jung has not only shown that it is an empirical reality which affects man, but that it also demands a religious approach from him. There are penalties for ignoring, remaining unconscious of these realities that seek expression in man. Today's problems of psychic illness, of drugs and violence, suggest that the priest, if he can become aware of the need to deal with spiritual reality, is called back to a function which has become crucial in our social economy.

WHICH VIEW?

In the world view which takes non-material reality seriously and considers this realm very real, there is no doubt that the priest has an important function. He is to know this part of reality, and then mediate it to men. But when we do not seriously believe in the existence of such a sector of reality, where do we leave the priesthood? Being a priest in a universe where the non-material does not exist is like trying to run a waterwheel in a dry stream bed. One feels more as if he were working in a magnified Rotarian fellowship, or sometimes an existentialist Browning Society, than in a church.

Unfortunately, we live in a time when most men seriously doubt the existence of any reality beyond the material world, or the validity of any knowledge without objective verification. Rational materialism has become dogma, not only in Marxism, but unofficially on Main Street, U.S.A. This belief is so prevalent that it pervades the very intellectual air we breathe. Even the existentialist ends by incorporating this very belief which he set out to deny. In fact it is almost pitiful when people finally realize that one does believe in another realm, and come timidly forward to tell of experiences of the non-physical which they have had, but were afraid to share for fear of being considered off their rocker.

This timidity is understandable. If there is no non-material reality, or if one exists with no way of contact, then how can our religion be anything but illusion or a sickness? The psychiatrist who believes only in the rational and material aspect of reality, if he is consistent, is forced to look upon religion in this way. The priest, holding the same belief, comes to deal with ideas about spiritual reality rather than the reality itself, with theology instead of religion, and there is quite a difference. One transmits ideas; the other mediates reality itself. The ideas are ours, and generally influence only those who already agree with us. The spiritual realities are God's, and have the carrying power that comes from and transmits conviction.

It was Dr. Jung who called my attention to the meaning of the word conviction. It comes from the verb "conquer" and means being conquered by. One cannot argue himself into conviction; ideas seldom convince. Instead one must be brought into the presence of something that conquers him—something of reality, which alone gives true conviction. If the job of the priest is to help people find religious conviction that will carry over into their lives, and even beyond, then this has to come from some reality which can touch individuals. Unless the priest has come to know this reality with which religion is concerned, how can he expect others to take it seriously, let alone be convinced by it himself?

Jung offers a way that is possible for men today to come into contact with such a reality. He gives us moderns a method of confronting and genuinely believing in the realm of spiritual reality, a method which can help us understand the spiritual leaders of other times. Jung's own experience made him know that these men, far from being deceived or sick, were in fact dealing with a deeper level of reality than ordinary people. It is not the really religious people who are sick, he saw, but the non-religious and those whose religion is neurotic and rigid. They are the ones who are out of touch with reality. Jung offers us a way of approaching reality that can help avert much of the neurosis and sickness of modern man. It is not important how, as priests, we learn of this spiritual world, whether by analysis or spiritual direction or overwhelming experience. What is important is that we come to know it, deal with it and, as mediators, help others to do the same.

Thus the priest and the therapist will both work with this same realm if they are trying to approach the whole man, but in different ways. The therapist will deal with this area of the unconscious in sick people, using special techniques to improve their relation to it. But the same realities also move through the unconscious in healthy people, and the important thing is to find our relation to them in health. The task of the priest, then, is to mediate this reality for healthy people, through word and action, in pastoral contact, sacrament and ritual, and through spiritual direction.[4] In counseling his concern will also be to help the individual recover a healthy contact with it when this has been disrupted. And finally he will be sure enough of his own standpoint to work with the doctor and support him in his effort to rid patients of specific ailments.

A knowledge of psychotherapy is a help in the priestly role. It offers ways that enable us to reach people, to evaluate their situations, and also to make more intelligent referrals of the problems that fall outside our function. It is valuable to understand the special techniques of the therapist, and to use many of them. But if the priest is to speak with authority of these realities which are the concern of religion, he can hardly take on the role of the permissive and non-valuing psychological healer as well. Instead of priests who try to do so, or psychologists who try to become religious experts, each profession needs to understand and work with the other.

As priest, however, one needs to be quite certain of the difference between being an authoritative mediator and being authoritarian or judgmental. There is a big difference between definitely standing for something and judging, which nearly always has an element of hostility and insecurity in it. The clergyman can stand for a great deal and still seldom judge.

Indeed, so far as one genuinely knows the spiritual realm, just so far can he be secure and accepting of others, free of the need to judge and reject the person who falls short. The clergyman knows something real, and he hopes by an understanding and accepting attitude to open the other person to this realm. From the psychological professions he can learn much about caring and accepting in concrete practice; the psychologist can help us operationalize the command of Jesus that we love one another as he has loved us. Still, one cannot pretend that spiritual realities make no claim upon the individual, or that this realm does not set standards from which the person can fall short.

We have in the New Testament, as one friend who is an analyst has reminded me, the best handbook on integration or psychological maturity ever written. Taken seriously as it is and not picked apart, the New Testament is a description of the spiritual world and the encounter with it. The task of dealing with this realm is hard work; it demands the total man. It is also dangerous work; one can be sucked under by this realm of being. Yet this is the task to which the priest is called, the religious task of meeting and drawing life from these realities of which Jesus spoke. There is no higher calling, none more needed.[5]

Notes

1. Suggested by Fr. Raymond Hostie in *Religion and the Psychology of Jung*, New York, Sheed and Ward, 1957, pp. 9 ff.
2. C. G. Jung, *Collected Works*, Vol. 11, New York, Pantheon Books, Inc., 1958, p. 334. Dr. Jung did not change his view on this subject, as was impressed on me some years after he wrote this, when I had a chance to talk with him and exchange a letter or two.
3. This kind of process is only now being investigated intensively, using some of the new techniques developed for the study of sleep and dream-

ing. The possibility and advantages of learning a certain voluntary control of brain waves, involving specifically the alpha wave state, the
images that arise in it, and also the healing process, are being studied in
several places. One major project is going on now at Sepulveda Vet-
erans' Hospital in Los Angeles under the direction of Dr. Barbara
Brown, Chief of the Experiential Laboratory.

4. In spiritual direction the clergy will need to work with dreams, visions,
and other such experiences, and this is quite possible without becoming
analysts. It is a matter of using the same materials for different purposes, much as the builder puts together a house out of the same materials which a chemist might subject to analysis. See my book *Dreams:
The Dark Speech of the Spirit*, Garden City, New York, Doubleday &
Company, Inc., 1968; also Maria F. Mahoney, *The Meaning in Dreams
and Dreaming*, New York, The Citadel Press, 1970.

5. John Sanford in *The Kingdom Within*, Lippincott, Philadelphia and New
York, 1970, has shown clearly our understanding of the sayings of Jesus
within this context. Also a short bibliography will be helpful for the
interested reader; these books give a background for understanding the
religious point of view of Dr. Jung, and they should be read in this order.

C. G. Jung, et al., *Man and His Symbols*, Garden City, New York, Doubleday and Company, Inc., 1964; also Dell Publishing Company.

———, *Memories, Dreams, Reflections*, rec'd. and ed. by Aniela Jaffe,
New York, Random House, Inc., 1963.

———, *Modern Man in Search of a Soul*, New York, Harcourt, Brace &
World, Inc., 1933.

———, *Two Essays on Analytical Psychology*, Cleveland, The World Publishing Company, 1956.

———, *Psychology and Religion: West and East*, Princeton, N.J., Princeton University Press, 1969.

Patrick Vandermeersch

The Archetypes:
A New Way to Holiness?

It is difficult to assess the true value of the work of C. G. Jung. So far as psychiatry is concerned, at least here in continental Europe, his influence seems very marginal. The man whom Freud called his heir apparent and who was the first president of the International Association of Psychoanalysis has left little trace. People still use some of his concepts, or rather, terms—complexes, introverts, extraverts—and they still know vaguely that he is the author of a typology. But that is not much. They have long since forgotten that he was Bleuler's first assistant and played a decisive role in the research into schizophrenia. Of course, it is some time now since the old sage of Zurich died, alone with his soul, that anima which in the end retained only a vague memory of animosity.

Among people concerned with religious life and inner experience however, Jung's name is mentioned more and more frequently. The reason is probably that at first sight his thought seems to be less rebellious to a religious conception of life than that of Freud. Freudian "pansexualism" is contrasted, sometimes over-hastily, with Jung's vision of the world, which seems to take better account of spiritual values and the higher strivings of the human soul.

This situation poses a problem. Truth is not to be played with. One may say that psychiatry and theology are two different things—though even that statement needs nuancing as a theory, and still more in practice—but even so, it seems suspicious that a system which is so outmoded or even false from the point of view of psychiatry and psychoanalysis should be so fertile for the religious life. Psychoanalysis, however, may be wrong in rejecting Jung's work, for it is a fact that the rejection is often accompanied by ignorance and misunderstanding. I wish therefore to look at the main ideas that structure Jung's work, see what are his main divergences from Freud, and try to clarify the issue. To what extent was Jung right or wrong? That is the first question to be asked.

There is also another question. Why do those who are concerned about religion take an interest in Jung? And why just now? For this interest can hardly have fallen from the skies. Looked at more closely, it seems to have come from the Himalayas. Jung was several decades ahead of our present interest in Yoga and Zen. Today's mystical seeking is tinged with orientalism, and Buddhist monasteries seem to be for some a higher equivalent of what a trip to Katmandu is for others. Certainly, it is in itself a good thing that ecumenism should extend beyond the borders of Christianity. We must seek truth everywhere, and there is no fragment of the universe from which the Spirit of God is completely absent. But there is a hidden danger here, a confusion into which it is easy to sink. The East, like the West, has its religion, its inner life, its mystical experience. But do these words cover exactly the same things for both of them? It may well be that the word "religion" means, for East and West, two realities that are each interesting and enriching but that are radically heterogeneous and have nothing to gain by being mixed together. Here again, it is a question of truth and of clarifying issues. Our second question will therefore be this: given our assessment of Jung's thought, what contribution can it make to typically Christian religious life?

JUNG'S LIFE

C. G. Jung was the son of a pastor, and his decision to become a doctor and a psychiatrist was the result of a compromise between his taste for science and his passionate interest in religion. For nine years, from 1900 to 1909, he was the assistant of the great Bleuler and seconded him in his research. Much of Jung's genius should be situated here, although the works of his

that date from this period are the least known of all. At the beginning of this century the endeavour was being made to syste-
matize and clarify all the nosographical entities that lay tangled
under the highly inadequate label of "mental illness". Bleuler gave
Jung the task of studying, in particular, schizophrenia, or *dementia
praecox* as it was then still called. In order to do so, Jung developed the technique of association tests, though he did not invent
them himself but borrowed them from Kraepelin and Aschaffen-
burg. This led to his becoming acquainted with Freud's work, the
aspect which interested him being the mechanism of repression.[1]
He went to Vienna to see Freud, and the two men soon became
closely associated. Bleuler too joined the group of "Freudians"
which was then beginning to get organized, and when the International Association of Psychoanalysis was founded, Jung became
its first president almost as a matter of course. However, all was
not for the best in the best of all possible worlds. Jung, Bleuler
and Freud very soon diverged from each other. Whatever the personal motives involved, it is interesting to see that on the theoretical level the divergences arose over the following questions: on
the one hand, the interpretation psychoanalysis gave to mythology and to religious phenomena in general, and on the other, the
problems raised by comparing hysteria and schizophrenia.

The break was not long in coming. Everything happened between 1910 and 1912. First, Bleuler left the psychoanalytical movement. The relations between Bleuler and Jung had already grown
cooler shortly before. Then came the rupture between Freud and
Jung. Almost simultaneously, each of the three published an important work giving his own views. For Bleuler it was the famous
book *Dementia Praecox oder Gruppe der Schizophrenien*, which gave the
name of schizophrenia to *dementia praecox*. Jung published in 1911
and 1912 the two parts of his *Wandlungen und Symbole der Libido*.[2]
Here he used parallels from mythology and the history of religion
to analyse a young American woman's fantasies and poems, which
contained a mass of self-analytical material. He also attacked Freud's
conception of libido, basing himself on an analysis of the differences
between hysteria and schizophrenia. As for Freud, in 1912–1913 he
wrote *Totem and Taboo*, dealing with the origins of religion, and introduced the concept of "narcissism" in order to distinguish psychosis from neurosis.

As is obvious, this confrontation between Freud, Jung and Bleuler is highly significant. One cannot but deplore the fact that the work Jung did at this period is so little known, even, paradoxically, by those most interested in his thought. They concentrate on what he wrote after the rupture with Freud. In fact, both sides are apt to study an abstraction when it comes to the history of the relations between psychoanalysis and religion: Freud without Jung, and Jung without Freud.

Where Jung is concerned, this can be explained by the fact that the part of his work dating from after the break with Freud is of quite a different kind from his earlier writings. That is where the problem lies. The earlier Jung was interested in nosography, the differential analysis of the different forms of psychic disturbance, very concrete psychiatric material, and casework; all this disappears from the second part of his work. We hardly find in it a single complete study of a case, or any concern about precise psychiatric diagnosis. What we do find is a great deal of mythological, gnostic and alchemical material to illustrate the influence emanating from the collective unconscious. The abundance of this second sort of material is no excuse for the relative lack of the first, and the reader used to the first Jung cannot but be puzzled. There is a world of difference between the two Jungs.

This world of difference between the two parts of Jung's written work is borne out by a blank in the bibliography. In the years immediately following his break with Freud, Jung published hardly anything. What was happening? Jung speaks in his autobiography of his confrontation with the unconscious. Of this self-analysis we know little except that in it he discovered his anima, and that one evening in 1916 he managed to free himself from the unbearable pressure of the unconscious by writing the *Seven Sermons to the Dead*. In the same year he gave a lecture at Paris on "The Structure of the Unconscious" (Coll. Wks. vol. 7) which is the nucleus of his later thought.

These *Seven Sermons to the Dead* are important, for they reveal the whole mystical system that Jung was later to develop. They are seven poems dealing with God and not intended for publication. In them we can easily see the path along which his self-analysis had led him. It should also be noted that at this time Jung kept a journal, his "red book", which has unfortunately been withheld from publication. The sermons begin as follows:

The Seven Instructions for the Dead. Written by Basilides[3] at Alexandria,
the City where East Meets West

Sermon I

The dead came back from Jerusalem, where they had not
found what they sought. They asked to come into my house to
be instructed, and I taught them this:

"Listen: I will begin with emptiness. Emptiness is the same
thing as fullness. In infinity, the full is also the empty. . . . We
call this emptiness or fullness the pleroma. . . ."

Then Jung goes on to speak of creatures, of the pairs of opposites
that form the pleroma, and of God.

At night, the dead lay among the dead and cried: "We
would know God. Where is God? Is He dead?"

God is not dead, He is as alive as ever. God is a creature,
for He is something concrete and therefore different from the
pleroma. God is a property of the pleroma and all that I have
said about creatures applies also to Him.[4]

Then Jung deals with good and evil, the Church and the communion of saints, and finally man. The rest—highly interesting—
can be found in the German edition of the autobiography; the trans-
lators of it have not been authorized to publish these sermons.

The rest of Jung's thought went on from there. We find there
the fundamental question: where is the unconscious leading us? We
will go into his theories more deeply later on; for the moment let us
mention a few landmarks. Jung was seeking cultural parallels that
might cast light on what was going on inside him. The unconscious
was fulfilling its function by bringing to consciousness the archetypes, which for Jung at this point were still primarily mechanisms
of compensation. In 1928 he received from R. Wilhelm a Chinese
treatise on alchemy called *The Secret of the Golden Flower* (Coll. Wks.
vol. 13), and wrote the preface for its publication. This was the start-
ing-point of his studies on alchemy, which he compared with religious symbolism. Here the archetype becomes an image, or rather,
the power of an image by which a man is impelled towards his final
harmony, the "self". After having lost at birth his immediate unity

and then trodden the path of the differentiation and reconciliation of the antinomies thus created, man regains a richer unity. This is the ideal of every human life and differs from culture to culture only by the way in which the differentiation and reintegration are carried out. But it will always remain an ultimate ideal: the process can go on for ever, which is why one of the last texts Jung wrote, shortly before his death, deals with eternal life.

I shall not say much about the part of Jung's work that dates from after the break with Freud, since it is better known. What I am mainly anxious to do is to stress its difference from the earlier writings. Nor shall I tackle the problem posed by the blank between the two periods. We have too little data on this self-analysis that the unconscious imposed on Jung, and what I have already mentioned will be enough for readers who like conjecture. We will go on now to ask ourselves what contribution Jung's work has made to psycho-analysis and to religion, and what problems it raises.

THE EGO AS A PRODUCT

What strikes one, from the beginning of Jung's earliest writings, when he was only starting to assimilate Freud's thought, is that he always considers the ego as a product, the result of a process. It is not, as it is for Freud, an agency.

It should be noted that this is not something peculiar to Jung. Romantic philosophy, which had not waited for Freud before speaking of the unconscious, interpreted the unconscious as a sort of psychic substance spreading throughout the cosmos but a little denser in some spots than in others, and particularly in human beings, for there—a miracle!—an ego emerges. The physiological psychology of the end of the nineteenth century was too materialistic to accept this idea of an autonomous psychic substance, but it continued to see the person as a mere product, the effect of associations carried out in the brain, with no value of its own. Bleuler was a representative of this school of thought, and he did not hesitate to compare the ego, which he reduced to self-consciousness, to the ticking of a pendulum—which exists simply because no silent clockwork has yet been invented.

We find the ego as a product throughout all of Jung's work,

without, of course, the materialistic reduction of positivism. The "self" is the hoped for and expected result of the ultimate evolution of the whole cosmos, or at least, of the activity of the unconscious. The ego is therefore a result, a product, an effect. It does nothing; or, more often, it makes the mistake of doing too much, whereas it would do better to let the unconscious do things to it.

This contrasts strongly with Freud's presentation. For him, the unconscious was originally produced by the ego, that is, by repression. For Freud, the ego is the principle of activity and life; for Jung, it is lived.

This ambiguity can be seen even in Jung's earliest writings. His interest in Freud was because of Freud's discovery of repression. He took up the idea, which seemed helpful for explaining the results of his word-association tests. But right from the beginning he added a qualification: repression is not necessarily an active function. He accepted the fact that there is opposition between the agreeable and the disagreeable and that this corresponds with the opposition between the conscious and the unconscious; but he would not agree that there is always a deliberate and intentional process involved in it. How could he, since, like Bleuler, he could only think of the ego as a product?

It is therefore not surprising that he began to speak more and more of "compensation" instead of "repression". When one sees that the unconscious contains something that the conscious does not want to accept, one can say with Freud that it is something that has been conscious but that has later been repressed by the ego (I am speaking in terms of Freud's thought prior to 1912). However, Jung was to say that it is a potentiality of which we have the seed within us (for we have the seed of everything, good or ill), but which has so far been neglected in favour of opposite potentialities. At some time or other such forgotten germs tend to rise to consciousness and enrich the ego, for the ego should be able to contain everything, even opposites—that is what the return to our original integrity means. That is what Jung means, too, when he says that virtue as well as vice may be repressed: we have opposing potentialities within us which we must manage to reconcile. If one of a pair of opposites is lived out consciously, the other will make its compensatory effect felt from the unconscious.

One may say that in the end, for both Freud and Jung, it comes down to accepting something in us that is disagreeable. However, there are important differences. For Freud, repressed material is hidden to avoid a painful clash with consciousness. It must be traced and recognized, and this necessitates going through the process of analysis. We may add, too, that it always comes down in the end to a question of interpersonal relations. For Jung, what makes its compensatory influence felt is something that has never yet been known and therefore cannot be recognized. All one can do is get to know it, by means of an image. Here a number of questions arise: what is the relation between the image and the compensation? Where do interpersonal relations come in?

THE ARCHETYPE: A MECHANISM OR AN IMAGE?

The term "archetype", which appears as a prolongation of the concept of introversion, is primarily meant to indicate a mechanism. In *The Relations Between the Ego and the Unconscious* (1928: Coll. Wks. vol. 7), Jung describes how the life-task of every human being is to realize first his "persona" and then his soul ("anima" or "animus"), and finally work towards the gradual realization of his "self". These are the major archetypes guiding human destiny. We need not linger over the "shadow", which represents the personal unconscious, or the "old wise man" and "great mother", which are connected with the self, or all the various forms that the archetypes can take (the anima can appear as a fairy, a witch, a prostitute, etc.). The essential thing is the dialectic between the persona, the soul and the self.

What exactly does this mean? Every human being is born with a whole array of potentialities, many of which, such as masculinity and femininity, are opposed to each other. This is the collective unconscious, which contains not only the instincts but also the germs of the spirit; and Jung supposes that it is genetically transmitted. Under the influence of education and environment some of these potentialities are developed while others are left untouched. A child wants to be "someone", a "grown up", and he identifies with the models and roles that he sees around him. He plays a part, like the ancient actors who put on a "persona", i.e. a mask, to play the part allotted to them. The archetype of the persona is the source of this movement of identification.

As has been said, for Jung the ego is a product. The persona is the first phase in the constitution of the ego. Thanks to the dynamism exerted by the persona, certain of the potentialities contained in the collective unconscious are realized, forming the first stratum of the ego.

Every realization implies a choice. One cannot be everything at once, play every role at once. The persona is constituted by means of realization and exclusion. To realize one potentiality inherent in the collective unconscious implies relegating the opposite potentiality which was also there. Roughly speaking, we may therefore say that by the constitution of the persona, the collective unconscious has been split in two: one part has found its fulfilment and the other has remained in an embryonic state. Jung calls this latter part the soul of the individual.

However, the soul refuses to stay put. It exerts its rights when the conscious attitude becomes too exclusive. In *Psychological Types* (1921) Jung develops this central idea of the compensatory action of the unconscious (the soul) on the conscious (persona). For example, he shows how a man of the extravert type, that is to say, drawn towards external objects, is forced by his unconscious to limit himself and attach more importance to his subjectivity:

> This is the extravert's danger: he gets sucked into objects and completely loses himself in them. The resultant functional disorders, nervous or physical, have a compensatory value, as they force him into an involuntary self-restraint. Should the symptoms be functional, their peculiar character may express his psychological situation in symbolic form; for instance, a singer whose fame had risen to dangerous heights that tempt him to expend too much energy suddenly finds he cannot sing high notes because of some nervous inhibition.[5]

In *Psychological Types* Jung shows for each type the opposition between the conscious and the unconscious and the compensatory effects that result from it. In *The Relations Between the Ego and the Unconscious* he situates this problem in the course of life: the realization of the persona occupies the first half of the life of each individual. During this period the soul may indeed make its compensatory effect felt from time to time; but it is chiefly when the graph begins to descend and the age of forty has been passed that it makes its demands felt. The realization of the persona goes with the creative, vital and instinctive aspects of life. When it has been achieved, the soul demands that the opposite aspects should be realized: the values of acceptance, and of a more cultural and spiritual life.

Roughly speaking, we may say that the persona is the archetype which sets going, from the collective unconscious, a process of differentiation; whereas the soul, by compensatory growth, leads the psyche towards integration through the realization of all its potentialities, even those that are mutually opposed.

I have been speaking so far of the dialectic of the persona and the "soul". To be correct, I should have used the word "anima" or "animus", for from *The Relations Between the Ego and the Unconscious* onwards these words replace the more general expression "soul" in Jung's work. But a problem lies behind this change of vocabulary.

Jung's reasoning is as follows: in the persona, the role that the child learns to play, femininity or masculinity holds a big place. Every human being has both femininity and masculinity as innate potentialities, since every human being participates in the same collective unconscious. Masculinity is part of a man's persona, therefore his soul contains the feminine potentialities which his persona left in the unconscious. Man has a feminine soul, an anima. For a woman, the opposite process has taken place and she has a masculine soul, an animus.

There are many problems here, and commentators have already raised them. What are masculinity and femininity? There are passages where Jung says that they are the roles allotted to man and woman in any given culture; hence, a dichotomy whose content is pretty arbitrary from the biological point of view. There are other passages where Jung ventures into speculations on the genetic material and all that may be hidden in it. I shall not go into these questions, for there is another point that seems to me to be even more problematic: the ambiguity that slips in when Jung moves from the idea of the anima as the whole of the potentialities that were excluded from the realization of the persona and can therefore be called the feminine in a man, to the idea that the anima is the image of femininity transmitted in every man by heredity.

Whereas in the beginning the concept of the archetype was considered as a mechanism of differentiation and integration, ruling the turning points of life, the archetypes now become innate virtual images that anticipate cultural situations where man will have to realise his instinctual heritage. The first explicit definition of the term "archetype" Jung gives in his work shows this very well already: the archetype is a scheme of action, that as an *a priori* is linked to the instincts (1919, in the article "Instinct and the Unconscious" Coll. Wks. vol. 8). Jung gives the example of a moth, the *pronuba yuccasella*, which manages to lay its eggs in the centre of the yucca flower, which opens only for one night, and does so in an astonishingly well-planned and complicated manner, without having learnt by imitation. Why then should there not be similar patterns innate in all human beings and correlative to the instincts? For the anima, this would mean that every man has an innate image of woman, and this would explain the passion when he finally finds the sister soul who corresponds with it.

To do Jung justice, one must emphasise that for him the archetype is not an image, but a virtual image. The anima gives no clear idea of the woman one needs, but confers a numinous power on some particular image of a woman one meets. However, the fact remains that the power is transmitted by the image. And in Jung's work there is no answer to the question: what is the relation between that image and the mechanisms of differentiation and compensation earlier described?

If one looks hard enough, with plenty of good will, one can find a connection. As early as *Wandlungen und Symbole der Libido* (1911–12), Jung spoke of the "imago" of the mother, into which are packed all the needs and potentialities that the child feels in himself but cannot fulfil. In this sense, the imago of the mother (= the anima?) could be interpreted as elaborated on the bases of what the child has experienced and what was left behind once the persona-differentiation had set in. However, it must be added that later Jung was to see the image of the mother as a manifestation of the innate anima, which contradicts what I have just said. One could think up other ways of passing from compensation to the power of the image, even involving Freudian notions, e.g. one could relate the theory of identification to the archetype of the persona. But Jung himself does not solve the problem, and indeed hardly seems to notice it.

The idea of the power of the image is most important, of course, for the archetype of the self. The self is the final state of the ego which has recovered its unity after the process of differentiation by a perfect integration of all the aspects that can go to make up life. The archetype of the self therefore appears after the anima has been integrated. It may appear as the Old Wise Man for a man or as the Great Mother for a woman (unless one prefers to see these images as autonomous separate archetypes which manifest themselves between the anima or animus and the self, as a resumption of the persona at a higher level). The self can also appear in a more abstract form, as in the mandalas which Jung himself drew in 1918 when he was military commandant at Château d'Oex; it was these that made him discover that the self is the final goal of the process of individuation.

The process of individuation, at least for the individual, ends with the self, an ultimate state never completely attained. The cycle from the undifferentiated collective unconscious through the persona and the anima is completed with the self. But for Jung that is not the last word. Each individuation enriches in its turn the culture and the collective unconscious, which therefore also grows even as such. It is thus that Jung distinguishes several eras in the collective unconscious, comparable to the stages through which the individual must pass. Cosmic history, like the history of the individual, is therefore the result of a spirit moving the whole universe by a process of differentiation and reintegration repeated on a number of levels.

RELIGION

Everywhere—in art, alchemy, gnosticism, myths and religion—Jung finds archetypes in the very varied forms that they can take. In fact, his genius lies in his insight that the representations found in these different domains can be related, and in his having shown that there is a certain continuity between the great symbolic systems such as art and religion and the more obscure and peripheral symbolic systems such as gnosticism and alchemy. The analysis of the great religious symbols occupies an important place in Jung's work, but to treat of it in detail would lead us too far afield. Suffice it to say that we find, in particular, studies on the Trinity, the transubstantiation that takes place in the Eucharist, Christ as the symbol of the self, the place of the Virgin in Christianity, and St Ignatius

Loyola's *Exercises*. Jung's interpretation is always the same: all these symbols are the expression of archetypes active within us. They are powerful representations that shape the destiny of each individual man and of all mankind.

Here a word must be said about what is usually called Jung's agnosticism. Several theologians have written about Jung or collaborated with him, and he liked to have representatives of religion around him. He was often asked if he believed that there was any objective reality corresponding to the religious symbols. Usually it was accepted and presupposed that Jung had successfully shown that on the level of human psychology the representations used by religion are produced by the archetypes. What the questioner wanted to know was whether Jung also believed that on the metaphysical level these symbols existed in themselves. It was in this Platonic form that the question was asked and that Jung understood it. He always answered that he limited himself to the psychological plane and that the question of the ontological reality of the religious symbols was a matter for the theologians. Jung's agnosticism therefore concerns the question whether there is a metaphysical plane corresponding to the plane discovered by human psychology. What he had no shadow of doubt about was that the archetypes do really lead man towards a hidden destiny. For Jung, the whole cosmos is traversed by a psychic current which, through the individuation of individual lives, strives to attain its fullness.

GOAL-DIRECTEDNESS

The idea of goal-directedness is the key to Jung's work. It is also the principle theme of *Wandlungen und Symbole der Libido*, the work that completed his rupture with Freud. Of course, the archetypes do not yet appear in it, but we do find the following fundamental idea: it is obvious that with sufficient analysis we can find sexuality everywhere; what is important is not merely to see that there are repressed instinctive impulses, but to ask what purpose they serve and whither the process is leading mankind. And that question will not be solved by analysing the individual only, but by analysing history and human culture and thereby seeing what meaning the unconscious processes may have for the individual. Jung says this explicitly:

> It seems to me that one must contemplate this strange journey of the libido with the admiration of a philosopher, and seek to find the purpose of its détours. The fact that the roots of it have been unearthed and belong to the erotic order tells us little, and in any case does not exhaust the problem. If there were not in all this some secret goal of the highest biological importance, the last twenty centuries would surely not have supported all these détours.[6]

In short, Jung had the impression that Freudianism led straight to cultural nihilism, religious iconoclasm and a return to pure instinct. The idea that the things of the spirit were only a gigantic farce was unendurable to him and seemed in any case to disregard reality. For there *is* culture, and there *is* repression. Have they no purpose? They cannot have dropped from the skies!

The way Jung answered this question in *Wandlungen und Symbole der Libido*, in 1911–12, was very different from his later conceptions. He saw that in fact, in religious and mythological representations, one can find erotic and incestuous tendencies. But why all this camouflage? Whence comes this repression of animal sexuality on the collective level? The answer Jung then gave (1912) was the idea of the death-instinct. However, that does not make everything clear, for this death-instinct seems to cover for him two different things. The death-instinct asserts itself primarily as a resistance to animal sexuality, which is thereby forced to discharge itself by side-paths. This brings about a sexualization of secondary objects, that is to say, a structuring of the world and culture and thought. This innate resistance to pure sexuality is the reason why man cannot satisfy himself simply by the sexual act, but must create myths, rites and religion. However, the death-instinct also means the tendency to regression, the return to the formless and undifferentiated, which shows itself on the sexual level in the desire for incest. In this way, Jung arrives at a very complicated relation between regression and desexualization, in which, as in a "dialectic moment", spirit arises out of nature.

CRITICAL REFLECTIONS FROM THE
POINT OF VIEW OF PSYCHOLOGICAL THEORY

Now that we have had a look at Jung's work, let us go on to
some critical reflections. First, let us mention some aspects which
we shall not deal with in detail. There is first that troubling fact of
the heterogeneousness of the two parts of Jung's work, with, between them, his self-analysis. We know little about this except that
Jung felt impelled to write a journal—the famous red book—to clarify his thought; and the *Seven Sermons to the Dead* are all we have to
enable us to imagine its contents. Some authors have not minced
their words and their diagnoses in describing this period after the
break with Freud. They have spoken of neurosis and even of an attack of psychosis. And it is true that for the reader of Jung I, the
texts of Jung II sometimes seem bizarre. That does not mean however that there is no continuity and that one can speak of a schizo-
phrenic production—a term which anyway would not have greatly
alarmed the patient in question. In any case, if Jung managed to
come through a phase of near-psychosis, that would be a feat to ad-
mire and a reason for studying his work all the more avidly.

A second aspect which poses a problem but with which we will
not deal in detail is the way Jung sees the link between biology and
psyche. For example, the anima's growth in opposition to the persona takes place around the age of forty; this implies a link between
biological maturity and psychic development which is far from having been proved.

Let us go on to what seems most doubtful and least confirmed
by experience: Jung's faith in the power of the image, and of the
image alone. It is here, and not on the point of sexuality or culture,
that the paths of Jung and Freud diverge radically.

What is important in Freud's so-called "pansexualism" is that
everything in it contains some interpersonal value. To reduce everything to sexuality in the brute biological sense is precisely what
Freudian analysis does not do. Though it links with the body and
sex the representations with which it deals, it always shows that
they bear an interpersonal meaning. Whether it be a question of
shame, guilt, hatred, love, perversion or anguish, for the Freudian
these never concern ourselves alone, but always our relations with
others as well, often in a much more concrete way than is imagined.

If some representations are attractive and others repulsive, that is because of the interpersonal value that they may have. For the Freudian, the power of the image is an interpersonal power.

This interpersonal aspect has no place in Jung's conception, or at least, in his system. Jung seems to take it for granted that the power of the image is bound up with what one can only feel in one's own depths. The collective unconscious seems to lead in the end to solipsism.

It should be noted that from this point of view there is no real opposition between Freud and Jung: in his theoretical concepts Jung simply does not deal with the problem of interpersonal relations. For him, it goes without saying that everything that happens in the human psyche is the result of a process of growth that comes from within, without there being any need to attach much importance to interaction with the outside world.

Freud laid ample stress on the reality of the outside world and all the interpersonal relations that it involves. In particular, he showed how it structuralizes the necessities that biology imposes. Clinical experience shows regularly that, as a recent French song puts it, "Elle court, la maladie d'amour", without its being a purely biological problem.

The difference in the importance Freud and Jung attach to the outside world is matched by the divergence between their concepts of the ego. Jung was the heir of romanticism and the ego was for him a product, a result of the processes in which it is steeped. It is not without cause that Jung was chiefly interested in the maternal symbols in religion. The collective unconscious is for him the matrix of everything. Freud on the contrary, sees the ego as an act. The ego manifests itself in the fact that we act and react, and if necessary, we repress; but always in relation with the desires, aspirations, prohibitions and obligations that bind us to others. Freud therefore also attaches greater importance to the father, who is precisely the symbol of the importance other people have for us outside our vital biological needs.

It is understandable that psychology and psychiatry, constantly confronted with problems of an interpersonal nature, have abandoned Jung's work because of this lacuna which, to tell the truth, lowers its value considerably. This does not mean that there would be nothing to be gained by rethinking Jung's work. It may be that besides the symbols connected with the interpersonal order, there is a more primary dimension of experience of the body and of life, which is not yet structured by interpersonal desires. The archetypes would then express an infra-personal human reality. Here we may think of Jung's favourite field of research, the understanding of psychosis. But in any case, Jung's data need to be completely reworked; as it stands his thought does not deal adequately with what is essential for mankind and interpersonal relations. For to say that Jung's work may be useful for understanding more primary strata does not mean that these strata are deeper and more august. I make this remark for a very practical reason: to follow out Jung's ideas thoroughly is to run a risk of solipsism, though it is never—or fortunately, hardly ever—real solipsism. Relational problems that are disregarded have a way of coming back by a roundabout route, and the clinical fact of neurosis is there to remind us that it is dangerous to disregard this objective aspect of our human nature.

FROM THE POINT OF VIEW OF RELIGION

What attracts the theologian and the believer to Jung's work is the fact that one feels less disparaged by it, that it seems to attach more importance than Freud's to the reality of psychic life and of culture, and that it seems to provide psychological grounds for belief in mystical experience. It is reassuring. But does the believer need to be reassured? It is not long since articles on the relation between science and religion formed a flourishing field of literature. They used to show that the two were not contradictory and that sometimes science can even contribute to the Faith. Perhaps Jung's popularity comes from an analogous problematic, with psychology taking the place of "science". But Jung's work is far from being a solid science accepted by all, on which one can safely base oneself.

On the other hand, is Freud's work incompatible with the Faith, as is sometimes said? Here the answer is clear: certainly not. There are indeed passages where Freud reduces religious phenomena to very little (or to all too much for some people); but the main idea in his work is that instinct always develops within an interpersonal relationship. This way of seeing things is certainly not less pertinent than Jung's for meditating on the meaning of human life and culture.

It is true, though, that Freud is primarily interested in analysis. He dissects the human phenomenon and looks for its deepest roots. He was first and foremost a clinician, continually faced with pathology and used therefore to lifting off the upper strata in order to get down to a hidden fault. His vision of culture in general is indeed tainted with pessimism. From this point of view Jung is perfectly right in saying that to seek hidden instinctive sources does not answer the question of the meaning of life. We still need to know: where is all this leading us? As Jung says, the fact that a cathedral is made of stones does not mean that it poses only a minerological problem.

The believer is prepared to face this problem of the meaning of life, and it is understandable that he should respond to Jung's thought. Only, let us not go too fast. To believe, with Jung, that regressive analysis cannot tell us all there is to know about the essence of the human being, and to give a primordial importance to the meaning of life, does not imply that one must accept the power of the image, the archetypes and the whole Jungian theory. The problem of meaning can equally well be posed using Freudian categories of thought.

One can even wonder whether Jung's thought is compatible with the Christian view of things. So far, I have indicated what seems to me problematic in Jung's work simply from the standpoint of philosophy and psychology. If we now move to the Christian standpoint, we shall find analogous lacunae. Religion as Jung understands it is much closer to the Eastern type than to Christianity. In fact, his whole system of thought is closer to the East than to the West, and it seems to me that one cannot accept it as it stands without losing one's identity as a Christian.

THE TWO TYPES OF RELIGION, AND HOW JUNG'S WORK CAN BE USED

We cannot go into the subject properly here, but it must at least be mentioned that the word "religion" can cover two rather different things. Christianity, with its faith in a God who is Father and its themes of sacred history, the freedom of the sons of God, the brotherhood of man and the resurrection of the dead, is a faith that accepts life in all its aspects. Life, as an autonomous position, is lived as a gift of God, who is relational life and the supreme act. Christianity is a religion in which things happen, and happen for a reason.

The religion or wisdom of the East, on the other hand, preaches detachment, the aspiration to the purely spiritual by the abolition of the body and its desires. The spiritual and the earthly are opposed to each other, and man must deliver himself from the shackles of his present condition by a process of asceticism. In this perspective, time, history, activity and even interpersonal relations lose their importance. It is a matter of finding the eternal in the temporal, the spiritual in the material and the divine in what is not divine.

For the Christian this way of looking at things is incomplete. In its relation with the divinity the East, like the West, accepts life as a gift; but it reduces that life to mere givenness, to what is outside its control. It does not believe in the value of its own creativity, it does not believe in the power of its activity as a possible means to salvation. The Christian too knows that he cannot do everything and that there are in life many aspects of illusion and of dependence. To deny that would be to tend towards Pelagianism, and from this point of view the Christian has much to learn from the East. But when all is said and done, the difference remains radical: for the Christian, the autonomy, the will and the creativity of each individual are also a gift of God. He does not see why these aspects must be eliminated from the human constitution. Is not God the Creator of them all? The Christian accepts his action and his interpersonal relations as a sharing in the supreme act and interpersonality: God. His faith, accepting both dependence and autonomy, is synonymous with responsibility.

These two types of religious sentiment can be found also in the way religious symbols are envisaged. They can be envisaged in the order of concordance: each religious symbol representing a metaphysical reality which exists in itself and which transpires partially in the symbol. This conception is usually accompanied by a fairly marked dualism, as is shown for example by Platonism, which for the West is its prototype. This is the world of the icon. But besides this order of concordance, there is a more dynamic conception in which the reality of the religious symbol is not sought in some correspondence with a higher order but in the dynamism coming from the interaction of all the various religious symbols. According to this way of thought, what matters is the truth of the dynamic and interpersonal movement which we recognize in living out the religious rites and symbols taken as a whole. I must admit that I have always been attracted by Origen's idea of the "pedagogical ruses" of God. He says that of course hell does not exist in itself; but God makes us believe in it because that is good for us. The truth of the symbol, according to this point of view, resides in its efficacy.

It would be simplistic to contrast these two orders as opposites and link them with an equally over-simplified opposition between an Eastern and a Western type of religion. These are not complete opposites, since for the Christian the wisdom of the East is not false but merely incomplete. However, one cannot help contrasting accepted responsibility, the interpersonal efficacy of symbols, psychoanalysis as a scrutiny of relations that exist by means of the body, and faith in the Fatherhood of God and in the Trinity, on the one hand, with asceticism and the abolition of desire, the purely iconographic value of symbols, analytical psychology as a transformation that takes place in us by the innate power of the image, and a more maternal divinity on the other hand. I repeat, this second line is not false; but for us Western Christians it ought to seem incomplete without the first. And that brings us to a very practical question: is the present Western infatuation with the East simply an effort to recover forgotten values which we can assimilate, or is it a regression?

CONCLUSION

The fact remains that Jung's work is fascinating. It has genius about it, even if it lets itself get carried away. If I have taken the trouble to analyse what seems to me deficient in it, it is because I am convinced that we have here a whole collection of material that demands to be elucidated. The work of understanding it needs to be re-done, but at least the problem has been posed.

Meanwhile, we can learn much from Jung. Not technical knowledge, but a certain style of respect, understanding, and faith in the efficacity of the truth. In short, a certain wisdom.

Notes

1. He had his own particular interpretation of repression, but we cannot go into it here. In any case, he wanted to see whether the mechanisms that Freud had discovered for hysteria could also be found in schizophrenia; in 1907 he published *The Psychology of Dementia Praecox*, a pioneer work.

2. An English translation by B. M. Hinkle was published in 1916 under the misleading title (also given to a work of 1943) of *Psychology of the Unconscious*, Moffat Yard & Co., New York. The work translated as *Symbols of Transformation* (The Collected Works of C. G. Jung, Routledge & Kegan Paul, London, vol. 5) is the completely revised edition of 1952, which in German bears the title *Symbole der Wandlung*.

3. Basilides was the leader of a Gnostic movement in the second century.

4. C. G. Jung, *Erinnerungen, Träume, Gedanken* (Rascher, Zürich, 1962), pp. 389–91.

5. C. G. Jung, *Psychological Types*, Coll. Wks. vol. 6, p. 336.

6. Translated from C. G. Jung, *Wandlungen und Symbole der Libido* I, in *Jahrbuch für psychoanalytische und psychopathologische Forschungen* III (1911), p. 178.

Thayer A. Greene

Persona and Shadow: A Jungian View of Human Duality

Clergy who seek the counseling services of a psychotherapist present the normal range of human problems and conflicts. They are not unique in their humanity. What is singular about the clergyman's situation is the extent to which expectations about his social role and identity can obscure and oppress his experience of personal reality. One wonders whether any other social or professional role so requires the appearance of virtue and perfection.

The synoptic gospels provide ample evidence that Jesus himself was clearly aware of the stark contrast between outer appearance and inner truth. His characterization of the moral and spiritual condition of the pharisees in contrast with publicans and sinners made plain his perception that the very potential for religious transformation was intimately related to the issue of who one appears to be and who one truly is. The depth psychology of Carl Jung offers an approach to this problem, even for those who do not seek or need help for some situation of personal conflict. Jung developed two concepts which are very useful in providing some differentiated understanding of what separates the way we relate to the world from the way we experience parts of ourselves that seem hidden, unacceptable, shameful, and often frightening. He defined these dual dimensions of our human psychic experience as the *persona* and the *shadow*. In what follows each concept will first be presented and discussed in some detail before dealing with their particular and practical implications for the life and work of the clergy.

167

PERSONA DEFINITION

The persona is a basic archetypal structure of human personality, the purpose of which is to provide a medium of adaptation between the individual and the collective environment experienced through persons, events, and objects. This persona or social role provides a bridge of identity between one's private experience and public performance. It is one's part in the social drama which meets the demands of convention and tradition, while protecting and preserving that which is unique and hence subject to collective misunderstanding and judgment.

HISTORICAL BACKGROUND

In arriving at an appreciative understanding of the persona concept in Jungian theory, a brief exploration of the historical roots of the word itself can be helpful. It stems from a Latin word which has the components, *per-sonare*, namely "to sound through." The term leads us back in time to the masks worn by the actors in the ancient Greek theatre who employed them to reveal more clearly and amplify the essential nature of the roles they were portraying. In the Roman tradition we find the word used in the definition of the trinitarian doctrine, "tres personae, una substantia," and it also serves as the root of such familiar English words as person, personal, and personality. Jung chose the term in order to stress the collective or social "mask" which every individual must wear in order to play his or her role successfully within society. By doing so a particular man or woman is able to adapt to the social order with its collective expectations while yet concealing or veiling those dimensions of experience which are singular, intimate, or unique.

DEVELOPMENTAL ORIGINS

The initial sense of identity, of "I-ness," in the experience of the very young child is closely related to the earliest development of the persona. It is as though the delicate gelatinous stuff of the immature psyche comes in contact with the reality of the outer world and causes a hardening process to take place which we speak of as adaptation. This emerging "face" is that which mediates between inside and outside, between the precariously emerging sense of self and the "others." To "lose face," therefore, is to feel exposed, shamed, vulnerable, in effect to be in the situation of the small child who has not yet developed adequate adaptive capacities which allow him to venture beyond a highly protective and supportive environment. One of the reasons that the clown, the jester, the comic fool have always evoked such laughter from children and the child within the adult psyche is because of the tenuous character of the early adaptation and the chaotic impulsivity of instinctual energy which lies just behind this mask of socialization. So much of the role playing of the child with his toys, animals, peers, and often parents or other significant adults can be viewed as experimentation with a variety of behavioral personas, a trying on of adaptive identities which later at the stage of adolescence will be taken up again with more serious consequences and greater anxiety.

The character and quality of parental perception and response to the early experiments of adaptation by the child will be a major environmental factor in the particular evolution of the persona of each individual. Shame and blame methods of child rearing can be very damaging to the acquisition of a trustworthy face with which to confront the world. For Jungian psychology the introversion-extraversion polarity of attitude type is another factor of at least equal importance. Jung contends that the predominance of introverted or extraverted qualities of behavior in the young child is a consequence of his basic psychic constitution. It is nature rather than nurture which determines whether the libido of a particular individual will carry him out into relation with the world of objects with a relative ease of adaptation or whether his psychic energy will cause him to draw back from the object into the primacy of his own internal subjective experience. In terms of persona development it need only be said that the introverted child will almost certainly experience much greater difficulty in acquiring appropriately flexible and varied adaptations to varied and ever-changing outer circumstances due to the highly subjective character of his sense of identity.

Early ego development is significantly connected with that of the persona. So much of a person's identity is conferred by the perceptions and responses of the environment it may be said that ego development is rooted not only in instinctual progressions but also in stages of social experience and adaptation. The experience of a new or changed persona can precede or evoke a new stage in identity. All major transitions, in the first half of life at least, involve a persona transformation followed by a subsequent ego adaptation. The transition from home to school to college to job to marriage is experienced first as a new role and social status and only later does it become assimilated as part of one's ego identity. Rites of passage and the conferring of changed social roles such as priestly ordination and hence of changed identity can be seen perhaps more clearly in the social organization and ritual practice of primitive culture than in our own but the pattern is similar.

The failure to develop both a differentiated persona and functioning ego leads commonly to the formation of a pseudoego, that is, a weak or deficient ego structure which draws vicarious strength and energy from the social role of the individual. The personality pattern is then based upon stereotyped imitation or a merely dutiful performance of one's collectively assigned part in life. The pseudoego leads one to *become* the professor, the doctor, the clergyman, the housewife, the mother rather than an individual who gives the role its proper due at the necessary times. Such a pseudoego is not only rigid but also extremely fragile and brittle since it is dissociated from the unconscious energies and intentions of the true ego potential of the personality.

One of the characteristic crises of the early stages of Jungian analytic therapy is the separation of the ego from identification with the persona. This is normally accompanied by feelings of depression, loss, and distress and by dreams or fantasies in which clothes, facial disguises, or even parts of the body undergo significant change. Very often some unattractive, threatening, or even repulsive aspect comes out of hiding and reveals itself. The dream of a pretty young introverted woman who was anxiously preoccupied with her own attractiveness and unwilling to confront her repressed dark qualities is clearly illustrative: "I am sitting on the floor of an apartment fifteen stories above Manhattan. Suddenly the outermost layer of my skin hardens into a clear plastic mask with sharp aquiline features of an extremely good looking woman and drops away from my face. I exclaim, 'I'm not me!' and start to cry. I feel as if I now have a vacant stare where there should be a face. There is a white screen in the darkened room. I now notice that projected on it is the face of a man in his fifties. His skin is drawn tightly over his cheekbones; he has a white bristling crew cut, feverish eyes, and two front fangs which protrude over his lower lip. His aspect is fierce and frightening. Although it is only two-dimensional, not three, the face projected upon the screen appears alive. I realize with shock and dismay that this projected face is my true face, which until now has been concealed by my exterior, attractive mask." Such a dream of course has implications beyond the persona problem but it does etch graphically the shock to ego consciousness when the inner face of the unconscious behind the outer mask must be confronted. Dynamically this process usually involves a withdrawal of energy from social role involvement and goals in order to give repressed conflicts of the personality the needed attention and concern of ego consciousness.

In contrast to the hardened mask of ego identification with an inflexible and rigid persona is the plight of those persons who are unable to establish any adequate relationship to collective standards. One woman who refused to grant any legitimacy to the claims of social convention and rebelliously insisted that the world accept her rather deviant behavior without reproach had a brief dream in which she was walking through Grand Central Station totally naked and very annoyed that she was attracting the attention of the crowd.

Distorted persona development can become extremely limiting, if not in fact pathogenic at either extreme; an ill-formed or nonexistent persona is just as restricting to full human functioning as its opposite, the over-developed and rigidly conventional mask. An inadequate relationship to the persona archetype may range from a fixation in its purely collective aspect to a rebellious refusal or inability to accept any collective adaptation or demand. Examples of dreams that portray the confining and overdeveloped persona are those of being unable to take off one's clothes, of being stuck in heavy armor, of being overdressed or having unusually tough skin. The underdeveloped persona may express itself in dreams of nakedness in public and social occasions or places, or wearing a transparent gown, of being a turtle without a shell, or wearing only underclothes to a formal reception.

Perhaps the most common and organic representation of the persona is the human face and skin of the body. In the most elemental way it is the skin which mediates between inside and out-side. It sweats, it shivers, it burns in response to an ever-changing environment. One finds that some skin disturbances are symbolic and psychosomatic in character, expressing an unconscious conflict in the adaptation of the ego to the social community. The simplest example is that of a spontaneous blushing reaction which has no di-rect relation to conscious feeling or outer stimulus. More serious skin problems can have a similar basis. One Jungian analyst tells of a young woman who had a severe skin eruption on her face, which resisted all attempts at treatment. She discovered in the course of an analysis undertaken for an entirely different reason that she had a serious adaptational conflict; she had always hidden the fact that she was Jewish when she had applied for a job, in order to save face, as she expressed it. Psychologically speaking, it was as if she masked her true identity, did not show her real face. The unconscious re-action to this deception was expressed in the actual skin eruption which ceased when she was able to risk exposure of her face psy-chologically.

SHADOW

"The brighter the persona, the darker the shadow" is a maxim familiar to any Jungian psychotherapist. It points to the dynamic and compensatory relation between persona and shadow in the structure of the adult personality. Peasant wisdom and common sense have always recognized those people who are "too good to be true." Wherever an individual falls into unconscious identification with an overly good or righteous persona, those energies and be-haviors which are excluded from any social expression will accu-mulate in the shadow with compensatory strength.

DEFINITION

Jung's psychological concept of the shadow represents that part of the personality which has been repressed from consciousness for the sake of maintaining a certain idealized image of the conscious ego identity. For the sake of the person we wish to be we deny from self awareness elements of ourselves that would contradict that wishful image. Such denial does not of course remove these darker energies from the personality and hence they accumulate in the unconscious forming a "dark brother," an inferior, primitive sub-personality which functions autonomously and often quite destructively as long as the conscious ego refuses to confront it.

HISTORICAL BACKGROUND

In western Christendom the origins of our personal psychic experience of the shadow are historically rooted in the ancient and yet continuing image of the Devil as the archetypal representation of Evil. An examination of both Old and New Testament materials indicates that the image of Satan became more and more separated from the image of God until there emerges in the book of Revelation an absolute and cosmic split between good and evil. (See *Satan in the Old Testament* by Rivkah Scharf Kluger, Northwestern University Press for a fine treatment of the Old Testament material.) The tendency of Christianity to polarize good and evil has had severe psychic consequences for all those generations of men and women who have been nurtured and conditioned by such an orientation. In regard to this Jung writes,

> "The splendour of the 'light' god has been enhanced beyond measure, but the darkness supposedly represented by the devil has localized itself in man. This strange development was precipitated chiefly by the fact that Christianity, terrified of Manichaean dualism, strove to preserve its monotheism by main force. But since the reality of darkness and evil could not be denied, there was no alternative but to make man responsible for it. Even the devil was largely, if not entirely, abolished, with the result that this metaphysical figure, who at one time was an integral part of the Deity, was introjected into many, who thereupon became the real carrier of the *mysterium iniquitatis:* 'omne bonum a Deo, omne malum ab homine.' " (Coll. Wks. Vol. 9.1, p. 189)

In myth, legend and literature one finds many examples of this same polarity of light and dark, good and evil. In Egyptian religion there is the conflict between Set and Osiris, in the Gilgamesh epic from Mesopotamia there is the struggle between Gilgamesh and Enkidu. Fairy tales and legends of all lands are filled with evil figures who oppose the hero's efforts to win the treasure. The compact with the devil as portrayed, for example, in the Faust legend is a common theme of western literature. In our own century we see striking literary examples in Robert Louis Stevenson's *The Strange Case of Dr. Jekyll and Mr. Hyde*, William Golding's *The Lord of the Flies*, and such works of Joseph Conrad as *Heart of Darkness* and *The Secret Sharer*.

Alan Watts in his book, *Myth and Ritual in Christianity*, criticizes the West's radical polarization of light and dark in these words:

> The tragedy of Christian history is that it represents a consistent failure to draw life from the Christian myth, and unlock its wisdom. This whole failure is epitomized in the problem of Lucifer who should have remained the symbol, not of deliberate malice, but of the necessary dark side of life, of shadow, revealing light by contrast. He would correspond to what the Chinese call *yin* as distinct from *yang*—the dark negative and feminine aspect of life in complementary opposition to the light, positive and masculine: the two represented together as the interlocked commas or fish—one black and one white, one ascending and one descending. In the West, the same symbol is found in the Zodiacal sign of Pisces, as the two opposed fish are the common motif of early Christian gems. Christ himself being the ascending fish, and very often the descending fish was associated with the Anti-Christ.

DEVELOPMENTAL AND SOCIAL ORIGINS

The formation of the personal shadow begins in very early childhood through the interaction with parents and significant others in the immediate environment. Negative parental reactions towards a child's instinctive spontaneity, bodily functions, rebellious feelings and autonomous impulses can seriously impair capacity for later expression in adult life. Children who are required to be "nice," "good," and never be seen as dirty, bad or angry learn very quickly that they can best survive by presenting a bright and shining face to the parental world and hiding those instinctive urges and feelings which are rejected. Very soon the child is hiding those same feelings from himself. My observation as a therapist is that the Church very often encourages this same repressive response to the spontaneity and instinctive energy of the developing child through its programs of Christian education. The horror stories one hears in the consulting room of so-called Christian teaching from Christian teachers makes it quite clear that much psychic damage to individuals is a consequence of damaging religious attitudes and methods of relating. Developmentally much of the personal shadow has already been formed by the time a child is six or seven, not so much by what parents and teachers say as by how they behave and relate to the child. Hence the parental persona and shadow influence profoundly the particular quality of those structures of personality within the developing child. When the parent or teacher allows for a wide range of feeling reactions and expressions of instinctive energies, the child quite naturally develops a more flexible and less rigidly controlled manner of relating both to himself and to others. When, however, perfectionist expectations are imposed upon the child, the polarity between the idealized persona and the totally denied shadow becomes so extreme that it often leads to severe psychological pathology. The denied shadow energies seek revenge, either upon the individual or upon others. Jung writes,

> "A man cannot get rid of himself in favour of an artificial personality without punishment. Even the attempt to do so brings on, in all ordinary cases, unconscious reactions in the form of bad moods, affects, phobias, compulsive ideas, backslidings, vices, etc. The social 'strong man' is in his private life often a mere child where his own states of feeling are concerned; his discipline in public (which he demands quite particularly of others) goes miserably to pieces in private. His 'happiness in his work' assumes a woeful countenance at home; his 'spotless' public morality looks strange indeed behind the mask—we will not mention deeds, but only fantasies, and the wives of such men would have a pretty tale to tell. As to his selfless altruism, his children have decided views about that." (Coll. Wks., Vol. 7, p. 307.)

PROJECTION OF THE SHADOW

The most characteristic phenomenon associated with the presence of the shadow within the psyche is that of projection. Whatever we cannot discern or confront within ourselves inevitably projects itself onto others since the energy in the shadow refuses to lie dormant for long. We are then free to have strong, even sadistic reactions to the faults in others which escape our inner vision. Jesus' telling image of the mote and the beam revealed clear understanding of this dynamic. One of the surest signs of a personal shadow projection is a strong, obsessive, affective reaction, positive or negative, to another person, especially if that other person is relatively unknown. The person we "can't stand," who "bugs" us, whose behavior is "disgusting" is almost always carrying a part of ourselves that we refuse to acknowledge. The shadow manifests itself also in our passionate reactions to social groups and social causes. Clergy are particularly susceptible to this form of projection because of their genuine concern for social betterment. The clergyman who is unaware of his own dark side may become polarized in his social and political standpoint so that he unconsciously identifies with a rigid moralism that does more to alienate than to transform other people's attitudes. Some years ago a clergyman joined with other clergy to take a strong stand in behalf of a major civil rights movement fighting racial segregation. Following a night during which he had stood vigil before the Lincoln Memorial in Washington on behalf of this cause, he had the following dream: "Governor George Wallace is standing in a doorway and I have just handed him a loaded rifle. He is shooting at me." Wallace was at that time the symbol of segregation and had in fact stood in a university doorway attempting to halt federal integration of higher education for blacks. What the dreamer had to face with his analyst's help was the discovery that there existed within his own unconscious psyche a segregationist attitude that insisted upon absolute separation between his own light and dark sides. All his political and moral efforts in support of legal integration of blacks and whites, however legitimate and necessary, could serve as a screen behind which a George Wallace shadow within his own soul was being handed a loaded gun to enforce a deep split between two sides of his own nature.

The shadow is most dangerous and destructive when it is expressed at a collective level. Racial and religious conflict, repressive totalitarian regimes, organized systems of torture and imprisonment all embody collective shadow behavior in which individuals have lost any individual discrimination of values and become identified with the collective values of the group. A tragic case of such an identification is the story of a young Nazi fighter pilot who lost his ability to differentiate colors. He suddenly saw everything as either black or white. Grounded for this reason from his flying, he came to a clinic for help. He began having disturbing dreams in which the Nazi leaders, whom he admired and blindly supported, had blackened faces, and the people he had been taught to hate and despise always had radiant white faces. The dreams reversed his conscious standpoint, but his identification with the values of the Third Reich would not permit him to accept their testimony. The dreams persisted and continued to disturb, so that finally he had to test their truth by visiting personally one of the concentration camps for Jews. Shortly afterward his analyst in Berlin received a letter from the distressed young man saying, "I believed for too long that black was white. Now the many colours of the world won't help me anymore." He had committed suicide. When individual consciousness becomes identified with such one-sidedness, the discovery of the collective shadow can overwhelm us. Lest we see the Nazi horror as a special case, let us remind ourselves that conservatively over three million women were burned at the stake by Protestant and Catholic clergy between 1450 and 1750 under the authority of Father, Son, and Holy Spirit.

In a time when we stand collectively on the edge of the nuclear precipice, human civilization may well be destroyed by the power of the collective shadow. Jung foresaw our tragic plight years ago and offered a modest hope if individuals would struggle to carry consciously the weight of their own shadows. He writes:

> If you imagine someone who is brave enough to withdraw all his projections, then you get an individual who is conscious of a pretty thick shadow. Such a man has saddled himself with new problems and conflicts. He has become a serious problem to himself, as he is now unable to say that *they* do this or that, *they* are wrong, and *they* must be fought against . . . Such a man knows that whatever is wrong in the world is in himself, and if

he only learns to deal with his own shadow he has done something real for the world. He has succeeded in shouldering at least an infinitesimal part of the gigantic, unsolved social problems of our day. (Coll. Wks. Vol 11, p. 140.)

CONCLUSIONS

For religious professionals certain useful insights can be drawn from Jung's treatment of the persona-shadow duality. The predisposition of the general public to idealize the religious professional in his or her role can lead to a state of ungrounded and unrealistic psychic inflation. Anyone who is the object of enormously positive, idealizing projections has a very hard time keeping his feet on the ground. All too easily one is seduced into an identification with the persona, partly because no one wants to disappoint those who esteem him so highly and partly because we are naturally inclined to esteem ourselves more highly than reality allows. In either case we lose contact with the shadow which alone can give us an anchor to prevent being blown away into a weightless state of spiritual purity which lacks adequate substance or contact with earthy human reality.

It is striking that throughout history the most creative spiritual leaders have been deeply in touch with their own shadows. Jesus, himself, responded, "Why callest thou me good?" Dealing honestly with one's personal shadow leaves its mark upon the human spirit, a mark which is psychically apparent to others. Before Jacob could cross the river Jabbok he first was required to wrestle with the dark stranger who only later was revealed to be an angel of God. He was wounded in that struggle so that forever after he limped. That encounter also changed him. His name was no longer Jacob but Israel. His identity had been transformed. The new land, promised by God years earlier, was now open to him. Religious authority does not ultimately derive from the outer trappings of a social role but from the struggle and suffering of inner transformation. Our ministries, our vocations, whatever they may be, have their origins not with the multitude but on the mountaintop. Jesus was perceived by those who gladly followed him not like the scribes and the pharisees but "as one having authority." He did not have the socially recognized role, i.e., persona, of a religious professional. What he did have was a spirit that had struggled with Satan in the wilderness, and a human consciousness that had searched so deeply into his own depths that other human beings could not hide their inner truth from him. He did not bring judgment upon those who openly carried the burden of their shadows, rather he offered compassion and hope. Only those psychically inflated by their religious roles and their own pretensions received his critical wrath.

CREATIVE POTENTIAL OF THE SHADOW

It would be an unfortunate misunderstanding to equate Jung's concept of the shadow with the traditional Christian concept of sin. Whereas sin connotes spiritual alienation and destructive behavior, the shadow is not necessarily destructive or negative. Rather it has a primitive, archaic, undifferentiated quality. Jung believed that to be disconnected from the shadow was to lose contact with the source of creativity and renewing life energy. That part of life and of the psyche which is despised, rejected, and ignored is exactly where the saviour will choose to be born. Pain, depression, humiliation are the seedbed for growth, according to Jung. The unconscious is a treasure house as well as a garbage pile.

> "If the repressed tendencies, the shadow as I call them, were obviously evil, there would be no problem whatever, but the shadow is merely somewhat inferior, primitive, unadapted, and awkward; not wholly bad. It even contains childish or primitive qualities which would in a way vitalize or embellish human existence . . . (Coll. Wks. Vol 11, p. 134.) The unconscious is not just evil by nature, it is also the source of the highest good: not only dark but also light, not only bestial, semi-human and demonic but superhuman, spiritual, and, in the classical sense of the word, 'divine.' " (Coll. Wks. Vol. 16, p. 389.)

The essence, then, of Jung's contribution to the resolution of the persona—shadow split is not that our dual nature can be abolished or even healed in any final sense. Rather we can come to appreciate the polarity of our social and private reality as a necessary and creative tension of opposites. We can begin to listen to and learn from the voices of the shadow which whisper hope and courage as well as painful truth. The masks we wear can become less rigid and brittle, more revealing of our true natures, and thereby assist the essential human task, not to be perfect but to be complete.

Jung and Scripture

I can remember that as a young boy in Ireland I frequently attended Mass with my parents. During the Mass the word of God was read. In those days it was all in Latin and meant very little to me. The sermon that followed however, was in English, and most often involved the retelling of the story by the priest, who embellished it in accord with his own emphasis. For me, at that time, Jesus was a hero figure, not very different from some of my other hero figures such as those from cowboy books. I don't think he was quite as exciting but at the same time he did capture my imagination. When I went to high school I continued to hear the gospel stories. Now they were read to us by retreat masters who frequently told these gentle stories with power filled voices, who rushed through them, and then got down to the real meat of what they wished to say to us. It seems, as I look back, that a subtle change came over my hero. Now he seemed to be against everything that I was for, a negating God rather than an affirming one, a God who seemed to get in the way of having a "good time."

I entered the major seminary in Ireland at the close of the fifties, and again the scripture stories were read. This time they were frequently used as a text book, or a reference book, or a proof book. We were surely encouraged to use them in prayer but I spent a lot of time reading the lives of the saints and other works. The scripture stories were nice, but, I had a difficult time understanding Paul and the Old Testament had not yet entered my world. In the seminary however there was a man who seemed to me to have a great love of scripture. It was evidenced in the way he held the book, reverenced it, and spoke of it. Scripture seemed to be important to him and a source of sustenance for his life.

Somewhere during these years this same man was instrumental in providing an opportunity for students to enter the "outside" world. He suggested we participate, on a voluntary basis, in the religious activities of the local community. Gradually this spread to educational activities. I volunteered to be part of this "missionary" activity, more I believe for the opportunity it afforded me to buy candy, etc., while we were out, than for any other reason. I volunteered to attend St. Dymphna's Mental Hospital. It was my first entry into the world of the strange and the different. It was awesome to me and frightening. I was shocked at what I encountered. Many of the people who were there had the most "weird" beliefs about God, Jesus, and church. Many of them had strange religious (compulsive) habits and their lives were filled with religious imagery. Their psychotic behavior troubled me but it was nice to have "them" as psychotic sick people. I could conveniently pass on to them all kinds of things that were unacceptable to me. In their eyes I could see my own suspiciousness, craziness, paranoia, etc., but at that time I could not acknowledge it. I had not yet come to realize the wisdom of Harry Stack Sullivan's observation "We are all the more same than different." The return to the seminary on a Wednesday evening was often a painful moment. I lived in two worlds without a bridge, or so it seemed.

The experience, however, in time brought me to Iona College and to the study of Pastoral Counseling. It was here that I first really came into contact with the writings of C.G. Jung although I had heard of him previously. He excited me. He seemed to talk of the inner life, about getting in touch with your own story and its unfolding. He spoke of a self beyond the ego, a self that is deeper than the normal everyday self that I am conscious of when I see, understand, judge and act. He spoke of getting in touch with this self through dreams and images and symbols, etc. He talked of emerging into an awareness of this self out of an identification with the collective. I was attracted to these ideas and to this world that spoke to me. One of the ideas that captured my imagination was his whole emphasis on symbols. Without even knowing it I think I had somehow absorbed the Freudian notion that all symbols that emerge from our dreams, etc., could be reduced to wish fulfillment. Jung spoke of another dimension. Symbols allow not only for an archaeological reading but for a teleological reading, that is, for a reading which allows not only desire to arise but also for a reading which allows a future to enter. Peter Mann was later on to introduce me to another notion, namely, the possibility of an eschatological reading which allows the symbol to be deciphered in terms of an ultimate meaning. There is then this multidimensionality to symbols although they can always be reduced to one dimension. This will be important to recall later in this article. Jung however did not just stress the importance of symbols. He wanted to help us understand that some symbols came out of our personal history and have meaning particular to us but others come from the history of all mankind, from our collective history. They are the "deposit of mankind's typical reactions since primordial times to universal situations such as fear, danger . . . love, birth . . . and death." The images and symbols that come out of this collective history of mankind he considered to be extremely important.

Jung believed we should pay attention to the symbols because they would lead us to wholeness. Images and symbols in dreams, he said, give us information that we do not have but that we should have if we are to become whole, and if we listen to them they will guide us. In short they will lead us on a journey. Paul Ricoeur has spelled out in a little clearer light the stages of that journey. He speaks of processes of change undergone by the meditator as he confronts the symbol. These have been synopsized by Peter Mann as follows: We face the text initially as spectators with a narcissistic consciousness. As we consent however to enter the world of the text we move away from the spectator stance to the scientific analytic stance. We begin to take the text apart, discover its inner structure and relationships, and explain it. This explanation, and the structure it uncovers, are already mediating the deep questions which move us, the existential depth situations of origin and end, birth and death, and the key figures, such as father, child, mother, etc., in terms of which we discover who we are. Thus we are moved from the spectator through the scientific observer to the existential participant. The final stage of reading is by way of entry into the horizon of the text, its way of projecting a world. Entering into the second order reality of the text is to understand the text, appropriate it existentially, become its disciple, see according to the text, become a seer by understanding yourself according to its vision. The meditator then would be going on a journey through these different stages from being a spectator to being a visionary. Jung I believe would welcome such an understanding and explanation and find it consistent with his views.

In elaborating my contact with scripture from childhood through seminary I have been in effect showing how symbols can be and are reduced to mere signs. The scripture had become for me, by and large, signs of institutional Christianity. In the process they had lost the power to mediate the holy and the numinous. In discovering that the refusal of the journey to which they invite me is the refusal of the holy, I had begun to find my way back. I come back to them now however, not as one reading only of the historical Christ, hero of the victory over the Romans by his death and Resurrection, but as one who believes that the Christ of the scripture is indeed a symbol of an inner reality. I am not saying that is all he is, but that as a symbol of an interior reality he is a guiding image for my life. In this process, which I believe is prayer, there is, as Thomas Kane suggests, "a coming to know myself. But there is also a coming to know Jesus as he is presented in the gospels," and, "if we are faithful to the gospel stories, if we don't impose our meanings on them, but slowly let them disclose their meanings to us . . . then the Lord of the gospels will have become the Lord of our lives." In short we will begin to see according to his vision, or to put it another way, we will have moved from being the spectator of the scriptural text to being a visionary of the world it projects through the symbols. In the language of theology life will have become sacramental.

Jung insisted that man's "self" desperately tries to communicate with him. His inner self sends him messages through symbols, stories, myths, etc. These establish an interaction between the self and the ego, between the objective psyche and the ego, between the unconscious and the conscious ego. The interaction is generally established through dreams, fantasies, artistic expressions, etc., which reveal to the person the attitudes, impulses, etc. that are now seeking attention and realization. Dreams as Jean Gill notes "reach up toward our conscious self from our unconscious inner depth" but then she adds "in meditation we consciously reach down to contact our inner unconscious self. The two approaches are complementary." The stories and symbols of scripture then can lead us on a journey to our inner depths.

By way of example of what I have been saying I would like to share a few reflections on the Baptism of Jesus from my forthcoming book. In Mark the story of Jesus' Baptism is conveyed through a series of symbols which are combined to form a theophany. These symbols are 1. coming out of the water, 2. heavens open, 3. Spirit comes like a dove, 4. voice speaks, 5. Jesus alone sees the vision. These elements, all taken from the roots of Jesus' own received tradition, serve to convey to the reader the knowledge that Jesus is the beloved, the Messiah, etc. Nothing however, in the general course of events, has happened to the reader other than the reception of information, which is important. There is no transformation however, and the purpose of the scripture is that we might have life, that we might be transformed. When I begin to enter this event of Jesus' Baptism via its symbols then maybe something else can occur.

I begin in my meditation and imagination to meet John the Baptist at the seashore. I set out to meet him and as I go I see that I carry a lot with me. I am aware that as I go I bring with me a lot of "stuff," a lot of not only material things but also a lot of assumptions, expectations and the like. Some of them I carry in bags and some in ice buckets. I carry books to occupy my mind, food to satisfy my hunger, drink to ease my thirst, a radio to keep in touch with everyone else, a hat for protection from the sun, footballs to play with, etc. Gradually as I look at myself going to the water I realize that I am well protected against silence, against stillness, against anything happening. Nevertheless I am also hoping against hope that this trip, this time of relaxation, this one day will change the way my life is. I come in short in need of conversion and willing to be identified with the call to conversion.

My eyes begin to focus on John. He challenges my existence, my way of life. He stands on the sand, the barren sand, the hot sand. In fact he is in my meditation the sand. He makes life uncomfortable. He is the host to gnats and flies, the different bugs and insects that bite and chew and scratch at my comfort. He is the sand that gets into my hair and eyes and ears, that causes me to move from one side to another, to slap at myself and tear at my extremities. He is the comforting sand of illusion that initially calls me and then is too hot to lie on, too bumpy to rest on, too dazzling to look upon. He is the sand that knows my life. He has received the flotsam and fragments, the drifting strands of kelp, the broken twisted weeds, the gnarled wood. The sand is message, the sand is call, the sand is salvation, the sand is John.

My eyes in my imagination move out to the sea and I hear the words of the poet John Masefield, "I must go down to the seas again to the lonely seas and the sky." As if in answer to the words I leave the sand and move to the water. Entering the water, in my imagination, I let it speak. I feel its coolness first, its distinctive difference from the sand. I feel it surround me and take my shape. I leave behind me all the symbols of my expectation lumped together on the beach. I cannot take all my past into the water. They will be too heavy and I will drown. The water will not support them and me. My first steps in the water are taken carefully. I look into the water, watching for stones and holes and sudden changes in the sand level. Looking into the clouded waters I realize I cannot see much and that I have not left all my past on the beach. Some of it is still with me in my fears, cares, worries, etc. How can I go beyond this history? Is the water beloved lover or cruel judge? Is it merciful upholder or destroying power? Will it devour or nourish life?

In the water a shuddering, a shivering, a feeling as my feet leave the safe ground. It is an instant and a lifetime. It is like the shattering of the world, like the rending of the sky in me. It is a space between my mind and my feeling. For one moment this ripping apart of me that anxiety is sweeps in upon me and holds me. Then a moment like no other. Somewhere beyond my fear, beyond my control, beyond both my desire and terror, I know that I am afloat. Something in me is held by something even greater. The self that I am is supported by something greater that I am not. In my imagination I am addressed by this other that I am not; a voice speaks and a heart without ears hears, "you are my beloved son, on you my favor rests."

I suggest that this Jungian reading of the Markan text can be further developed so as to expose the inner experience of the reader as he grows and develops. Thus following a typical day which could be seen as the everyday work of the disciple, there are the five conflict stories which lead from identification with the collective to a sense of self, the call of the four apostles which might help to establish the preferential types, the six crossings of the lake as a way to begin the negotiation of the shadow and the contrasexual opposites, the journey from the blind man of Chapter Eight to the blind Bartimaeus of Chapter Ten as descriptive of the key question and work of mid-life, and the five conflict stories in the temple as life's battle with meaning. This of course is only a rough schema which cannot be pursued here but which I have tried to develop in the work now awaiting publication.

Robert A. Repicky, C.S.B.

Jungian Typology
and Christian Spirituality

In recent times there has been much written and discussed around the topic of integration. One hears of the need to integrate one's daily experiences into one's prayer and the need to grow as an "integrated person." There is also much more emphasis today among theologians and writers on Christian spirituality on the *relationship* between God and the individual Christian, speaking of the Father precisely as a father, the Son as brother and companion, and the Spirit as that love which unites all human beings and transforms their lives as each progresses on his or her own spiritual journey.

In all of this, I see a very serious attempt to overcome that subtle form of dualism which all too often in the past has crept into personal spirituality causing a real separation between the so-called *sacred* and the *profane*. Such a separation inevitably gives rise to a mentality which compartmentalizes one's life in such a way that certain areas are seen to be completely divorced from others due to the apparently vast difference between them. As a result, the individual winds up living a fragmented existence without even being conscious of it.

In particular, this has often been the case in the relationship between psychology and theology. It is only quite recently that it has been possible to use psychological studies to enrich our understanding of theology and personal spiritualities. I propose to do just that in this article by looking at the results of some studies on the psychology of the individual and his or her personality and its relatedness to the relationship which develops between God and the individual Christian, as well as the manner in which this relationship transforms the Christian into the "new creation" of which St.

Paul speaks. In order to do so, I will focus upon prayer in the life of the individual in such a way that it takes into account the *whole* of the person and relates to his or her psychic constitution, understood in terms of Jungian typology. Furthermore, I also hope to show how that relationship, established in prayer, gives rise to a Christian *giftedness*, what St. Paul describes as the gifts of the Spirit, in such a manner that we can more easily understand their role in the lives of *all* Christians rather that simply confined to members of the charismatic or pentecostal movements.

In his article, "Prayer and Celebration In the Christian Community," Gerard Fourez makes a very important distinction between Prayer (the profound attitude of heart of the Christian in the presence of God) and prayer (those particular behaviors through which the Christian tries to foster Prayer).[1] Although I will be dealing most of all with prayer as that particular manner in which the individual relates with God, I think it first appropriate to comment upon Fourez's notion of *Prayer*.

Prayer as an attitude or stance before God, says Fourez, can be expressed in our lives in many ways. It can be expressed in a stance of openness, acceptance, intimacy, silence, awe, respect, and so forth. But it is always expressed with an awareness of the presence of God. He maintains that our Prayer is not meant to make God aware of us, but rather to help us to foster and retain an awareness of his presence in our lives.[2] This awareness is a conscious realization that there is a transcendent meaning in our lives, a dimension to human existence which goes far deeper than our own understanding. Prayer, then, is an attitude of an individual before the Divine who seeks to draw that individual into an ever deeper relationship with himself and give meaning to that transcendent dimension on a personal level. And it is precisely because Prayer is an attitude of an *individual* that we must deal with the conscious awareness of the individual. Prayer as a conscious event is also a psychological event.

The central question in the life of the Christian is: Who am I in relationship with God? In his little book, *Depth Psychology and Religious Belief*, Christopher Bryant leaves no question as to the importance of bringing one's whole personality to bear on one's attitude toward one's relationship with God. There is an essential unity in one's psychic life which cannot be ignored if one is to strive for an integrated existence. "The secret of success, or at least of getting the best out of yourself . . . lies largely in getting your unconscious to work in harmony with your conscious mind."[3] To do so, it is very important for the individual to come to some realization of how he or she functions as a conscious, intending subject. This is a very great responsibility for the individual, for only such an awareness will create the possibility of bringing the unconscious into harmony with the conscious. Only in this way may the individual relate to God in a holistic rather than fragmented manner; and only such a holistic prayer can make one's essential stance in Prayer authentic.

In speaking of prayer, then, we are speaking of the individual relating naturally and spontaneously with God in such a way that he not only clarifies for him the basic attitude he has in the presence of God, but that his prayer also becomes formative of that stance. It is only natural then that how the individual relates and functions in his or her everyday life will have some bearing upon how that same individual relates to God.

In C.G. Jung's psychiatric practice, he was struck by the fact that his patients not only displayed individual differences in their lives, but typical differences as well. It was thus that he began to formulate his theory of psychological types, a theory which was intended to help facilitate an understanding of how individuals perceive and relate in their lives. In general, he was able to distinguish between two basic attitudes or orientations with which the individual approaches life: *extraversion* and *introversion*. He made the further distinction that, within each of these basic attitudes, there were also two quite distinct modes of perception (*sensation* and *intuition*) as well as two ways of evaluating and ordering that which was perceived (*thinking* and *feeling*). The use of any one of these four functions, he held, necessarily excludes the use of its opposite within the pair. It is important to note, however, that, while every individual has access to all of the functions, it is the *habitual* use of one to the *habitual* exclusion of another which will constellate the psychological type of the individual. It is my conviction that a proper understanding of these basic dispositions of the personality and these four functions will contribute greatly to a healthy understanding and directing of one's personal giftedness, prayer and spirituality in general.

THE ATTITUDINAL TYPES:
EXTRAVERSION AND INTROVERSION

As with the "functional types," it is the habitual preference of orientating oneself either extravertedly or introvertedly which determines the "attitudinal type" of the individual. That attitude which is not habitually preferred will recede more or less into the individual's unconscious.

When I speak of an extravert, then, I am speaking of one who consciously is primarily interested and at home in the world of people, material things, and action.[4] In his adjustment and reaction pattern, the extravert orients him or herself predominantly by the outward, the collective norms, "the spirit of the times."[5] Being so outwardly directed, one's actions have a character that is always adapted to the actual circumstances in which he finds himself, and the moral laws governing his actions coincide with the demands of society or the prevailing moral standpoint. The extravert is the individual who always appears to be "normal" due to his ability to fit into existing conditions with comparative ease. He does what is needed or what is expected of him and refrains from all innovations the demands for which are not entirely self-evident, or which exceed the expectations of those in the immediate environment.[6]

The danger of which the extravert must beware is that the more extreme his extraverted attitude becomes, the more likely it is that he may lose himself in his attachment to the outer world. Neglect of unconscious introversion may compensate in a display of childish egoism which may become ruthless and brutal in one's dealings with others and the environment.

"The introvert, on the other hand, is more interested and at home in the inner world—the world of ideas and reflection."[7] For this person, the ego and the subjective psychological process are primary. He insists upon being a codeterminer of the world in which he lives, selecting his own, subjective determinants as being the decisive ones. Whereas the extravert may be described as one who keeps things "up front," the introvert is classically the "deep" person. This person is often misunderstood by the extravert as being two-faced because so much goes on "behind the scene." This generally forces upon the introvert the psychology of the underdog.[8]

Because of their differences, the introvert can also mistakenly view the extravert as "shallow."

The danger which the introvert faces is that his unconscious extraversion makes itself felt as an absolute and irrepressible tie to the objective world. Thus,

> the more the ego struggles to preserve its independence, freedom from obligation, and superiority, the more it becomes enslaved to the objective data. The individual's freedom of mind is fettered by the ignominy of his financial dependence, his freedom of action trembles in the face of public opinion, his moral superiority collapses in a morass of inferior relationships, and his desire to dominate ends in a pitiful craving to be loved.[9]

THE IRRATIONAL FUNCTIONS: SENSATION AND INTUITION

The "irrational functions" are those functions through which one perceives, or registers, the input of data from the outside world. Whatever they do or do not do is not based in any way upon a rational judgment, but simply upon the intensity of the perception. As functions of the conscious mind, they can take upon themselves quite a distinct twist in their manner of operation, depending upon which attitudinal preference is utilized.

According to results from the Myers-Briggs Type Indicator, 65–79% of the population of the United States use "sensation" as either the main or as an auxiliary function,[10] sensation being that function which basically relies upon the perception of the five senses. The sensate most easily perceives concrete objects and facts (how things are) and focuses primarily upon the present moment. When presented with a problem, he or she most often seeks to arrive at a practical, workable solution.

If sensation is combined with an extraverted attitude, the person will be a master for noticing details and will be unequaled as a realist. "Value" in the objective world is dependent upon the stimulation of sensations and their intensity. This individual experiences a great need for enjoyment, and his or her morality is oriented accordingly. Because of their capacity for enjoyment, the sensate make for very good company and, if "normal," will be conspicuously well-adjusted to reality.[11]

The danger with such a type, however, is that if sensation is allowed to "run wild," the person can become a crude pleasure-seeker or an effete aesthete who ruthlessly exploits the object, squeezing it dry, since its sole use is to stimulate sensation.[12] Repressed intuition may erupt in a mood of melancholy, or a feeling of dark and sinister possibilities lurking in the background, whose source is impossible to locate.[13] In the religious sphere, such an emerging shadow will quite often take the form of pharisaism or religious superstition.

If sensation is accompanied by an introverted attitude, a somewhat different picture emerges. Marie-Louise von Franz compares the introverted sensate to a highly sensitive photographic plate which absorbs every detail coming to it from the object.[14] In processing the data subjectively, this individual often acts as a sort of "equalizer," raising what is too low, lowering what is too high, dampening enthusiasm, restraining extravagance—in general, keeping all influences within necessary bounds.[15] Due to the introverted nature of the sensation, such a person gives the impression of being rather slow. One simply is not aware of all that is going on within him or her. The subjective influence of the introversion does, however, give the person the ability to perceive the mythological and archetypal components of reality. If the individual can learn to convey his or her impressions in some form, he or she can become a great artist, either in painting or in writing "psychological" novels, because of such a keen impression of reality.

The dangers inherent in this type also stem from overindulging in sensation and from an explosion of underdeveloped intuition. Overindulging in sensation can lead one to become trapped in an inner world of either benevolent deities or malevolent demons.[16] Underdeveloped intuition may erupt in the form of prophecies marked by a sinister and pessimistic character which may either accurately fit the situation or miss the mark by miles.[17]

"Intuition," the other irrational function, is characterized by its perception of possibilities in things and situations rather than in details *per se*. It looks toward the inner meaning of events and their possible implications and effects, bringing the dimension of the future into focus.

If this function is accompanied by extraversion, the individual will be very creative in the outer world, possibly as one who can create the future, either for his own environment or for the others in it. This person is the type who will recognize the value inherent in another and be able to direct sufficient attention toward it. As such, the extraverted intuitive can be a maker of great men or women and a tremendous promoter of new enterprises. The only problem is that quite often, before a particular enterprise has time to reap its benefits, he or she is off on another venture. Thus, one may

> fritter his life away on things and people, spreading about him an abundance of life which others live and not he himself. In the end, he goes away empty.[18]

An overextension of intuition could also lead to not attending to one's own physical needs and quite often results in exhaustion. Following one's nose, one exempts oneself from all laws of reason, only to be victimized in the end by neurotic compulsions which give free reign to a low order of pleasure-seeking on the sensual level.

The introverted intuitive is one who perceives the slow processes which go on in the collective unconscious and archetypal changes, and communicates them to society.[19] Because of the future direction of intuition, however, this person can usually be understood only in later generations as a representative of what was going on in the collective unconscious of his time. Such a person does experience a moral problem when trying to relate himself to his vision, attempting to participate in its life:

> He feels bound to transform his vision into his own life. But since he tends to rely most predominantly on his vision, his moral efforts become one-sided; he makes himself and his life symbolic . . . but unadapted to present-day reality. He thus deprives himself of any influence upon it because he remains uncomprehended.[20]

The shadow of this type will be characterized by intemperance, difficulty in controlling the appetites of the body, and ignorance of its true needs.[21]

THE RATIONAL FUNCTIONS:
THINKING AND FEELING

Thinking and feeling are considered "rational" functions because they assess the data brought to the individual through his perception. They organize what has been perceived and indicate to the
individual how to act upon it. Thinking seeks to apprehend the
world and adjust to it through an evaluation by way of thought or
cognition. Feeling apprehends the world through an evaluation
based upon one's scale of values.[22]

Thinking involves logic, systematic thought-processes. One
whose main function is thinking will be one who likes things well-
ordered and systematized. Solutions to his or her problems are always very logical. Such a person is a great planner, for he or she can
outline a particular project step-by-step and is always very fair.

The extraverted thinker is the one who can clarify the objective
situation and keep things well-ordered. This is the one whose constant endeavor is to make all activities dependent upon intellectual
conclusions which have at their basis external or objective facts or
generally accepted ideas.[23] The ruling principles which this one obtains from these conclusions are extended by him to cover his entire
environment. Being so governed by logic and principle, the extravert thinker is the least personal of all the types.

The shadow of this type comes into play as personal formulas
become more and more rigid and the individual attempts to form all
things and people in the same mold. Repressed feeling may emerge
in the form of a subtle, self-seeking twist which distorts one's own
search for truth and value. The end begins to justify the means, or
"the guardian of public morals" discovers himself in a compromising
situation.[24] Another problem which such a one might face is that
after a life-time of settling problems and stating things clearly, he
may well wake up one morning in despair, wondering what it all
really meant.

For the introverted thinker, new views rather than facts are
the main concern. He is concerned with logical ideas. This is the
philosopher who is trying to return to basic concepts and discover what the subject is really doing mentally. This person is
usually very impractical, and his subjective bent drives him or

her away from any form of publicity. He makes a poor teacher, due to his preoccupation with the material rather than its presentation.

Because the repressed feeling in this type is extraverted, its shadow may come forth in the form of devastating emotional attachments to persons and things. The individual becomes brutal and vicious when someone or something for whom there is such an attachment comes under attack or criticism. If thinking is over-extended, the introverted thinker will tend to form very black and white judgements about the reality of things based upon the abstractness of his or her ideas.

The final function with which we must concern ourselves is "feeling." "The feeling function is the instrument with which we sort out the genuine and the spurious."[25] Persons, situations, objects, or moments are appreciated in terms of value and, as such, it is the most "personal" of all the functions.

If feeling is accompanied by an extraverted attitude, then it will seek to establish harmony with objective values, with traditional or generally accepted values. Such persons make for great patrons of the arts, and they move amiably in society. They spread an atmosphere of acceptance, making people feel wonderful in their presence, often sacrificing themselves for the benefit of others.[26]

Since thinking will tend to be repressed, such a type dislikes dealing in the abstract, with philosophical problems or ideas. When thinking is called into use, it will often come forth in a negative manner, becoming very critical or even cynical. Thus, paradoxically, the warmest of all types can also be the coldest. Where feeling is pursued to an extreme, this type can become very fickle, unreliable, and moody, indulging in whatever may strike him to be of value at the moment.

When feeling is introverted, we have one of the most misunderstood types in our culture. Introversion causes this one to seek his values within, and it is thus that he may seek after his own vision, finding great difficulty in giving outward expression to it. The outward demeanor is "harmonious, inconspicuous, giving the impression of pleasing repose, or of sympathetic repose, with no desire to affect others, to impress or influence, or change them in any way."[27] In order to communicate with others, this type must be able to arouse similar feelings in them and relate on that level. Such being the case, the introverted feeler exercises a very strong, but hidden, influence on those around him and quite often will be the ethical backbone of the group.[28]

Such an influence, however, can also be extended to become rather cruel and domineering in the individual's frantic effort to remain on top of the situation, or superior to other people. Because his thinking tends to remain rather primitive, it can become fixated around one or two thoughts or facts. If kept in check, however, such a person could develop a real gift for being very clear, simple and intelligible.

THE INFERIOR FUNCTION AND SPIRITUALITY

Within the explanation of the various types, it has already been mentioned that the habitually repressed or undeveloped function (the inferior function) may suddenly burst forth at times, making its presence known in most undesirable ways. Due to its lack of utilization, it remains the least differentiated of the functions and thus tends to have a rather primitive or archaic nature. Such being the case, the inferior function has a natural ability to act as a bridge to the unconscious, often through its role as a major factor in the constellation of the individual's "shadow" and other neurotic complexes.

> Many people discover relatively soon in life that the realm of their inferior function is where they are emotional, touchy and unadapted and they therefore acquire the habit of covering up this part of their personality with a surrogate pseudo-reaction. . . . You can always observe these "covering-up" reactions by the fact that they are impersonal and banal and very collective. They have no convincing personal quality about them.[29]

When any one of the conscious functions is overdone, the inferior function will arise to thwart and falsify it, making its presence unmistakenly felt and calling the individual to the realization that there is more in his or her life which needs to be integrated. Within the life of the Christian, this is often experienced as the "call to conversion." It is inferior function which reveals that person's cross, which points to shallowness and a need for greater personal growth in the individual's life.

In keeping with Bernard Lonergan's notion of the particular grace which we all need at the point where we experience moral impotence, keeping in mind, too, Sebastian Moore's reflections on the self within that is hated because of the discomfort it causes, I would say that it is precisely in the realm of the inferior function where the depth of one's commitment to his relationship with God, in humble acceptance of himself and desire for transformation, meets the real test. The religious experience of conversion will always be accompanied in some manner by an eruption of the inferior function as it reveals the individual's state of disintegration, rendering him helpless and in need of the healing of God's love and acceptance in grace.

This aspect of the inferior function is most important for the individual in his or her spiritual journey because it enlightens the personal meaning of that biblical phrase which again and again appears in the Old Testament, the "two-edged sword." All human giftedness (including God's Word) in the hands of our fragile psyches can either be life-giving or destructive, depending upon the balance which exists in our psyches. As a compensating factor within the structure of the psyche itself, the inferior function helps to maintain the balance between personal inflation and self-depreciation which is essential to human growth and development in all facets of human relatedness.

Donald Gelpi maintains that the Christian experience is the experience of the Jesus event and the Pentecostal experience which came out of it.[30] This experience is central to the life of each Christian. It is the experience of religious conversion, and the broadening of one's horizon as a result of that experience. The overall effect of living within this experience is that one's natural gifts and potentialities are raised to a new level and become "spiritualized" by attaining a new dimension in the realm of meaning.

St. Paul, in reflecting upon the Pentecostal aspect of the conversion experience, speaks of the gifts of the Holy Spirit as an integral part of the Christian's life, flowing from prayer and his new relationship to God through Christ. Such gifts are an essential part of the transformation of the individual into a son or daughter of God. However, one must really exercise a good deal of caution in speaking in such terms, for such a change cannot be seen as "miraculous" in the common-sense notion of the word. Rather, the "miraculous" nature of this transformation derives more from the gifted awareness of the transcendent nature of *all* human giftedness.

If these reflections are applied to typological considerations, there are tremendous implications for our whole approach to spirituality which do not only affect one's approach to prayer, but the responsibility attached to the concretization of one's faith life as well.

We have already seen that *intuition* is more concerned with potential and possibility than with concrete reality. This being the case, in the light of faith and the individual's relatedness to God, such a natural tendency to perceive potential would be further developed to the perception of the potential good in people and situations. Traditionally, we have referred to such an ability by saying that the individual had the gift of wisdom.

If the individual tends more toward introversion, the focus of intuition will be interior, toward the inner self. In prayer, this will reveal itself in a natural bent toward contemplative prayer, or types of prayer experiences which will yield a sense of the permeating presence of God. The ability of the individual to perceive archetypal changes at work will be refined in the light of God's grace and yield a realization that such changes have a profound influence and are very intimately connected with the presence of God in the working out of salvation history. In such a move from the archetypal to the anagogic the person of the prophet emerges.

To be a prophet carries with it its corresponding shadow over the individual, however. The light of grace does not automatically take care of the individual's struggle with the disintegrated inferior function. In this case the "future scope" of the prophet's vision must be tempered by his extraverted sensation which will cry for attention to the immediate details of his situation, restraining him from becoming lost in a future vision on the positive side, and overwhelming him with insignificant details on the negative side. In such a negative case the individual is called upon to struggle with the shortcomings of the present in a loving manner rather than to merely condemn them and walk away feeling superior.

The extraverted intuitive's prayer will be more "outward" in scope, and will realize itself more in concrete service to others. Such an individual will be drawn more to a "prayer-in-action" type of spirituality in which private prayer will assume the character of meditation-seeking-insight for future action or direction. Such an individual's wisdom, having an extraverted orientation, will tend to be more practical, and thus, this person makes for an excellent leader who can rally others to his or her cause, which cause will be characterized by his or her relatedness to God. The danger for such an individual can either come from his sense of inflation (in which he begins to try and become God, rather than remain in relationship to God) or from the interference of his inferior function (introverted sensation), which may distort his activities with a neurotic compulsiveness which will finally lead to exhaustion.

Turning to the *sensate*, we have an individual who is much more in touch with concrete reality than the intuitive. The special feature which this individual may bring to his life is a simplicity of life and life-style.

As an introvert, this individual will tend toward the use of religious icons, pictures, rosaries, etc., in prayer.[31] Such types of devotional prayer find their meaning within the individual, and his giftedness will be marked by a deep sensitivity to others and the various situations in which he may find himself. Simplicity, and the ability to act as an "equalizer" in extreme situations give way to the virtue of prudence in this individual. In the case where extraverted intuition makes itself felt this prudence may give way to a type of "prudishness," causing the individual to cling to a static rather than simple way of life for fear of the possible dangers in anything not already integrated into that pattern.

Due to the reliance of the extraverted sensate upon the five senses, he or she will be the type to revel in the presence of God in the beauty of nature or other sensual experiences. For this person, prayer will focus more around liturgical worship, and the sacraments will provide a center for the development of his spirituality. Practical, meaningful, sacramental ministry, in whatever capacity the individual may be able to exercise it, will mark the giftedness of this individual. Repressed intuition may result in this case with the individual having to struggle with a tendency toward Jansenism. If sensation becomes inflated, on the other hand, the danger of a tendency toward pharisaism or superstition will have to be dealt with.

The *thinker* with his natural inclination to logic and reasoning will find theology very important. Such a one will naturally be given to meditation and will tend to show concern for justice in the world because of the value which reason and fairness hold in his or her life.

When thinking is introverted, the inclination to deal with ideas and concepts will give way to prayerful meditation upon the mysteries of the faith. This prayer gives rise to the gift of knowledge in the person of the theologian. The inferior function, feeling, may well make its presence felt in his attachment to his own thought and speculation such that the introverted thinker becomes trapped in the systems and structures which he has helped to create. Thus, the individual may lose all creativity in his attempt to defend his thought, warping all other facts and ideas to fit into it rather than by adapting it to whatever new knowledge may have come to light.

The extraverted thinker is more naturally suited to teaching than would be the introverted thinker due to his or her natural orientation to the outer world. He or she is also quite gifted with respect to the organization of the community. Because of his rational sense of fairness, this person is also more geared to deal with matters of social justice. Ethics and moral behavior would be of great interest to such an individual. The sense of duty and obligation which this person displays would also extend somewhat into his prayer and, combined with the extravert's general interest in the traditional or generally accepted, his prayer tends to be more traditional with an emphasis on vocal prayer (traditional or spontaneous). A very good example of this is the individual whose private meditation consists of "talking to God." The Divine Office, as the Prayer of the Church, would also be very important, and as a priest or religious, he could develop scruples about "getting-it-in." A definite advantage for this person is that his tendency to have a well-organized life also reaches over into the regularity of his prayer. But, just as rigidity can become destructive in other spheres of his life, so too can it interfere with the natural flow of life here. Much anger and tension may result if a spontaneous situation calls for some rescheduling of either prayer time or some other important activity.

A *feeler's* sense of value finds its expression in prayer most often in "meditation through intercessory prayer, prayer with others in prayer groups and such rituals as the Eucharist, which emphasize intimate relationships in the presence of God."[32] Because of the "personal" nature of the feeling function, the feeler has the ability to sense in others and to give joy to others.

When feeling is accompanied by introversion, the individual naturally tends toward becoming a mystic, seeking solitude to explore and bask in the intimacy of his or her relationship with God. As earlier stated, the introverted feeler is one of the most misunderstood types in our culture because of his inability to articulate his experience. Thus, the mystic who cannot always articulate himself nevertheless can develop the facility of being truly "present" to others. This gift of presence is of vital importance to the community because of the joy, peace, and standard of values which he or she non-verbally radiates outwardly to those to whom he or she is present. When inferior thinking interferes, however, one must be cautious not to center his joy and peace around one or two experiences. This can result in a mindless, naive, and basically empty joy which is satisfied with saying: "Jesus loves me and all is right with the world." The genuine joy and peace which this individual must share with the world must be such that it can be sustained in the face of unpleasant truths as well as those which are pleasant.

Because of its sensitivity to atmosphere, sense of rightness, sense of appropriateness, and the sense of the values inherent in a given situation, extraverted feeling will have a marked tendency toward affective prayer, very often manifesting itself in intercessory prayer. This individual's spirituality will grow out of his or her ability to read situations in the light of value and, focusing upon what is addressed to the heart, such a spirituality will give rise to the gift of discernment. If, however, the primitive thinking of this individual should emerge, the most natural thing for it to do is to distort discernment with a "plotting" character, degenerating it (and his approach to intercessory prayer as well) into manipulation.

It is extremely important to note that these tendencies associated with each type are not exclusive. In one's psychic constitution, the main function will always be accompanied by auxiliary functions which, although not developed to the same proficiency as the main function, also operate within the conscious intentionality of the individual. Thus, there are a number of possible functional combinations which together make up one's psychological type, and these combinations will also affect the individual's natural inclination toward an increasing variety of spiritual experience.

THE USE OF PSYCHOLOGICAL STUDIES

Many insights are to be gained from the use of psychological studies which definitely can be of value to the individual in his spiritual journey. Our concentration upon Jungian typology, as it has been summarized here from Jung's writings as well as from the work of Marie-Louise von Franz, helps one to see that the Christian religious experience has a very human foundation. The manner in which one relates to others and the world around one says a great deal about what it means for that particular individual to relate to God. The considerations of typology also help one to be a little more aware of those areas in which he experiences a need for conversion. Furthermore, they enable the individual to see that the transformation of the ego through faith does yield certain gifts or talents which are in accord with the natural bent of his personality. He is enabled to see that, due to his natural tendency to delight in what he can do easily and well, ongoing conversion is necessary not only in newly emerging areas of his life, but in order to avoid inflation as well.

Lastly, because groups of people are made up of human individuals, one cannot ignore the role which typology plays in the communal setting as well. The most recurring type among the individuals in a group will have an impact upon the character of that group and will determine the "type" of the group. Those individuals whose type may well be in the minority will definitely feel the effects of such a situation and may well be called upon to act as the "inferior function" of the group. Thus, within the group there is still a great need to look for the complementary to be found in other types in order to avoid that inflation or degeneration which can occur in a group just as well as in an individual.

Christianity, as a communal religion, cannot afford to overlook this fact. Specifically with regard to prayer, Fourez states:

> . . . prayer is a celebration leading to a growing awareness of God's presence in our lives. It will be expressed in various ways according to individual psychologies, educational background, cultural heritage. To realize that there are different ways of praying—and that they are all limited—is, perhaps, an essential aspect of the experience of God. But any celebration, any aware-

ness, would be unfulfilled if it were only an individual experience. That is why there must be communal prayer, i.e., a
communal celebration culminating in a communal awareness of
God's presence among us.[33]

It is essential that one realize the limitations to each particular
gift or form of prayer, just as there are limitations to any individual
personality. There is therefore a need for the communal aspect or
communal complementary to our individual lives. Christian prayer
needs to be communally celebrated as well as individually. This
means that our diversity of approaches to prayer, as well as the diversity of our giftedness, must also be shared in order for each person to relate more fully to God.

> Remembering the categories of personalities proposed by Jung,
> we can see that a good communal celebration will try to provide
> a variety of symbols so that each type of person can find some-
> thing to which to relate: there must be silence for the *feelers*, some
> vision for the *intuitives*, something to understand for the *thinkers*,
> and something to *do* for the "pragmatists."[34]

CONCLUSION

There is still much work to be done in this area. Such considerations as I have tried to provide here can only be seen as founda-
tional at best. Even so, there is much which has been omitted and
condensed. However, I believe that the relevance of such matters
for personal growth within the Christian context is clear. Naturally,
as with all knowledge, one may attempt to manipulate psychological
studies and thus increase the already present fear of their relevance
to the area of spirituality. But in a world such as ours today, Christians must begin to value knowledge (especially self-knowledge)
over ignorance and begin to assume the responsibility for directing
their own self-development through insights gained from that
knowledge in humble and intimate companionship with God.

Notes

1. Gerard Fourez, "Prayer and Celebration In the Christian Community," *Worship:* Vol. 46, Number 3, 1972, p. 141.

2. *Ibid.*, p. 142.
3. Christopher Bryant, *Depth Psychology and Religious Belief* (Wakefield, England: West Yorkshire Printing Co. Ltd., 1972), p. 28.
4. Morton Kelsey, "Personality Types and Meditation," *Transcend*, Number 13, 1978, p. 2.
5. Jolande Jacobi, *The Psychology of C.G. Jung* (New Haven: Yale University Press, 1973), p. 18.
6. C.G. Jung, *Psychological Types*, The Collected Works, Vol. 6 (Princeton: Princeton University Press, 1971), p. 334–5.
7. Kelsey, p. 2.
8. Jung, p. 392–3.
9. *Ibid.*, p. 378.
10. This figure was quoted by Barbara Kelsey at a workshop entitled: "Christian Education for Wholeness," given in Toronto, through the Center for Christian Studies, in June, 1979.
11. Jung, p. 364.
12. *Ibid.*, p. 365.
13. Marie-Louise von Franz, "The Inferior Function," *Jungian Typology* (Irving, Texas: Spring Publications Inc., 1979), p. 23.
14. *Ibid.*, p. 27.
15. Jung, p. 397.
16. *Ibid.*
17. von Franz, p. 29.
18. Jung, p. 369.
19. von Franz, p. 33.
20. Jung, p. 402.
21. von Franz, p. 34.
22. Jacobi, p. 12.
23. Jung, p. 346.
24. *Ibid.*, p. 449.
25. James Hillman, "The Feeling Function," *Jungian Typology* (Irving, Texas: Spring Publications Inc., 1979), p. 82.
26. von Franz, p. 43–44.
27. Jung, p. 389.
28. von Franz, p. 48.
29. *Ibid.*, p. 11–12.
30. Lecture given by Donald Gelpi on "Jungian Personality Theory and the Theology of Gifts" at Berkeley, California, April 28, 1977.
31. Kelsey, p. 6.
32. *Ibid.*
33. Fourez, p. 147.
34. *Ibid.*, p. 148.

Ernest Skublics

Psychologically Living Symbolism and Liturgy

Symbolism has always been understood to be basic to liturgy, in the sense that the symbolic character (*Zeichenhaftigkeit*) of the ensemble of liturgical worship was a key to the understanding of its working. This fact has led scholars in every age to discuss this aspect of liturgy and sacramentality copiously. But often these discussions remained on a purely theological, or even predominantly philosophical level. The present-day reader of these discussions is struck by their strongly aprioristic approach and sometimes sheer arbitrariness.

In his *Images and Symbols*, Mircea Eliade speaks of a contemporary rediscovery of symbolism.[1] This rediscovery is not limited to his own discipline. Beside the names of Van der Leeuw, Lévy-Bruhl and Lévi-Strauss, one is immediately reminded of Ernst Cassirer, Karl Rahner, Paul Tillich and, of course, the depth-psychologists, particularly Freud and Jung. That contemporary art, drama and cinema are thriving on symbolism and on the taste the public has for it, needs no better proof than the experience of Expo 67 in Montreal.

The last few decades have presented us with an extremely interesting phenomenological account of what role symbolism plays in man's life. The findings of modern depth-psychology are particularly valuable for the theology of worship, for our improved understanding of sacramentality and also for our approach to liturgical reform, this ongoing process of day-to-day change.

Thus it is disappointing that, e.g. a Vagaggini, in his classic, *Theological Dimensions of the Liturgy*, or a Verheul, in his *Introduction to the Liturgy*, or a von Allmen, in his *Worship, its Theology and Practice*,[2] just to mention three of the best known works on the theology of worship, should completely ignore this contribution, when treating the sign or symbol character of liturgy. There are also a number of systematic theologians who have much to say about symbolism, or in whose theological methodology symbolism plays a major role. The obvious examples are Paul Tillich, Karl Rahner and John MacQuarrie. Although some of these symbol theories are in effect remarkably close to the depth-psychological one I shall be speaking of, they really fail to make any systematic use of it or even acknowledge its usefulness.

SYMBOLS AS OPPOSED TO SIGNS

The present rediscovery of symbolism brought with it a fine distinction between "signs" and "symbols" which is very important for the theology of worship. Both a sign and a symbol are understood to be perceptible realities related to hidden realities. This relationship of the perceptible to the hidden is one of both identity and distinction. The perceptible reality is, in a way, both distinct from and identical to the hidden reality. The most important difference between a sign and a symbol is that the former is more distinct, the latter is more identical.

While the two words, and a score of other synonyms, were often used interchangeably in the past, the ancients tended to insist more on the unity and identity, the continuity between the perceptible and the imperceptible reality, while the moderns insist more on the distinction. This may have much to do with the more integrated world view of oral society, as opposed to the fragmentation resulting from alphabetic script, and later print culture.[3] Whatever the case, the earliest Christian ideas about sacramental celebrations originate from a period when integrality and symbolic identity rather than distinction were stressed. Cipriano Vagaggini, in his *Theological Dimensions of the Liturgy*, points out how the ancient way of looking at symbolism prepares us much better to understand and appreciate the liturgy. If we can believe Marshall McLuhan and Walter Ong, the fast unfolding electronic age with its "new orality" and its consequent overcoming of fragmentation should once again render us more capable of the right kind of approach to and appreciation of liturgy.

Vagaggini says:

> If . . . we insist on the difference between the sign and the thing
> signified, to the point of considering them as belonging to two
> worlds foreign to each other, we shall obviously be tempted to
> regard the liturgy as a pointless, sterile game, in which the play-
> ers are simply shaking rattles, to no effect. We shall find it hard
> to believe that God can, or at any rate will, fulfill the mystery
> of Christ in us through signs, and that through these same signs
> man can render an authentic worship to God.[4]

The well known controversy between the symbolic and real
presence of Christ in the eucharistic bread and wine is cited as a typically false, and relatively "modern" question. The present-day Roman resistance to "transsignification", as if it opposed the proper
meaning of "transubstantiation", is still symptomatic of the same
state of the question. Signification is not seen as involving identification. There is, of course, no opposition between the two, if the
unity and identity of the symbol with the reality symbolized is
stressed. Symbolic presence is real presence. The eucharistic bread
and wine are not signs but symbols of the body and blood of Christ.
Since this distinction will be very important, let us see more precisely how signs and symbols are distinguished, particularly by
Jung.

By way of simplification one could say that a sign according to
this terminology is rather distinct from what it signifies while a symbol is more radically identified with the imperceptible reality it manifests. Of course there is no clear-cut demarcation. Even a
conventional sign can have some deep-seated natural relationship
with what it signifies, this being part of the reason why it was chosen
for its function.

But to pursue this differentiation between signs and symbols,
let me describe briefly C.G. Jung's respective notions. A symbol he
defines as the "essence *and* image of psychic energy".[5] If we leave
aside for now the meaning of "psychic energy", or provisionally substitute "grace" for it, it will be easily seen that "essence *and* image"
corresponds perfectly with the ancient notion of a sacramental sign
or symbol. This correspondence becomes more and more pronounced as we follow Jung's description. Although the symbol is

"essence *and* image", it merely suggests without unveiling. This suggestion appeals both to feeling and to thinking, it stimulates sensation as well as intuition.[6] A symbol and its way of "getting across" is not simply an affair of the intellect. While addressing our conscious, it points beyond it, to an obscurity that would be completely inaccessible to us were it not for the symbol. The symbol thus mediates between conscious and unconscious, known and unknown, rational and irrational, intellectual and emotional, concrete and abstract. It always belongs to both of these respective realms simultaneously. That is how it can mediate, correlate, focalize in one, two different realms of reality, and become an event of revelation and integration.[7] Since the unconscious is seen as largely collective, the symbol also correlates individual and collectivity.

As it is of the essence of the symbol to contain both known and unknown elements, it can never be the product of free choice or agreement. In this sense Jung distinguishes the sign from the symbol. The sign stands for a thing fully known, while the symbol expresses something "as yet unknown or only relatively known". This means that a symbol cannot function properly unless "we are prepared to accept the expression as designating something that is only divined and not yet clearly conscious".[8] Symbols cannot be invented like signs. They are not the products of reason and free will but of a process of psychic development which spontaneously expresses itself in symbols. This development is not merely individual but collective, so that Jung sees symbolism as the spontaneous product of the unconscious psychic activity of countless generations.[9]

We can apply all of this to our sacraments without in any manner denying their institution by Christ, whatever way "institution" is to be understood. Some comparative study of rites will convince anyone that the symbols actually used—or better, the symbol-actions performed—by Christ have indeed developed spontaneously through thousands of years and were not his arbitrary inventions. As a matter of fact their continuity with ancient rituals, Jewish and otherwise, warranted the Christian conviction that those ancient rituals had been figures of the new sacraments, with the meaning attributed to them in the Christian dispensation.

Neither Christ, the founder, nor the present-day reformer of Christian worship can simply design arbitrary new symbols from known associations, for what would thus be manufactured, could contain no more than was put into it, and could consequently not function as a living, revealing symbol.[10]

If sheer rational thinking cannot create a living symbol or symbol-act, nor can it, of itself, ever penetrate a symbol it encounters.[11] Since the symbol is the most complete possible expression of a reality partly unknown or even unknowable, any attempt to "translate" a symbol into concepts does the worst service in an effort to uncover the obscurity: by dissecting and fragmenting it, such an attempt destroys the symbol and renders it incapable of carrying out its integrating, revealing and mediating function. The obscurity of the symbol is inseparable from its vitality and richness in meaning. We cannot eliminate the symbol's ambiguity without mutilating it.[12] Thus one must accept inexactitude and lack of clarity as no less characteristic of the symbol than meaningfulness and complexity. The core of the symbol is unknown. It encompasses not only forgotten elements but also elements which have never yet entered consciousness.[13]

In the specifically religious context Van der Leeuw defines the symbol as a participation of the sacred in its shape here and now. There is a substantial communion between the sacred and its shape. This substantial communion—Lévy-Bruhl's "participation"—alone makes the symbol. Symbolizing and symbolized, manifesting and manifested thus flow into a single image. The image is what it is the image of, the symbol the symbolized.[14]

From what has been said it will be clear that sacraments or liturgical acts in general will have to be considered symbol—rather than sign-actions, if we are to take this terminology into account. This choice does run counter to the usage of many, and not only the usage, which, after all, could be a matter of indifference, so long as it is well clarified. Ambrosius Verheul, e.g., is of the opinion that "because liturgical signs are wholly dependent on Christ and his Church, it is at once plain that here we have to do not with natural signs but with free cultural signs", although he admits that "in general we can say that Christ and his Church did not create a completely new symbolism. In the choice of symbols they took into account the already existing natural meaning of things".[15] From the way Jung describes the emergence of symbols, we would have to say that liturgical symbol-acts are indeed culturally conditioned (and thus also subject to change) but at the same time they are closer to what Verheul and others term "natural signs", with an archetypal signification that is not a matter of free choice or agreement, than to conventional signs.

If below we shall describe the divine institution as specification of the given symbol-event in the particular faith context, that, in my opinion does not make the symbol-event into a "free cultural sign". On the contrary, this institution or specification exploits precisely the fact that the given symbol-event already has a deep-rooted inalienable signification which is already psychologically functional, and thus lends itself to be the effective sacramental vehicle of the salvation reality of which it becomes the memorial.

THE DEPTH-PSYCHOLOGICAL CONTEXT

If the above description already suggests the dynamic, rather than static character of symbols, this aspect becomes quite clear when we inquire into the context in which Jung observed the function of symbolism. This context is the "individuation process" as Jung termed the development of the personality. It is a process of self-realization, integration or maturing, during which the identity of the person gradually becomes clarified. The individual becomes what he has always been implicitly and first unconsciously.[16]

The name *individuation* process should not mislead us into conceiving this development as an *individualistic* way of defining our identity by means of isolation from society. Indeed Jung has been accused of an introversive ideal of becoming oneself,[17] but then the realization of oneself will always be interpreted with an emphasis corresponding to the character of the individual. The process itself is equally susceptible of the opposite emphasis. Rather, we must see the importance of individuality in the fact that this process is described basically in terms of emerging consciousness: "*Bewusstwerdung*," which is the properly personal individual element in man, while the unconscious is predominantly collective.

During this process man's conscious ego is confronted with his total personality, in particular the unconscious. Through this confrontation the unconscious, as far as possible, becomes conscious, or at least is "felt out" and harmonized with the conscious life. This of course implies the constant adjustment of the conscious to the gradually emerging givens of the total personality. Through this process the first unknown identity of the self emerges and the conflicts arising from lack of understanding and integration within and without subside.

The crucial issue in this process is the coming to terms between conscious and unconscious. Surely no sheer intellectual effort alone can unearth and comprehend the unknown. It is here that the unique mediating role of symbolism enters the picture. We have seen that a symbol is always the co-incidence of conscious and unconscious, inner and outer, personal and collective. It is only in this function of blending that the structure of the symbol becomes evident. The origin of a symbol is always (at least) twofold, and only when the two corresponding elements meet does the symbol result. In fact the symbol is nothing other than this happening of co-incidence (*syn-ballein*) itself.

This statement will be enlightened by Jung's *archetype* theory. In the course of the treatment of numberless patients, he observed that the unconscious always manifested itself in images and symbols which, naturally, could not be deciphered by any simple logical procedure. They were always multivalent, and only when a long series of dreams and other spontaneous symbolic representations of the patient were cumulatively taken and conferred with the known history and situation of the patient, did they begin to suggest possible "messages". But even then, varying interpretations were possible. One fact however offered a clue. A large number of the symbolic representations bore a striking similarity to ancient mythological ones, even when it could be established with certitude that the patient could have no knowledge of the myths in question. Further, it was discovered that these motifs not only *occurred in some* mythologies but indeed were the common stock of practically all mythologies, appearing with only slight modifications in very similar accounts bearing a very similar relevance for the lives of the respective peoples. As a rule, neither the patients depended on the mythologies, nor the mythologies on each other. Yet the symbolic representations were sometimes almost identical. The message of the dream-images in question could then be surmised through a comparative study of similar occurrences. The results thus obtained did fit into the pattern of the individual case, and the critical deadlock in the individuation process could be overcome.

Thus Jung came to postulate the existence of a deeper and essentially collective layer in man's unconscious. This collective unconscious contained, so to speak, sedimentary traces of age-old collective human experience, crystallized, as it were, into nouminous structural elements of the psyche.[18] These structural elements which became manifest through the typical, symbolic patterns they projected into the conscious, Jung came to term archetypes.

The archetype theory is merely a working hypothesis, which by no means claims to have discovered a new species of beings, and for all the tentative descriptions of the archetypes Jung offers, they remain a large X-factor, which is, by definition, unknown and unknowable. It is therefore a vain discussion for us to enter, whether archetypes are unchangeable, as one would be inclined to presume from their name and from some of the descriptions Jung offered, especially in his earlier works, or whether they are susceptible to gradual development, as the typical situations of human life can undergo a modification of connotations, while retaining their identity. (Or is it precisely that which constitutes their permanent identity, if they have one, that is called *archetype?*)

In any case, we can say that there is a certain X-factor, respectively an undeterminable number of X-factors in man's unconscious, which possess a certain specific energy, whereby they can attract contents of the conscious having a potential kinship with them.[19]

> The "archetype as such" is an irrepresentable factor, a disposition which begins to operate in a given moment of the development of the human mind, arranging the material of consciousness into definite figures.[20]

The X-factor is latent until, at a certain point of the person's development, a certain characteristic vital situation brings it into resonance, arouses and activates it. Then it asserts itself with its "psychic energy", projecting itself, as it were, as "structural disposition" into the conscious material hitherto unrelated to this aspect of the unconscious, and organizes it, constellates it into a symbolic representation, which connects known and unknown, intellectual and emotional, personal concrete and primordial collective. The symbol, then, is the event of this dynamic coincidence. The archetype is "always a potential symbol and its 'dynamic core' is at all times . . . ready to be actualized and thus appear as symbol".[21]

> The unconscious supplies, so to speak, the archetypal form which, as such, is empty and thus unimaginable. But it is immediately filled up by the conscious with related or similar image-material and thus it becomes perceivable.[22]
>
> For as soon as the collective human core of the archetype, which represents the raw material provided by the collective unconscious, enters into relation with the conscious mind and its form-giving character, the archetype takes on "body", "matter", "plastic form", etc.; it becomes representable, and only then does it become a concrete *image*—an archetypal image, a symbol.[23]

In this sense does Jung define the symbol as "the essence as well as the image of psychic energy".

Jung's symbol, then, is not statically conceived. It is, by definition, always *in actu*, happening and functioning, or otherwise it is not considered a *living* symbol at all.

CONDITIONS OF LIVING LITURGICAL SYMBOLISM

It is important to note that neither the archetype, nor the available conscious material of itself is a symbol. We may in both cases speak of potential symbols, but not in the sense that they possess all the constitutive elements of a symbol and are merely awaiting the appropriate moment to be activated. Both the archetype and the related conscious material are, of themselves, constitutively incomplete. They are merely potential elements of a number of possible symbols, and only when the corresponding elements actually co-incide, do real, living symbols happen. Thus objects observed, persons encountered, actions performed, the external rites of liturgy are all potential symbols which *can become* actual, living symbols, through co-incidence with some corresponding unconscious configuration.

Thus static, potential symbol elements commonly referred to as signs or symbols are not considered symbols at all. The Jungian symbol is a happening, and corresponds very closely to what Schillebeeckx or Powers call sign-act, sign activity, symbolic action or symbolization.[24] In some instances the context of their usage almost echoes Jung's even if no direct dependence is indicated. Thus, e.g., Powers writes:

> The process of human growth, then, which is the existential functioning of the human person, is, in its essence, a process of sign-acts, acts in which man expresses his own personal reality to his world and thus grows into his own personal reality.[25]

Now, when we speak of religious, sacramental symbol-events, a third, explicitly theological dimension enters the dynamic coincidence of unconscious disposition and conscious material, namely the divine institution or specification of the given symbol-event in the particular faith context. Thus the religious, sacramental symbol fulfills its specific mediating, revealing-and-materializing function by focalizing the theologal meaning-content with the corresponding vital, psychological situation of the subject, in the consciously perceptible, shared symbol-event. In the ideal case of a successful, vital liturgical act the three dimensions coincide perfectly, having occurred in a situation of optimal correspondence.

This correspondence is very complex and multivalent, the same symbol-act encompassing a variety of simultaneous meanings. Immersion in water means destruction and re-creation, death and life, cleansing and refreshment. Sharing food and drink means nourishment, friendship, giving-and-receiving, celebration, covenant. Thus the same ritual event may be experienced with quite different overtones at different times, or by different individuals, within the same celebration, depending on the situation and predispositions of the individual.[26] This multivalence includes a coincidence of complementary opposite aspects, as the example of baptism by immersion illustrates particularly well. There is an interdependence and inseparability between these opposites and a symbol is always *a coincidentia oppositorum*. Evidently, perfect co-incidence may be regarded as a theoretical limit situation, which in fact is never completely attained.

But we may certainly say that the success of a liturgical celebration is in direct proportion to the degree to which this multivalent co-incidence takes place. It is obviously hard to measure the

degree of this co-incidence, partly because it involves the unconscious, the integration of which it promotes but not in a clearly de-
finable manner. A symbol-event is an event of revelation, but
revelation cannot be completely conceptualized. One cannot define
after a liturgical service what exactly was revealed to one during the
service, because the resulting insight-and-integration is not all fully
conscious.

A second factor has to do with the acceptance of the unknown:
openness to the unexpected is the only favourable disposition in the
face of revelation. Since the unknown—to some extent always subject to revelation—is an essential element of the symbol, any a priori
exclusion or limitation in this regard means resisting the revealing-
and-integrating function of the symbol. Such an attitude, whether
conscious or unconscious, hinders the possibilities of correspondence and co-incidence for the initially excluded strands of meaning.
Jung emphasizes that a living symbol is possible only if we are "prepared to accept the expression as designating something that is only
divined and not yet clearly conscious".[27] Every pretence or even innocent conviction that we know everything the symbol means spells
death to the symbol. If indeed the case could be made out that all
the elements of a certain symbolic reality have become fully known,
that would mean the symbol had fulfilled its function and thereby
disposed of a further raison d'être.

Finally the role of perception, or better, communication, incarnational participation, involvement, is obviously crucial to the vitality of the symbol. This concerns what we earlier termed "the
conscious material" patterned into symbolic representations. This
material is not always necessarily external, "incarnational", it can
take the shape of dreams or internal images, but when we speak of
liturgical acts, of course, we are dealing with ritual happenings
which are not merely perceived or imagined but actively engaged
in. A ritual may be perfect on all other counts, but if not engaged
in, at least by means of what might be termed the mental participation of "silent spectators", it cannot possibly be a real symbol for
the person in question. It will then only be a potential symbol in the
sense in which possibly all reality is potentially symbolic.

These three factors of a successful symbolic celebration, multivalent correspondence, openness to the unknown and involvement
with the ritual event can be broken down into innumerable details

which we need not go into here. Let me perhaps just explicitate somewhat the first factor, multivalent correspondence. All three dimensions ritual, theologal and psychic may be reduced in a manner which will hinder a successful celebration. The rite may have suffered from atrophy, like the medieval mass where not only active participation, particularly the sharing of bread and wine, but even visibility was practically extinct, through historical development. The atrophy of a rite, understandably often occurs hand-in-hand with a shifting emphasis in the acknowledged theological dimension. The history of the eucharist offers many good examples. The shape of the celebration itself, at various times, all but totally disregarded those sides of the sacramental meaning which were at the same time also theologically neglected. As long as such a one-sided emphasis corresponds to the dispositions of the community at the time, it does not destroy the vitality of the symbol, though it is likely to weaken it, and it also lessens the corrective function of liturgy. But any amount of tardiness in changing the one-sided shape of the liturgy as soon as the disposition of the people has shifted results in the growing inapplicability and irrelevance of the rite. But a rite can also be systematically reduced through a rationalistic approach to simplification, where lack of understanding of the complex nature of symbolism and of the fact that all aspects of the symbol in question are not fully known results in the mutilation of the symbol. This is precisely the pitfall of many a contemporary liturgical reform attempt. The simplification of rites is often necessary. But simplification must not be reduction. Its scope is precisely to uncover and even restore the symbol in its full integrity and multivalence so that it is not muffled by incongruous accretions. A misconceived "simplification", on the other hand, can mutilate the symbol. Since it is impossible to assess theoretically every possible shade and aspect of any dimension of the symbol, undertaking its "simplification", in such a way that a loss in the not fully knowable multivalence is risked, results in the narrowing of the symbol's vital applicability. In other words: it will lose some of its many possibilities to correspond to varied personal situations, or theological aspects. The theologal dimension can also be atrophied or reduced, due to a lack of theological culture, adequate proclamation and catechetical foundation. The complexity and multivalence of the theologal dimension of the mystery may be missed.

This case may also be an example of resistance to the unknown. The symbol event can be impaired by our refusal to remain open to unknown theological aspects, to new revelation. The theology of the sacrament in question is, by its *raison d'être*, oriented towards knowledge and understanding. This quest ought to open one's vistas to the innumerable possible aspects of the mystery which cannot be fully known, rather than describing it in closed categories, to the exclusion of presently unrealized aspects, thereby limiting the chances of its multivalent symbolic realization. A good example for such a priori reduction in theological content is the theoretical denial of one of the inherent meanings of the eucharist. Also, any rationalization of a symbol, pretending to *explain* its meaning, spells death to the symbol, because it reduces its multivalence as well as its revelatory potential.[28] Finally, the psychic situation of the person may be unfavorable. Mental wholeness, balance, adjustment, openness to oneself and the others, readiness to accept the less preferred aspects of one's personality, refraining from repression, all these make for a disposition where more of the totality of the whole person is capable to enter the symbol-event, so that its correlating function can be fuller and more effective. It is obvious that ideal co-incidence will also require a psychologically suitable time for the celebration.

THE CAPACITY FOR LIVING SYMBOLISM AND RITUAL

The problem of man's capacity for the fruitful performance and reception of living symbols (*Symbolfähigkeit*), and more particularly, the capacity for ritual or symbolic worship (*Ritualfähigkeit, Kultfähigkeit*) is often mentioned in connection with the liturgical movement, but one does not find any extensive, systematic treatment of it.[29] This is another neglected topic deserving more attention. The revision of texts and the reform of rites, in short, the endeavour to secure adequate forms of worship is only one side of the problem of a vital liturgy. But, as Romano Guardini pointed out with a touch of foreboding, all the spectacular, enthusiastic renewal in forms might pass like colorful distractions, but at the end, there is still the unanswered question: *is contemporary man still capable of worshipping* (*kultfähig*)?[30] Because if he is not, no amount of shaking the kaleidoscope will provide a lasting remedy.

I do believe that the darkest moments of suspense caused by the decadent rationalism of the ontological age are past. However, while we are getting used to the mannerisms of our new age, many a herald of the liturgical reform still entertains an extremely rationalistic idea of liturgy, which, of course, is a continued indication of an approach to worship which is not at all conducive to a renewed capacity for symbolism and worship. Humanity reduced to pure *ratio* can replace worship by philosophy. Although it is too early to form a complete image of the new breed, be it "functional" or "symbolic", and its capacity for worship may well remain problematical, it can be asserted with a fair amount of certainty that its predominant difficulty will not be rationalism. The spontaneous abundance of secular rites, of symbolically oriented art and of appreciation of symbolism in many realms in fact all support a more optimistic view.

A few valuable insights, though no satisfactory solution in regard to this problem can be gained from two articles of Erich Neumann.[31] In the primitive group-ritual, he maintains, a transpersonal element in man reacts to a transpersonal situation. This transpersonal element is the self of the individual responding to the oneness of the group. Thus the re-integration of the individual into the group is an essential function of any ritual, and especially of the primitive group ritual. The differentiation of the individual has to be reversed and lifted. The group is restored to its primordial unity and wholeness through dancing, singing and other communal cultic acts, and the individual experiences himself transformed and enlivened, as well as re-integrated into the community. His profane existence, which is to say his isolation, is lifted. He recovers his capacity for the ritual (*Ritualfähigkeit*) again, and is restored to his "transpersonality" which at the same time, coincides with the "transpersonality" of the group. Only one who is initiated can be capable of worshipping, i.e. one who, to some extent, has realized his transpersonality.

But the reintegration of the individual into the group and the restoration of the wholeness and transpersonality of the group is only the first step. This horizontal, inter-human event is followed by the integration of the now unified group with the world of the numinous powers. This vertical second instance is the central event

of the rite, tuning the group as it were to oneness with that numinous world which, for the Jungian psychologist, is the world of the
archetypes, governing the unconscious, for the theologian the *ko-*
inonia of men with their God.[32]

The genuineness of the group-ritual, however, becomes problematical to the extent to which humanity distanciates itself from the
original psychic situation, and the individual becomes differentiated
from the community. For as the individual consciousness of the person expands and the arbitrium of the ego increases its realm at the
expense of instinctiveness, the individual gradually loses his capacity to be reintegrated into the group. Thus, to the same extent, he
suffers loss of his capacity for worshipping.

Individualization and ego-development means an intensified
conflict also between conscious and unconscious: it is, in a certain
sense, a split in the psyche, resulting in a situation altogether other
than that of primitive man, who could enter a ritual easily as a
whole.

Also, while the more predominantly unconscious primitive celebration was characterized by the repetitious nature of instinctive
functions, for a more differentiated, conscious participation, effectiveness as well as repeatability becomes problematical. The symbolism of the rite is not entered forever on the same level. Conscious
activity gradually penetrates it deeper and deeper, interiorizing it
and assimilating it in a more personal, more spiritual manner. But
in a sense, for full effect, the original situation of the institution must
be recalled every time the rite is celebrated. This was easier for an
undifferentiated community which was not so far removed from
that situation, not only outwardly, but also in terms of the inner
distance travelled on the road of interiorization and particular spir-
itualization. This inner distance also complicates the capacity for
worship.

Thus, in a sense, the process of interiorizing gradually sup-
plants the elemental ritual action. Bodily action gives way to looking, looking to interiority which can render external action
unnecessary or even impossible. Significance, way of realizing and
effect of the ritual are conditioned by the overall psychic situation
in which the interplay of conscious and unconscious is determining.

The development described by Neumann seems to be irre-
versibly converging to the zero-point of the capacity for worship,

and thereby of the possibility of a relevant ritual. There is no solution offered for the crisis within the frame-work of the group-ritual; there is no salvation promised for the group ritual. For one who sees no *theological* necessity of carrying on, it is not pressing to find it.

Reference is made to three standard reactions this crisis usually evokes. One is the continued effort of the clergy to bring the secularized flock back to vital worship. This effort as far as the core of the problem, resurrecting the capacity for the ritual is concerned, is rather external, and the results are often theatrical mass movements rather than genuine recovery. At certain stages this reaction asserts itself in the form of rigid ritualism, where preservation of rites which have become meaningless becomes the chief concern. Obligation and legalism replace relevance, esthetical perfectionism is substituted for genuine religious experience. Neumann points out that at this point the ritual becomes deceptive, "opium for the people", since the people involved become victims to the illusion that they are integrated to the numinous world, or, theologically speaking, that they are leading an adequate, genuine religious life. The ritual transformation is celebrated by an untransformed people, imagining that the action is genuine. The requirement that the transformation represented through the rite be matched by genuine reality in the participants is not primarily seen as an ethical requirement, but as the criterion of a truly effective rite, once it is understood what it means that the whole man has to fully enter the rite.

According to Neumann the very take-over by a special priesthood on behalf of the people itself is a consequence of the above described development to individualism and interiority, rendering the capacity of the whole community for the ritual problematical.

Another reaction is the "illuministic" conclusion of rationalism, according to which a ritual in this stage not only does not lead to new awareness, but, in fact, hinders such, is regressive and detrimental to consciousness.

A third reaction is the "prophetical-mystical" one, objecting to the ritual for its own sake, no longer bringing about the transformation of the person.

Neither the "illuministic", nor the "prophetical-mystical" answer sets much store by a continued liturgy.

In Neumann's opinion this crisis is surmounted by the gradual supplanting of the group-ritual through the individuation rite no longer requiring the group. Here the re-integration of individual and collective—resulting in a recovered capacity for ritual—takes place within the person. The Collective Unconscious represents the group while the ego stands for the individual. This individual individuation rite can take place as a true, externalized action, or it can be the action of the imagination, unaccompanied by proper, external ritual.

While collectivity retains its—though somewhat altered—position in this individual rite, the problems created by differentiation in regard to the genuineness and repeatability of the group ritual are seen solved.

In all of these considerations the pattern of psychic development is the determining factor for the capacity for worship. But the consideration does not seem to be carried through consistently. It runs out where man finds himself in the stage of the battle with the dragon, in the stage where his self-asserting ego, often symbolized in the hero-image, tears itself out of the primordial unconscious, and divides the inner man into two belligerent camps. This stage corresponds to that sensitive, diffident, bewildered state of youth, when the young ego has to be on constant guard, but does not quite know how, against unknown dangers threatening his newly won, ill-fitting independence. In this stage a very explicit hero worship is about the only kind of cult man is capable of. Reason alone receives full confidence, and the obscurity of symbols, unpenetrable by pure reason is repugnant. So is any community not giving due respect to individuality.

The age of this division is not over once we "grow up" outwardly: it tends to arch over the better part of our life. It would be extremely interesting to study the progress of this development from the viewpoint of the capacity for worship. While the diffidence of the early part of this age may gradually subside, other qualities of youth favourable to worship, may also disappear. One must remember that youth is not pure and total opposition to the primitive, mythical stage with its capacity for worship but only a beginning of that opposition. Early "ontological" man is still greatly "mythical" at the same time.

The complementary point to be made here in any event is that this divided stage is not the final state of man. What Neumann calls *individualization* is to be sharply distinguished from what Jung called *individuation*. In the terms of dialectics, individualization is the antithesis of primordial unconsciousness, while individuation is the subsequent synthesis. Neumann says of man in the middle stage, which almost looks final to him:

> He has experienced his own precipitous depth and thereby lost to a great extent the possibility for an "integral reaction", which is the prerequisite for the truly redeeming efficacy of the ritual.[33]

The now following phase of the *individuation* however, is precisely a coming to terms with that "precipitous depth": an integration which, if successfully progressing, ought to be able to restore man's capacity for an "integral response" (*Ganzheitsreaktion*), and thereby for symbolism and worship. However, this is admittedly a hypothesis. But if the hypothesis is right it also means man's renewed capacity to rediscover himself as a member of "community". His inner integration represents the integration of individual and collectivity, that is: he discovers the community as an integral part of himself, which must mean that he discovers his organic belonging to the community, and consequently, he is again capable, and even in need, of realizing this community ritually. It is another question that on this level the respective communities will be more differentiated than the primitive tribal community was.[34]

The capacity for living symbolism and ritual worship, be it individual or communal, as well as for art and creativity in general, is intimately connected with the psychological journey of the human being, both as race and as individual, from the cradle to the grave. This capacity has a primordial virulence in the earliest, largely unconscious and mythically thinking age of man. It experiences a necessary crisis with the advancing growth of individual consciousness. This crisis may be long and to all appearances hopeless. But a healthily progressing development towards integration, in my opinion, is bound to recover this capacity, and recover it in new depths and with enriched meaning.

Now that both the conditions of living symbolism and the capacity of man to enter into such symbolism have been discussed, we can pass on to the last question: the theological significance of living symbolism or relevance.

THE THEOLOGICAL NECESSITY
OF LIVING SYMBOLISM

After all that has been said about living symbol-events and the factors contributing to their happening, one will want to ask the question: what is the theological significance of all of this? What if a celebration is "unsuccessful" on the above terms?

Of course it will be easy to concede that a celebration with obvious psychological appeal, experienced to be spiritually profitable, over and above being "valid" and technically "fruitful", has an undeniable advantage. But does this advantage affect the theological functioning of a sacrament, and if so, to what extent? Jung says that "a symbol that seems to obtrude its symbolical nature need not be alive. Its effect may be wholly restricted, for instance, to the historical or philosophical intellect".[35] This observation can very well apply to a Sunday eucharist which does not possess any psychological vitality. It is celebrated faithfully, as historical and theological meaning is recalled to the mind through the well-explained and intellectually exhausted external forms and embraced through faith. We would certainly have to say that the symbolism in this case has become mere sign function, but that does not exclude the possibility of genuine faith, devotion and, beyond unquestioned "validity", even technical "fruitfulness". What does it matter theologically speaking that there is no living symbolism in this rite?

To quote Jung just once more, "a symbol really only lives when it is the best and highest possible expression of something divined but not yet known . . . Under these circumstances . . . it advances and creates life".[36] In this statement a connection is asserted between the "revelatory character" and the life creating and advancing efficacy of the living symbol. This connection is as basic to our sacraments as it is to any living symbol. The sacraments have precisely this twofold function, they produce, realize, materialize, render present, incarnate that which they symbolize. They are salvation revealed in its realization or realized in its revelation. *Sacramenta significando causant* means that sacraments are "means of grace" only in their capacity of symbols and not apart from it. Johannes Betz says, "the meal, the matter of the sacrament itself already effects presence by virtue of its natural symbol-content".[37] Conversely, must we not say that what is not effectively symbolized, is not caused to be present and operative either?

The connection between manifestation and realization has been greatly obscured by the ontologizing theology of the past. The revelatory or proclamatory function of the sacraments was neglected to the point where their life creating and advancing efficacy—sanctifying—came to be regarded as practically the only effect. This effect was produced *ex opere operato*, and this security could be played up—advertently or inadvertently—vs. the revelatory or proclamatory function, which was more complex to understand. A synonymous development emphasized the sacrament at the expense of the word, which, as has been pointed out, led to the impoverishment of the sacrament itself.[38]

The intrinsic inseparability of revelation and redemption in the liturgical symbol action was, however, taken seriously by the Second Vatican Council. The Council undertook to reform the liturgy "in order that the Christian people may more certainly derive an *abundance of graces*" from it, and it hoped to enhance this sanctifying efficacy by disposing both texts and rites in such a manner that "they *express* more clearly the holy things which they signify, and that thus the Christian people might be enabled, as far as it is possible, to perceive them with ease . . . ".[39] There is then an interdependence between the capacity of the sacred symbols to *express*, to reveal on the one hand and to sanctify on the other. In short, when the symbolism of a ritual has lost its actual power to reveal, when it is no longer perceived, experienced as a revelation of "something divined but not yet known" (for what is already known need not be revealed), then it is also necessarily impoverished in its life creating and advancing efficacy, i.e. its sanctifying power, its fruitfulness. A eucharist then which, while "validly" and "fruitfully" celebrated, does not possess the qualities of a living symbol-event, in other words is not experienced as a revelation, does not communicate a deeper realization of the mystery of salvation in relevant terms, while satisfying the norms of the textbooks, in fact loses a great deal of its fruifulness. Nourishing the faith through relevant "instruction" itself is part of the fruit of the sacrament, and because sanctification is inseparably linked to this revelatory or proclamatory aspect, sanctification itself is diminished through lack of living symbolism. Psychologically living symbolism is then required of a liturgical celebration for the very success of its theological function.

"Fruitfulness", in the textbooks, is a quality which is either realized or not. It has no degrees. In this sense, of course, we could speak of a fruitful but irrelevant sacrament. This "fruitfulness", however, is regarded only as a minimum measure of a worthily celebrated sacrament. To what *extent* a "fruitful" sacrament is fruitful, is another question. Objective efficacy and the negative norms of a minimum of fruitfulness do not place any limitation on the varying degrees in which God can communicate grace through a sacrament. Yet, customarily, this variability has been made dependent solely on the free love of God and the inner response of the recipient, in other words on not in themselves sacramental realities. In other words, the degree of fruitfulness is made practically independent of the successful sacramental symbol-function which, in a sense, amounts to a de-sacramentalization of the encounter, in contrast to the principle of incarnation.[40]

The principle of incarnation underlying the whole sacramental economy states that all communication between God and man follows the pattern of the Incarnation. The "God-made-man" means that the divine word became human word, divine love human love, divine power human power.[41] This does not mean that it ceased to be divine, but it does mean that God now communicates with man through the natural realities of this world, into which he has incarnated his revelation and salvation. It means that sacramental grace operates according to the laws of symbolic realization. It means that the salvation event here and now incarnated in a symbolic rite is effective and real according to the intrinsic nature and proper operation of the symbolic rite. The principle of grace does not cease to be "supernatural", if one wants to retain this terminology, but the channels through which it operates are natural.

A sacrament, as symbol, by its very nature, necessarily involves in its operation human perception, conscious and unconscious, volition, free and unfree. Its fruitfulness in regard to revealing and nourishing the faith is radically bound up with its success as a psychologically living symbol. And so is, indirectly, its sanctifying power.

It appears therefore as an inevitable conclusion, that if sacramentality is taken seriously, the degree of fruitfulness cannot be imagined as independent from the psychological vitality via relevance of the rite. In this essay we have inquired into the nature and function of symbolism, and investigated what conditions are required for the realization of living liturgical symbolism. These conditions are not only external to the person entering the symbol action, his own capacity for its fruitful performance and reception is also of great importance. We have also found that the quality of vital relevance is a factor affecting the very theologal success of a sacrament, as a grace-filled encounter with God.

Notes

1. M. Eliade, *Images and Symbols*, New York, 1961, pp. 9 ff.
2. C. Vagaggini, *Theological Dimensions of the Liturgy*, Collegeville, 1959; A. Verheul, *Introduction to the Liturgy*, London, 1968; J. J. von Allmen, *Worship, its Theology and Practice*, New York, 1965.
3. Cf. the writings of Marshall McLuhan and Walter Ong.
4. C. Vagaggini, *op. cit.*, p. 24.
5. Quoted in J. Jacobi, *Complex, Archetype, Symbol in the Psychology of C. G. Jung (Bollingen Series, 57)*, New York, 1959, p. 75.
6. C. G. Jung, *Psychological Types, or the Psychology of Individuation*, London, 1923, 1964, p. 607.
7. J. Jacobi, *op. cit.*, p. 98.
8. C. G. Jung, *op. cit.*, pp. 602–603.
9. J. Jacobi, *op. cit.*, p. 105; cf. also P. Tillich, *Theology of Culture*, New York, 1959, pp. 54–58.
10. C. G. Jung, *op. cit.*, p. 602; cf. also P. Tillich, *The Protestant Era* (abridged Ed.), Chicago, 1957.
11. R. Hostie, *C. G. Jung und die Religion*, Munich, 1957, p. 55.
12. C. G. Jung, *Psychology and Religion: West and East* (Vol. II of *Collected Works*, edited by H. Read and others: *Bollingen Series*). New York, 1958, p. 254.
13. R. Hostie, *op. cit.*, p. 51.
14. G. Van der Leeuw, *Religion in Essence and Manifestation*, New York, 1963, Vol. II, p. 448.
15. A. Verheul, *op. cit.*, p. 110.
16. C. G. Jung, *Von den Wurzeln des Bewusstseins*, Zurich, 1954, p. 55.
17. H. Trüb, *Heilung aus der Begegnung*, Stuttgart, 1951, *passim*.
18. C. G. Jung, *Symbols of Transformation* (Vol. V of *Collected Works: Bollingen Series*), New York, 1956, p. 232.

19. *Ib.*
20. J. Jacobi, *op. cit.*, p. 53.
21. *Ib.*, p. 86.
22. C. G. Jung, *Von den Wurzeln des Bewusstseins*, p. 491 (Translation mine).
23. J. Jacobi, *op. cit.*, p. 75.
24. Cf. E. Schillebeeckx, *Christ, The Sacrament of Encounter with God*, London—New York, 1963, and J. M. Powers, *Eucharistic Theology*, New York, 1967.
25. J. M. Powers, *op. cit.*, p. 83.
26. A. Vergote, *Regard du psychologue sur le symbolisme liturgique*, in *La Maison-Dieu*, n. 91 (1967), p. 139.
27. C. G. Jung, *Psychological Types*, p. 603.
28. Cf. A. Vergote, *art. cit.*, p. 140.
29. Cf. *Ist der heutige Mensch liturgiefähig?*, in *Herder-Korrespondenz*, 1966, pp. 517–522, and Th. Bogler, Ed., *Ist der Mensch von heute noch liturgiefähig?*, in *Ars Liturgica*, Maria Laach, 1966.
30. R. Guardini, *Der Kultakt und die gegenwärtige Aufgabe der liturgischen Bildung*, first in *Liturgisches Jahrbuch*, 14 (1961), pp. 101–106, last in *Liturgie und liturgische Bildung*, by the same, Würzburg, 1966.
31. E. Neumann, *Zur psychologischen Bedeutung des Ritus*, in *Eranos Jahrbuch*, 19 (1950), pp. 65–120, and *Gewissen, Ritual und Tiefenpsychologie*, in M. Schmaus and K. Forster, Editors, *Der Kult und der heutige Mensch*, Munich, 1961, pp. 317–323.
32. E. Neumann, *art. cit.*, resp. E. Schillebeeckx, *The Church and Mankind*, in *Concilium*, Jan. 1965, pp. 34–50; p. 35.
33. E. Neumann, *Gewissen, Ritual und Tiefenpsychologie . . .*, p. 322 (Translation mine).
34. In all of these considerations we find a remarkable parallelism between C. A. Van Peursen's "mythical", "ontological" and "functional" man (*Man and Reality, The History of Human Thought*), adopted in Cox's *Secular City* and the "oral", "typographical" and "electronic" man of McLuhan and One (*Understanding Media, The Gutenberg Galaxy, The Presence of the Word*). With regard to man's capacity for ritual, it would seem that this parallelism confirms our conclusions. According to McLuhan we are now re-entering the tribal (ritual) dance, but this time with our eyes wide open.
35. C. G. Jung, *Psychological Types . . .*, pp. 604–605.
36. *Ib.*, p. 605.
37. *Eucharistie* in H. Fries, Ed., *Handbuch theologischer Grundbegriffe*, Munich, 1962–63, Vol. I, pp. 336–355. Cf. also H. M. M. Fortmann, *Abziende de Onzienlijke*, Vol. 3a Hilversum, Antwerpen, 1965, pp. 221–222.

38. Cf. H. Fries, Ed., *Wort und Sakrament*, Munich, 1966, pp. 11 and 15.
39. *Constitution on the Sacred Liturgy*, § 21. Cf. E. Lengeling, *Werden und Bedeutung der Konstitution über die Heilige Liturgie*, in H. Rennings, ed. *Die Konstitution des Zweiten Vatikanischen Konzils über die Heilige* Heft 5/6 (*Lebendiger Gottesdienst*), Münster i. W., 1965, p. 84.
40. Cf. C. Vagaggini, *op. cit.*, pp. 166–169.
41. *Ib.*, and E. Schillebeeckx, *op. cit.*, pp. 13–17.

Thomas E. Clarke, S.J.

Jungian Types and
Forms of Prayer

It is well known that Jungian spirituality—approaches to human and Christian development which draw on the insights of Carl Jung—is experiencing a high point of interest and influence.[1] More specifically, the Jungian psychological types are attracting many, especially as these types are identified by the Myers-Briggs Type Indicator (MBTI), a preference measurement perfected over several decades by the late Isabel Briggs Myers.[2] More particularly still, there is considerable interest in describing forms of prayer which correspond to the categories of the Jungian typology.[3]

In this context the present article seeks to identify and reflect on ways of praying which correspond to the functions and attitudes of the Jungian schema; it will also offer some suggestions and cautions towards the further exploration of such correspondences. It is written not only for those who are already acquainted with their MBTI types, but also for those seeking a basic explanation of this instrument in its usefulness for prayer.

These observations are based on a dozen retreat/workshop experiences of six days which have sought to aid Christian growth by correlating Jungian type-categories with Gospel themes and Christian practices. They are also meant to supplement what has been said in a recent book transposing the retreat/workshop into print.[4] The scope of this article is quite limited. First, it does not profess to know how people or groups belonging to any one of the sixteen types actually prefer to pray or, still less, ought to pray. Secondly, it does not seek to correlate each of the sixteen types with one or more forms of prayer. The basis of the correlations here suggested will be the four functions, with some consideration of the attitudes of introversion and extraversion.

The article does, however, go beyond the previously mentioned literature in three ways. First, it will speak not only of the prayer of individuals but also, though less in detail, of prayer in groups and in liturgical assemblies. Secondly, it will raise the question of prayer as a form of leisure, hence as a time for making friends with the shadow side of one's personality. And thirdly, it will raise the question of forms of prayer for individuals at different stages of life's journey.

A PRELIMINARY OBSERVATION

One final preliminary remark needs to be made, on the method of correlation followed in our retreat/workshop, in the chapters of *From Image to Likeness*, and in the present article. Jungian theory and the Christian Gospel are two quite distinct and heterogeneous interpretations of what it means to be human. The properly behavioral and the properly religious dimensions of life are irreducible one to the other. Even where common terms, drawn from either sector, are used, we must be wary of assuming a univocal sense. Carl Jung presented himself principally as pursuing the science of the soul. Jesus Christ is God's Word of salvation, the founder of the faith community which bears his name. Nevertheless there are between the insights of Jung and the teachings of Jesus significant affinities, likenesses, analogies. As in the case of Plato and Aristotle, Darwin and Marx, penetrating Jungian insights into the human condition can meet, and be met by, facets of the Gospel. The method employed here, then, is one which centers on such resemblances. My impression is that much of the energy generated within Jungian spirituality today derives from the exciting discovery that these two basic perceptions of our humanity often converge in remarkable ways. The convergence on which we will focus here is that which obtains between the characteristics of each of the Jungian functions and different forms of Christian prayer.

THE JUNGIAN TYPES

My guess is that most readers of this article have already been introduced to the Jungian types either directly or through some such instrument as the MBTI. But a brief summary may be helpful, at least to those not 'acquainted with the types.

Carl Jung's clinical experience acquainted him with the fact that while we all engage in common forms of behavior we also differ notably from one another in our behavioral preferences, and hence in the way in which we grow humanly.

He used two generic terms, *perceiving* and *judging*, to designate the alternating rhythm, present in each person, of a) taking in reality, being shaped by it, and b) shaping reality, responding to it.

Each of these two postures was specified, Jung postulated, in two contrasting *functions*. Perceiving (P) was specified as either *sensing* (S), the function through which, with the help of the five senses, we perceive reality in its particularity, concreteness, presentness; or as *intuiting* (N), the function through which, in dependence on the unconscious and with the help of imagination, we perceive reality in its wholeness, its essence, its future potential.

Judging (J) was also specified, in either *thinking* (T), by which we come to conclusions and make decisions on the basis of truth, logic, and right order; or in *feeling* (F), which prompts conclusions and decisions attuned to our subjective values and sensitive to the benefit or harm to persons—ourselves or others—which may result from our behavior.

All four of these functions, Jung affirmed, can be exercised by way of *extraversion* or by way of *introversion*. He invented this now celebrated distinction to describe the flow of psychic energy in any given instance of behavior. In extraverted behavior the flow of energy is from the subject towards the object of perception or judgment. In introverted behavior, the flow of energy is in the opposite direction, that is, from the object towards the subject. What makes the difference is not precisely whether the target of our perception or judgment is something outside ourselves or within ourselves, but which way the energy is flowing. Rather commonly, the impulse to share one's perception or judgment immediately with others or at least to give it bodily expression, signals the presence of extraversion (E); while a tendency to gather the perceiving or judging behavior and to deal with it within oneself marks introversion (I).

Working independently of Jung, and on theoretical foundations previously explored by her mother, Isabel Briggs Myers developed an instrument which, on the basis of a preference questionnaire, indicated how the respondent prefers to behave in given situations. The typology is based on four sets of polar opposites: extraversion/introversion; sensing/intuiting; thinking/feeling; judging/perceiving. In tabular form:

E - I
S - N
T - F
J - P

The four pairs of opposites in varying combinations yield sixteen types, each of which is identified with its code e.g. ESTJ; ISFP; ENFJ. In the process of decoding, which we cannot describe in detail here, one arrives at the order of preference of the four *functions* (described as dominant, auxiliary, third, and inferior), as well as the *attitude* (introversion or extraversion) of the dominant function. Thus one person's most preferred behavior will be extraverted feeling, another's introverted intuiting, and so forth. Also worth noting is that when the dominant function is a perceiving function (sensing or intuiting), the auxiliary function will be one of the two judging functions (thinking or feeling), the third function will be the other judging function, and the inferior function will be the perceiving function opposite to the dominant function. A corresponding pattern will obtain where the dominant function is a judging function. This is one way in which Jung's view of "compensation," or the tendency of the psyche towards balance, is verified.

Extensive research and testing, especially with respect to the professions chosen by people of various types, enabled Isabel Myers to construct profiles of the sixteen types. These in turn have won for the MBTI an extensive use in the fields of career guidance, personnel policy, and the dynamics of groups and organizations. The key psychological insight on which the MBTI capitalizes is that people's behavior, development, and relationships are strongly affected by their preferences in perceiving and judging, as well as by the extraverted or introverted character of the respective preferences. If one makes the assumption that persons are capable of enlightenment and growth through free exercise towards more human ways of living, this psychometric tool then becomes a vehicle of human development. Such is the conviction which has sparked enormous

interest in the MBTI in recent years. Out of the work of these two
American women has emerged the *Association for Psychological Type*,
whose membership has reached 1500, and which has sponsored five
biennial conferences for discussing numerous aspects of the typology. One of the interest areas provided for in APT covers religious
education, spiritual growth, prayer styles, missionary service, and
similar themes.[5]

With this brief outline of the various functions and the two attitudes which qualify human behavior, we now turn to correlating
each of the four functions with forms of Christian prayer. In the case
of each of the functions we will ask: What are some of the forms of
prayer—individual, group, and liturgical—which correspond to
this function?

SENSING FORMS OF PRAYER

Forms of prayer corresponding to the sensing function will be,
in general, those ways of praying in which we pay attention to present reality in a focused way, whether with the help of the five external senses or through a simple perception of interior reality. Here
are some examples of what we may call sensing prayer.

1) *Vocal prayer*, such as the recitation of the psalms or the rosary,
will be sensing prayer when the posture of the one praying is characterized by simple attentiveness, a certain contentment with each
passing phrase, and an eschewing of rational thought, imaginative
scenarios, and strong emotional investment. Sensing prayer tends
for the most part to be simple, quiet, undramatic, contemplative,
and down to earth. Vocal prayer, whether the words are recited
aloud, gently murmured, or just expressed within, are apt vehicles
for exercising this side of our personality.

2) The *"prayer of simple regard"* is a traditional term used to describe a kind of prayer which, I would suggest, has the characteristics of sensing prayer. It consists in just "being there," present to
present reality, especially to God within the mystery of divine presence. It needs no words (except perhaps to recall one from distrac-
tion) and does not involve strong yearnings of the heart, but in
simplicity accepts the "sacrament of the present moment."

3) The prayerful *"application of the senses"* may also be an exercise

of sensing prayer. But here I understand this term as referring to the use of the five exterior senses, or any one of them, on their appropriate objects. The first part of Fr. Anthony de Mello's widely read book *Sadhana* contains many such exercises which he lists under "Awareness."[6] The sense of touch, for example, may be prayerfully exercised just by letting myself become aware of bodily sensation, beginning perhaps with the shoulders and working down to the soles of the feet. Touch is also exercised when I attend to how, in breathing, I feel the air as it enters and leaves the nostrils.

Listening to sounds in a quiet posture of receptivity and enjoyment is another instance of sensing prayer. Provided I have entered this exercise with faith, I do not need to have recourse to the thought of God or to any devout feelings, even though, as Fr. de Mello suggests, a variation of this exercise might consist in hearing the sounds as God sounding in all the sounds made by nature and humans. Thus the chatter of voices, the purr of a motor in the basement, or the thunder of a ride on the New York subway, can be grist for the mill of sensing prayer.

Something similar may be said for gazing as a form of sensing prayer. I may look at objects of devotion, at pictures in a book or album, at faces in a crowd, at the beauties of nature. Even taste and smell can be vehicles of prayer for a person exercising faith with a heightened consciousness.

4) Sensing prayer can also draw upon the *interior sense,* our capacity for paying attention to what is going on within us. Focusing on our breathing or our heartbeat can be a point of entry. Then we may choose simply to attend to what is happening in inner consciousness, to the words, images, or feelings which spontaneously bubble up from the unconscious. Sometimes this kind of exercise can induce a gradual slowing or cessation of inner chatter, and we can for a while just listen to the silence within. We may even come to a happy interior verification of the Quaker motto, "Don't speak until you can improve on silence."

Sometimes people ask with regard to such exercises, "Is it really prayer?" Even if it were not, it would not be a bad way of disposing ourselves for prayer. But when it is situated within a life of faith and for the purpose of expressing and deepening our faith, it can be prayer—excellent prayer—even though we do not name God, converse with God, or experience any devout surge of the heart.

Sensing Prayer in Groups

So far I have been suggesting sensing forms of prayer for the individual. But groups can also pray with an accent on sensing. Various kinds of vocal prayer such as litanies or the Office in common, especially when they are engaged in with simplicity and even with a certain routine, enable the members of a group to meet God and one another through the sensing function. It is also possible to create prayer services in which each of the five senses has its place, as, for example, by listening to the tinkle of a bell or to a guitar quietly strumming; by devoutly kissing a crucifix or extending a handclasp of peace; by smelling incense or flowers; by tasting a sip of wine; by focusing on the lighting of a candle. Sensing prayer in common leaves aside what is highly cognitive or interpersonal or imaginative. It calls the group to be together with a great deal of simplicity and quiet awareness of God, one another, and the environment.

Sensing in Liturgical Prayer

There are times when people come together in larger groups to pray, and particularly to participate in the official or public prayer of the Church. When we celebrate the Eucharist and other sacraments and the divine Office in large assemblies, prayer takes on what I would call a societal character, in contrast to the interpersonal character of prayer shared in small groups.[7] The general thesis which I would propose is that a well-celebrated liturgy needs to attend to all four functions. Ideally, each participant and the congregation as a whole should have the opportunity to exercise both sensing and intuiting, thinking and feeling, in extraverted and introverted ways.

In the present aspect, sensing prayer, liturgical celebration will meet our humanity when it evokes the exercise of the five senses in a congruous way by inviting the participants to look, listen, touch, taste, and smell, all in a fashion which nourishes their faith and deepens their solidarity. There is no need here to detail how apt the celebration of the sacraments in the Christian and Catholic tradition is for meeting this need of human personality. My impression is that consequent upon Vatican II the effort to break out of liturgical straitjackets sometimes brought an "angelism" insensitive to the importance of the senses in good eucharistic celebration. Heightened attention to the homily tended to move celebration excessively towards the cognitive, to the neglect of the sensate elements of good celebration. To some degree we are today recovering the importance of the life of the senses in liturgy. This Jungian approach to societal prayer can assist in that recovery.

INTUITING PRAYER

Intuiting prayer may be described as contemplative prayer drawing upon fantasy and imagination, as well as what might be called the prayer of emptiness or the prayer of the vacant stare. The Jungian tradition uses the term "active imagination" to designate those behaviors in which we let images and symbols freely emerge from the unconscious and flow in consciousness. The term "active" could be misleading, if taken with a connotation of control or shaping reality. There is a sense in which this use of imagination is not active but passive, as the person's posture is one of receptivity. The orientation of such prayer is to what might be, to futures dreamed of rather than planned. As the five senses and the interior sense are the vehicles of sensing prayer, so the gift of imagination is what carries intuiting prayer.

But, in my opinion, the intuiting function can be at work in prayer even when images are not freely flowing. The vacant stare into space aptly symbolizes a contemplative posture in prayer which is aptly subsumed under intuiting prayer. In such prayer the mind is not occupied with thoughts, the imagination is not delivering images or symbols, and the heart is not strongly surging toward the good. Such prayer of emptiness appears to differ sharply from the prayer of a simple regard, even though both forms are characterized by an absence of thoughts, images, and strong feelings. The difference consists in the focused or unfocused character of the gaze. To use a playful distinction which I once heard Brother David Rast employ, in the prayer of simple regard we are *now/here*, fully present to the present actuality of life, whereas in what I call the prayer of the vacant stare we are *no/where* (recall that the Greek term for nowhere is *Utopia*).

Centering Prayer

In this context it is worth asking just where "centering prayer" as developed by Fr. Basil Pennington is best situated from the standpoint of the four Jungian functions.[8] My own inclination is to view it as a form of intuiting prayer. It is true that centering prayer makes use of a word in the journey to the center; and, as we shall see, the word in prayer belongs primarily to the thinking function. But here the word is functioning not as a mediator of rational meaning but as a carrier of the spirit to the beyond. Centering prayer has a predominantly unfocused character and brings us to a certain emptiness. Hence I would put it with intuiting prayer.

All of this having been said, here are some examples of intuiting prayer for the individual.

1) We have just discussed a first form, centering prayer in the proper sense.

2) The familiar "contemplations" of the *Spiritual Exercises of St. Ignatius* are appropriately listed under intuiting prayer. But it needs to be noted that these contemplations of the mysteries of the life of Jesus belong also to feeling prayer, as we will see. The imagination is exercised with freedom, but with a view to drawing the heart in love. It is the feeling function, we shall see, which relates to the past through reminiscence. Perhaps a large part of the power of the Ignatian contemplations consists in the fact that both the dreaming imagination and the heart are drawn on to energize the retreatant engaged in the process of "election." Something similar may be said of the contemplation of the mysteries of the rosary. The imagination freely recreates a scene which contains in symbolic form deep Christian values.

3) Various kinds of fantasy in prayer have an intuitive character. Anthony de Mello's book here again contains some interesting exercises, Christian and non-Christian, under the general heading of "Fantasy." Some which might appear at first to be quite macabre can be a source of intense joy and peace: attending your own funeral, or the "fantasy on the corpse" which Fr. de Mello borrowed from the Buddhist series of "reality meditations."

4) Ira Progoff's "Intensive Journal," both in the sections devoted to dealing with dreams and in the various kinds of dialogues, offers an abundance of forms of intuiting prayer. The dialogues may

be said to combine intuiting and thinking prayer, the latter because of the dialogue form of the prayer.

5) Praying with the help of *symbols* engages the intuitive function in a way that can energize us greatly. The journey, the cave, the house, the tree, the Cross, the City—these are just a few of the symbolic possibilities of intuitive prayer. Books of the Bible such as the Fourth Gospel and the Book of Revelation are a source of abundant Christian symbols which can be explored in prayer.

6) Finally, one may prayerfully explore God's call by asking the question, "What would it be like if . . . ," envisaging oneself in alternative human situations, dreaming of new ways of one's pilgrimage.

Intuiting Prayer for Groups

Many of the approaches to intuiting prayer just described for the individual can be adapted for groups which are praying or prayerfully reflecting together. For example, a community which has gone off to the country or to the shore for some time together might have a very meaningful time of common prayer by having each member bring back some nature-object which symbolizes something important for that person. In planning for the year ahead, a community might put to itself the question, "What would it be like if . . . ," making sure not to become too quickly pragmatic and sensible in dealing with the dreams of particular members for life in common. Another exercise of intuiting prayer in common might be to invite each member to select a Scripture passage which is symbolic of some aspect of the community's life, and to share the passages, taking care to be contemplative, without the need for discussion or response.

Intuiting in Liturgical Prayer

Lyrics from two well-known religious songs aptly characterize the intuitive element which ought to be present in any liturgical celebration. "Take us beyond the vision of this moment . . ." and "Look beyond the bread you eat. . . ." This note of "beyond," or (in Hopkins' poem, "The Leaden Echo and the Golden Echo") "yonder," corresponds to the eschatological quality of Christian faith. In sacramental celebration, it is the complexus of ritual gestures and of symbols which principally contains the invitation to dream, to be open to a limitless future which is God. Psychologically, this facet of good liturgy is effectively present when the congregation as a whole shares, in joyful hope, this unfocused contemplative expectation of future blessing. Though it may find verbal expression, for example within the readings of the celebration, its primary vehicle will be symbol, inviting to the "vacant stare."

FEELING PRAYER

Forms of prayer which correspond to the feeling function are rather easily described. They will be exercises of prayer characterized by affection, intimacy, and the devout movement of the heart. More specifically, feeling prayer takes place when the exercise of memory in gratitude or compunction brings us back to the roots whence our values are derived, when we come back home, so to speak, in the mysteries of the Gospel, the origins of a particular religious heritage, or the sources in our own personal life through which the gift of faith came to us.

The third section of de Mello's *Sadhana* contains an abundance of such exercises of prayer. Here is a briefer listing of some forms:

1) Any form of prayer in which affective dialogue takes place, with God, with Jesus or Mary or any of the saints, or with those who have been important in our personal life, verifies this kind of prayer. In the Spiritual Exercises of St. Ignatius, the contemplation of the mysteries leads to such affectionate "colloquy," in which the grace being sought includes a growth in intimate love.

2) Aspirations, when they are repeated with a view to stirring the heart, are a second way of exercising feeling prayer. The "Jesus prayer" of the Eastern tradition, when said with a view to engaging the affections, is a major example.

3) One can also wander "down memory lane" in one's own life, recalling the persons, the experiences, the behaviors, which have had great influence on one's growth. Such prayer of the heart can often be combined with the exercise of imagination, as we recreate a scene of childhood, for example, or tender moments later in life which make us grateful. Gratitude and compunction are the two dis-

tinctive graces of such kinds of prayer. For each one of us, the past contains both the gifts of God, especially in the form of the goodness of persons, and our failure to respond trustingly and generously to those gifts.

4) All of us have favorite hymns and songs, and sometimes in solitary prayer our hearts can be deeply moved by singing them quietly, or letting their melodies flow through our inner consciousness.

The Feeling Function in Group Prayer

When groups pray together with some regularity, it can help occasionally if the prayer is directed toward the heart. This calls for discretion, of course, for even when the members know each other well there will remain considerable differences in the ability and desire to manifest emotion in common prayer. But experience will show just what is possible and desirable. Music and song is an easy vehicle, usually unembarrassing. The group might listen to an endearing hymn, or to some instrumental music which appeals to the heart.

Story telling, the sharing of personal history about a theme important for the faith life of the group, is another simple and easy way of being together in an affectionate way.

Spontaneous prayer, in which people are free to pray aloud and from the heart, can also deepen the bonds of affection within a community, and strengthen the common commitment to shared values.

This is an appropriate place to mention the relationship of spiritual direction. At least in a broad sense it is part of the prayer life of both the director and the one being directed. It calls for the engagement of all four of the functions. But, inasmuch as it is an intimate relationship of two persons of faith and aimed at the fostering of Gospel values in the life of the person being directed, it calls particularly for the exercise of the feeling function. This is not the place to discuss the question of friendship within this relationship of spiritual direction, apart from observing that there are contrary views on the subject. But, whatever discretion may be called for to preserve the character of the dialogue as one of spiritual direction, it remains a situation where the feeling function is expressed interpersonally.

Feeling in Public Prayer

From what has already been said readers will be able to describe for themselves the aspects of liturgical prayer and other forms of public prayer which correspond to the feeling function. There is significant difference, of course, between the face-to-face prayer of a small group and the largely anonymous quality of public prayer in large assemblages. There will be corresponding differences, therefore, in the ways in which this side of our humanity finds expression.

In my opinion, one of the imbalances of recent years with regard to our expectations of liturgy is that we have often expected it to nourish intimacy in ways beyond its power. Concomitantly, we have tended to lose contact with the deep enrichment which can come to our affective life from such experiences of faith. However one may be personally disposed toward the large gatherings of charismatics which have become such an important part of public prayer and worship, it needs to be said that the charismatic movement is more effectively in touch with this facet of our humanity than most people are. Some of the scenes in which John Paul II has been involved in his worldwide travels provide a further illustration of the energy which flows from religious values through societal prayer and worship. In particular, hymns sung by thousands of voices can be memorable in their impact, as anyone who has been to Lourdes or Rome can testify.

THE THINKING FUNCTION IN PRAYER

I have left the thinking function till last for a few reasons. One is that I find it to be neglected and even, at times, disparaged. Why this is the case is understandable in relationship to the rediscovery of the life of feeling which has taken place in Roman Catholic circles in recent decades. Prayer had, in many respects, become too "cognitized," partly through a reduction of the Ignatian tradition to what was conceived as *the* Ignatian method of prayer as exemplified in the well-known schema of a nineteenth-century Jesuit general, John-Baptist Roothan. In any case the thinking function in prayer has a rather poor press nowadays. Even Anthony de Mello writes,

A word about getting out of your head: The head is not a very good place for prayer. It is not a bad place for *starting* your prayer. But if your prayer stays there too long and doesn't move into the heart it will gradually dry up and prove tiresome and frustrating. You must learn to move out of the area of thinking and talking and move into the area of feeling, sensing, loving, intuiting.[9]

Fr. de Mello is faithful to this conviction, for his book is divided into three parts, corresponding more or less to the sensing, intuiting, and feeling functions. There is no section on thinking prayer.

Doesn't something more positive need to be said about our capability of meeting God through the rational mind? Surely it is no less important a part of God's image in us than the life of sense, feeling, and imagination. And, within the unity of the person, it is intimately linked in its workings with the operations of these other facets of our humanity.

But instead of arguing theoretically for a place for thinking in prayer, let me offer some examples of how one may pray with the rational mind.

1) A clear instance of thinking prayer for the individual is the famous "First Principle and Foundation" of the *Spiritual Exercises* of St. Ignatius Loyola. I can ponder it during a period of prayer and, first, try to appreciate its simple logic in the linkage of purpose, means, and attitude. After savoring its truth I can then examine my life to see where there is order and where there is disorder, and just what area calls for the struggle to be free from inordinate affections. Knowing that I cannot free myself, I can turn to ask God's help. Then I can make a few practical resolutions touching some steps on the road to freedom. Such highly cognitive activities in prayer are really prayer, and not merely preliminaries to prayer.

2) Prayer may also take the form of setting down a personal charter or set of basic principles by which I wish to live, e.g., "Every human being I meet is worthy of my respect." Periodically I can review this set of principles in order to evaluate and improve my fidelity.

3) I may choose also to draw up for myself a plan of life, which would include a daily or weekly schedule of prayer, reading, pro-

visions for work and leisure, practice with respect to money, and so forth.

4) From time to time I may wish to take a book of the Bible, and, with the help of a good commentary, carefully and systematically over a period of some weeks seek a deeper grasp of God's word, attending to the structure of the work, its cultural setting, the precise meaning of terms, and so forth. I may wish to write my own paraphrase of the book, or use the text as the basis of my own reflections. Most of us are accustomed to contrast prayer and study. But when study of God's word takes place within a life of faith and for the purpose of fostering faith, I believe that it lacks nothing of the reality of prayer itself.

Thinking Prayer in Groups

Not all group prayer needs to be self-revelatory and strongly interpersonal in its character. The common recitation of the Office or prayer of the Church is a good example of communal thinking prayer. Such prayer is characterized by clear structure, orderly procedure, and the absence of strong emotions. While it would be untrue to say that affectivity is absent, what prevails is a sense of meaning and purpose. Especially when such prayer includes reading a passage from Scripture or from some other source, the mind's desire for meaning is being fed. Spiritual reading, which is another form of thinking prayer for individuals which might have been mentioned, can also take place within a group united in faith.

Thinking in Liturgical Prayer

Liturgical celebration, especially when it occurs in larger assemblies of people, takes on a societal or public character. The very term *liturgy* conveys this, of course. Inasmuch as the movement from the private to the public in all dimensions of our life involves a significant shift of behavioral attitudes, it brings to the fore the thinking side of our personality. As we begin to relate to people outside the circle of intimacy, it becomes necessary to create conventions, etiquettes, structures, which provide us with supports and safeguards as we relate to larger and more anonymous gatherings of people.

It is for such reasons that our liturgical celebrations contain a good deal of structure and ritual gesture, and tend to be less highly personal than informal prayer in small groups. More of the thinking side of our humanity needs to be engaged when we celebrate the Eucharist and other ceremonies on a large scale.

Similarly to what was said previously about sensing prayer in public worship, I think that we can be helped to understand both the tensions and the failures which have characterized our experience of liturgical worship during the past few decades if we bring to bear on them an understanding of personality types. At the risk of being simplistic one might say that the Tridentine liturgy had become ossified and institutionalistic in its absolutizing of the thinking mode of public worship. This made it understandable that, in the swing of the pendulum in recent decades, we experienced some loss of the basic sense of structure, decorum, and ritual which needs to preside over our public prayer. Some (not all) of the negative reactions to the kiss of peace probably stem from an uneasiness lest the distinction of private and public worship be overlooked.

The present juncture, I would say, is a time when we need to recapture, without returning to rigorism and institutionalism, the rich energies of a thinking kind contained in our sacramental and liturgical traditions. We will pray much better in public if we prize this aspect of our humanity and of our Christian prayer.

FURTHER CONSIDERATIONS

Up to now this article has offered principally a correlation of forms of prayer, chiefly individual but also interpersonal and societal, with the four functions of the Jungian personality types. As has already been said, we should be wary of too easy identification of any of the sixteen types with one or other preferred way of praying. It is not one's type alone but a variety of factors which affect our attractions in prayer. Two of these factors will now be discussed briefly. They concern 1) prayer as an exercise of leisure; 2) prayer in the stages of human development.

Prayer and Leisure

One plausible theory which one hears voiced in Jungian circles would have it that, when we turn from the areas of work and profession to the exercise of leisure, there is a spontaneous inclination in the psyche to move from a more preferred to a less preferred side of our personality. In terms of the functions this would mean, for example, that a person whose work or ministry calls for a great deal of extraverted intuiting—being with people in situations which call for a good deal of creative imagination—will spontaneously seek relaxation after labor by some quiet exercise of sensing: baking a cake with careful attention to measurements, or working at one's stamp collection, or hooking a rug according to a given pattern. Similarly, someone whose work is highly analytical and impersonal, let us say in dealing with a computer, might want to relax by sharing a Tchaikovsky concert or a TV sitcom with a few friends.

Such a suggestion makes a good deal of sense, especially in view of the natural mechanisms of compensation which seem to be built into our psychic life. If one then adds the similarly plausible suggestion that prayer is or ought to be an exercise of leisure, then we would appear to have a useful criterion for evaluating our forms of prayer, and for suggesting new approaches to prayer, particularly when we seem to be getting nowhere. In such a view, we might profitably ask ourselves from time to time whether our behavior in prayer does not tend to be too much a compulsive continuation of the kind of behavior which we prefer in our work or ministry. And we might, if such is the case, deliberately seek ways of praying which helped to disengage us from such compulsive patterns. Someone whose primary gift, for example, is introverted intuiting, and who spends a good deal of time in the course of the day exercising that gift, might deliberately choose some extraverted sensing forms of prayer, for example, praying the rosary with simple attention to the words, the touch of the beads, and so forth. Or someone whose ministry makes heavy emotional demands—caring for the senile or the retarded, or counselling disturbed people, for example—might find some interior exercise of thinking prayer to be balancing and eventually attractive.

One small suggestion regarding this experiencing of leisure in prayer. It should take place, like all prayer, not by violence but by attraction. It might well be that, though one appreciates the value of shifting gears when one approaches prayer, it is not so easy to disengage from one's favored behavior. One might have to make an entry through the preferred function, especially an auxiliary function, before learning to exercise a less preferred function, especially the inferior function, in prayer.

This use of the auxiliary function to wean us away from too exclusive a reliance on the dominant function is part of a Jungian strategy of individuation. It would seem to be applicable to strategies in prayer. For example, if thinking is my dominant function and I exercise it abundantly in my work, I may find myself attached to it even when I come to prayer. Instead of directly trying to rouse myself to feeling prayer, I might begin by letting my auxiliary sensing direct my gaze to particular objects, interior or exterior, which in turn and in due time may stir my heart to affective prayer. The philosophy of non-violence has an important area of application in prayer.

Prayer and Development

Numerous are the theories which, in the present century, have sought to plot the course of human development, in its cognitive, affective, social and ethical aspects. The well-known names of Piaget, Maslow, Erikson, Fowler, and others have provided rich insights into the various facets of growth. One characteristic of a Jungian perspective on development is that, in the light of the diversity of personality types, it will be wary of imposing a monolithic pattern on the wide variety of human preferences. When prayer is viewed in this light, there are some salutary cautions and perhaps some qualifications of long-standing assumptions about progress in prayer.

Dr. W. Harold Grant has, for some years, been investigating the hypothesis of our periods of differentiated human development, starting at age six and ending at fifty, with major switching points taking place at twelve, twenty, and thirty-five. In each of the four periods, according to the hypothesis, the person would be developing one of the four functions: the dominant in childhood, the auxiliary in adolescence, the third function in early adulthood, and, from the age of thirty-five on, the inferior function. The hypothesis includes also an alternation of introversion and extraversion in the successive periods. Prior to age six and subsequent to age fifty development would be taking place more randomly, and not selectively, as in the four periods between six and fifty.

If one accepts this as a plausible hypothesis, some implications for forms of prayer at the different stages of life would seem to be present. First, one would be open to the possibility that the spontaneous employ of sense, imagination, reason, and affection in prayer may not be uniform for all persons or types. Any such prevailing assumption that growth in prayer takes place first by the use of reason and imagination and then, in a darknight experience, by their cessation, might have to yield to a view which acknowledges more diversity in the way in which the attachment/detachment phenomenon takes place in different types of personalities.

Secondly, the hypothesis may help to throw light on crisis periods in people's prayer lives, by suggesting that the emergence of a new function—especially of the inferior function about the age of thirty-five—may be signaled through the decline or collapse of previously fruitful ways of praying. It might also suggest that the person involved in such a crisis might do well to explore some alternative ways of praying, ways which would be in keeping with whatever function was seeking to find its place in consciousness. Let us think, for example, of persons in whom feeling is dominant, experiencing something of a crisis in prayer around mid-life. They might do well, with the help of a director, to exercise their thinking side in prayer, for example, by keeping a journal in which reflection on the meaning of what they are experiencing, or meditation on the meaning of some scriptural passages, was cultivated.

It should be obvious that these two factors, touching the question of leisure and the question of diversity in human development, do not exhaust the sources which make for different experiences in prayer. Factors stemming from each person's unique personal history will be at least as important in deciding what course we wish to chart in prayer. And ultimately, as has already been said, it is the attraction of the Spirit of God at every juncture of life which is the primary determinant of how we choose to pray.

CONCLUSION

But if it all comes down at last to attraction, why bother consulting the Jungian types for help in praying? For two principal reasons. First, such a consultation will make us wary of being misled by stereotypes of prayer and of progress in prayer, and particularly of the monolithic character of many descriptions of growth in prayer, even among the great classics. And secondly, when persons are in a time of crisis or barrenness in prayer, they may be helped in dealing with the situation if they have had some practice in a variety of ways of praying, and if they realize the affinity between these various ways and the different functions within the Jungian personality types. With the reservations we have indicated in this article, acquaintance with one's type through the MBTI can help foster better praying.

Notes

1. See, for example, Morton Kelsey, *The Other Side of Silence*, (New York: Paulist, 1976); *idem, Transcend: A Guide to the Spiritual Quest*, (New York: Crossroad, 1981); John Sanford, *Healing and Wholeness*, (New York: Paulist, 1977); *idem, The Invisible Partners*, New York: Paulist, 1980); Wallace B. Clift, *Jung and Christianity: The Challenge of Reconcilation*, (New York: Crossroad, 1982); John Welch, *Spiritual Pilgrims: Carl Jung and Teresa of Avila*, (New York: Paulist, 1982); Robert Doran, "Jungian Psychology and Christian Spirituality," *Review for Religious* 38 (1979), pp. 497–510; 742–52; 857–66.
2. See Isabel Briggs Myers, *Gifts Differing*, (Palo Alto: Consulting Psychologists Press, 1980).
3. See Christopher Bryant, *Heart in Pilgrimage: Christian Guidelines for the Human Journey*, (New York: Seabury, 1980), pp. 182–195; Robert Repicky, "Jungian Typology and Christian Spirituality," *Review for Religious*, 40 (1981) pp. 422–435.
4. See W. Harold Grant, Mary Magdala Thompson, Thomas E. Clarke, *From Image to Likeness: A Jungian Path in the Gospel Journey*, (New York: Paulist, 1983).
5. APT publishes a newsletter, *MBTI News*, for its membership, and is based at 414 S.W. 7th Terrace, Gainesville, FL 32601.
6. See Anthony de Mello, *Sadhana: A Way to God*, (St. Louis: Institute of Jesuit Sources, 1979).
7. See Thomas E. Clarke, "Toward Wholeness in Prayer," in: William R. Callahan & Francine Cardman, *The Wind Is Rising: Prayer Ways for Active People* (Hyattsville, MD: Quixote Center, 1978), pp. 18–20.
8. See Thomas Keating, M. Basil Pennington, Thomas E. Clarke, *Finding Grace at the Center*, (Still River, MA: St. Bede Publications, 1978).
9. De Mello, p. 13.

Notes on the Contributors

M. ESTHER HARDING received her M.D. from the London School of Medicine for Women and the University of London. She worked with C.G. Jung at Zurich in 1922 and in subsequent years. She began her analytical practice in New York in 1923 and became a founding member of the Analytical Psychology Club of New York, the Medical Society of Analytical Psychology of America, and the C.G. Jung Foundation of New York. Her works include *The Way of All Women*, *The Parental Image*, *Woman's Mysteries*, *Journey into Self*, and *The I and the "Not-I"*.

EUGENE C. BIANCHI received his Ph.D. in History of Religion from Columbia College (1966). He is currently Professor of Religion at Emory University, in Atlanta, Georgia. His works include *Aging as a Spiritual Journey* and *On Growing Older*.

ERNEST SKUBLICS has a doctorate in Theology from the Catholic University at Nijmegen in Holland (1967), and a Diploma in Liturgical Studies from the Liturgy Institute at Trier (1966). He is currently registrar of St. Paul's College at the University of Manitoba, and lecturer in the Department of Religion. His publications include *Restoring the Icon* (Edwin Meller Press).

THAYER A. GREENE has an M.Div. from Union Theological Seminary (1958) and an S.T.M. also from Union (1964) in Psychiatry and Religion. He is author of *Modern Man in Search of Manhood* (Association Press). Other publications include "Jungian Group Therapy and Analysis" in *Jungian Analysis* (Murray Stein, ed.) and "Bicentennial Reflections: America's Loss of Innocence" (Psychological Perspectives). He is former chaplain of Amherst College, Amherst, Mass., and former president of the New York Association for Analytical Psychology. Currently Mr. Thayer is on the faculty of the C.G. Jung Institute in New York and is an analyst in private practice.

ROBERT A. REPICKY, C.S.B. is a doctoral student at the Graduate Theological Union in Berkeley, Cal. His publications include "Reflections on Spirituality and Bioenergetics" *(Bioenergetics Review)*. He is a pastoral counselor in the Berkeley area.

MORTON KELSEY is Professor Emeritus at the Department of Theology, Notre Dame. An Episcopal priest, Kelsey is widely published in the area of psychology and Christian spirituality. He has written *God, Dreams, and Revelation* (Augsburg). *Prophetic Ministry* (Crossroad), *Caring* (Paulist Press), and many other works.

ROBERT M. DORAN has an M.A. in Philosophy from St. Louis University (1965) and a Ph.D. in Religious Studies from Marquette University (1975). He is an associate professor at Regis College in the Toronto School of Theology, and on the staff of the Lonergan Research Institute at Regis College. His publications include *Subject and Psyche* (University Press of America), and *Psychic Conversion and Theological Foundations* (Scholars Press).

THOMAS E. CLARKE S.J. has an S.T.D. from the Gregorian University, Rome. His works include *Playing in the Gospel* (Sheed and Ward), and *From Image to Likeness: A Jungian Path in the Gospel Journey* with W. Harold Grant and Magdala Thompson (Paulist Press). He is a writer and speaker in New York City.

JOHN A. SANFORD is a Certified Jungian Analyst in private practice in San Diego. He is an Episcopal minister and a lecturer. His publications include *The Strange Trial of Mr. Hyde* (Harper and Row), and *The Invisible Partners* (Paulist Press).

DIARMUID McGANN has an M.Div. from the Immaculate Conception Seminary, Huntington (1979), and an M.S. in Pastoral Counseling from Iona College (1980). He is associate pastor of St. Frances Cabrini in Coram, New York. His works include *The Jour-*

neying Self: The Gospel of Mark through a Jungian Perspective (Paulist Press), and *Journeying Within Transcendence* (Paulist Press).

ANN BELFORD ULANOV has an M.Div. from Union Theological Seminary, a Ph.D. also from Union, and an L.H.D. from Virginia Theological Seminary. Currently she is Professor of Psychiatry and Religion at Union Theological Seminary, in New York City. She is author of *Picturing God* (Cowley Publications), *Receiving Woman: Studies in the Psychology and Theology of the Feminine* (Westminster Press), and *Primary Speech: A Psychology of Prayer* with Barry Ulanov (John Knox Press; British edition, SCM Press). She is a Jungian Analyst in private practice.

PATRICK VANDERMEERSCH received his doctorate in Theology and Philosophy from the University of Louveigne for his work on the writings of Carl Jung. He currently resides in Louveigne, Belgium.